$ 17.00

PROTEST & PRAISE

SACRED MUSIC

. *of* .

BLACK RELIGION

JON MICHAEL SPENCER

FORTRESS PRESS   **MINNEAPOLIS**

PROTEST AND PRAISE
Sacred Music of Black Religion

Scripture quotations unless otherwise noted are from the Revised Standard Version of the Bible, copyright © 1946, 1952, and 1971 by the Division of Christian Education of the National Council of Churches.

Interior design: Jim Gerhard
Cover design: Ned Skubic
Cover photo: The Bettmann Archive, copyright © Bettmann Newsphotos

Library of Congress Cataloging-in-Publication Data

Spencer, Jon Michael.
    Protest and praise : sacred music of Black religion / Jon Michael
Spencer.
      p.   cm.
    Includes bibliographical references.
    ISBN 0-8006-2404-1
    1. Afro-Americans—Music—History and criticism. 2. Afro-
Americans—Religion. I. Title.
ML3556.S8 1990
781.71'0089'96073—dc20   89-23573
                                        CIP
                                       MN

The paper used in this publication meets the minimum requirements of American National Standard for Information Sciences—Permanence of Paper for Printed Library Materials, ANSI Z329.48-1984. ∞™

Manufactured in the U.S.A.   AF 1-2404
94   3   4   5   6   7   8   9   10

To C. Eric Lincoln
"A Scholar Maker"

CONTENTS

PART TWO: PRAISE SONG

PREFACE

The ten chapters that comprise this book are divided into two parts—"Protest Song" (Part One) and "Praise Song" (Part Two). Insofar as the spirituals are the prototypical music of black religion, and black religion and the black church evolved out of black rebellion, it is fitting that this corpus of song constitutes the first part, "Protest Song" (Chapters 1–5). While the spirituals (Chapter 1) document the inside of slavery looking out, antislavery hymnody (Chapter 2) chronicles the outside of slavery looking in. In order not to interrupt the kingdom of God motif that connects antislavery hymnody (Chapter 2) to social gospel hymnody (Chapter 3) to civil rights song (Chapter 4), the segment on early blues closes Part One (Chapter 5).

Scholars have always concurred that antislavery hymnody, social gospel hymnody, and civil rights song were vehicles of protest. However, whether black spirituals were songs of empirical or spiritual liberation has been the subject of long-standing controversy. In telling the exodus story through the spirituals and the story of the spirituals through the exodus, I maintain that the spirituals were unquestionably the archetype of protest seen later in antislavery, social gospel, and civil rights hymnody. I also contend that early blues was a music of rebellion, namely, a radical affront to the hypocrisy of the church and the advocates of slavery.

Part Two, "Praise Song" (Chapters 6–10), is also ordered in historical chronology. The ring-shout (Chapter 6), having its counterpart in the spiritual, opens this section. Since tongue-song (Chapter 7), Holiness-Pentecostal music (Chapter 8), and gospel music (Chapter 9) constitute a continuum that evolved from the type of religious expression found in the ring-shout, the chapter on the chanted sermon closes Part Two (Chapter 10). While the ring-shout, tongue-song, Holiness-Pentecostal music, and gospel music are clearly songs of praise, the chanted sermon is included here not because black preaching has neglected to be a vehicle of protest, but because intoned declamation always tends to occur at a sermon's climax where adoration is emotionally expressed and salvation physically celebrated.

Based on the musical genres covered in the following ten chapters, it seems that the most inclusive designation for the whole is *the sacred music of black religion,* rather than *the music of the black church, black sacred music,* or *black hymnody.* Antislavery hymnody and the blues are not idioms of the black church; the former, along with social gospel hymnody, are musical genres written mainly by reformers of European descent. The aforementioned corpus of music is neither black nor of the black church, but music sacred to black religion. White antislavery hymnody addressed the real foundation of black liberation. White social gospel hymnody, essentially concerned with the social conditions of industrialized European immigrants, blacks adopted for their own means of kingdom-building. And early blues was a form of black rebellion existent on the periphery of Afro-Christianity.

The ten chapters of this book are bound together by means of a method I term *theomusicology,* which is musicology as a theologically informed discipline. The musical topics covered evolve out of differing historio-theological contexts, so each chapter has a distinct theological approach to analyzing its subject matter. Chapter 1, "Promises and Passages," extracts the meaning of the music by using spirituals to explain piece by piece a chronological lining of Scripture. In Chapter 2, "Songs of the Free," the hymnody of moral abolitionism is contrasted with the song of political abolitionism. In Chapter 3, "Thy Kingdom Come," the historical dissemination of "kingdom" hymnody into the Social Gospel movement is traced through the theological writings and correspondences of its great theologian and liturgist, Walter Rauschenbusch. Chapter 4, "We Shall Overcome," discusses the dispute between the nonviolence movement's theology of singing and the Black Power movement's "militancy of silence" (not singing). In Chapter 5, "Bluesman Adam and Blueswoman Eve," an ethical argument is made that blues life is a reliving of the parable of the Prodigal Son, so that blues songs are raw religious reflections of individual and ritually synchronized sojourns in moral maturity.

Opening Part Two, Chapter 6, "The Drum Deferred," traces the development of the ring-shout, beginning with a discussion of the theology of the African drum and the drum's deferment in the diaspora to North America. In Chapter 7, "The Heavenly Anthem," accounts of tongue-song extracted from the thirteen issues of the revival's newspaper, *The Apostolic Faith* (1906–1908), are assimilated to construct an authentic theological interpretation of this music. Chapter 8, "Isochronisms of Antistructure," specifically treats the singing of gospel hymns in the context of the testimony service, which liturgy helps sustain the larger black community. In Chapter 9, "Christ against Culture," the five-part theological typology formulated in H. Richard Niebuhr's *Christ and Culture* is used to locate the theological stance of gospel music amid Christian pluralism. And in Chapter 10, "Sermon and Surplus," a theology for musicality in preaching is construed alongside the chanted sermon as song.

The research for this book was made possible through a grant from the Eli Lilly Endowment, to whom I express my highest indebtedness. I express my appreciation to Professor William B. McClain of Wesley Theological Seminary, Professor Harold Dean Trulear of Eastern Baptist Theological Seminary, Professor William C. Turner, Jr., of Duke University Divinity School, and Professor Alton B. Pollard III of

Wake Forest University Department of Religion for reading
my manuscript and making insightful suggestions and improvements. I am also grateful to Duke University, especially
to the Divinity School, for allowing me four years of resi-
dency as a visiting professor and for the helpful suggestions
of divinity and religion faculty who read various parts of this
book—Professors C. Eric Lincoln (to whom this book is dedicated), George Marsden, Frederick Herzog, Stanley Hauer-
was, John Westerhoff, and Kenneth Surin.

—Jon Michael Spencer
Duke Divinity School

PART ONE

PROTEST SONG

1

Promises and Passages:
The Exodus Story Told through the Spirituals

THE   SPIRITUAL

Heavy Burdens

Now there arose a new king over Egypt. . . . And he
said to his people, "Behold, the people of Israel are too
many and too mighty for us. Come, let us deal shrewdly
with them, lest they multiply, and, if war befall us, they
join our enemies and fight against us and escape from
the land." Therefore they set taskmasters over them to
afflict them with heavy burdens (Exod. 1:8–11a).

It is not difficult to imagine how enslaved Africans
might have heard the above passage from Exodus: Now there
arose a new king over the South of North America—King
Cotton. And he said to his white people, "Behold the people
of Africa are too many and too mighty for us. Come, let us
deal shrewdly with them, lest they multiply, and, if civil war
befall us, they join our enemies and fight against us and
escape from the South." Therefore they set taskmasters over
them to afflict them with heavy burdens. They whipped
them into submission, lynched their men, raped their women,
and sold their children downriver. Their children "wringed
their hands and cried":

> Sometimes I feel like a motherless child (3X)
> A long ways from my home (2X).

3

Their women moaned "like a moanin' dove":

> Nobody knows the trouble I see (*3X*)
> Nobody knows like Jesus.

Their men groaned "a tremblin'":

> O Lord, O my Lord, O my good Lord,
> Keep me from sinkin' down.[1]

"Of the Sorrow Songs," W. E. B. DuBois's melodious lamentation in the immortal *The Souls of Black Folk* unmasks the "minor cadences of despair" in these songs of the homeless, the troubled, and sunken down. Though he knows that these penultimate cadences of despair "change often to triumph and calm confidence,"[2] there is weeping in DuBois's own soul. It is condolence that causes his heart to sing of the sorrow songs. They are "the music of an unhappy people, of the children of disappointment," moans that "tell of death and suffering and unvoiced longing toward a truer world, of misty wanderings and hidden ways."[3]

He Killed the Egyptian

One day, when Moses had grown up, he went out to his people and looked on their burdens; and he saw an Egyptian beating a Hebrew, one of his people. He looked this way and that, and seeing no one he killed the Egyptian and hid him in the sand (Exod. 2:11–12).

Moses' killing the Egyptian was "the first blow of liberation from Egypt."[4] The ensuing exodus, the type of liberation unattainable by one raised as a slave or by one unconnected with the slaves, was possible only by one brought up in the midst of oppressors and who had been educated in the ways of

[1] Respectively, "Sometimes I Feel Like a Motherless Child," "Nobody Knows the Trouble I See" (rare version), "Keep Me From Sinkin' Down." See also "Wring My Hands and Cry."

[2] W. E. B. DuBois, *The Souls of Black Folk* in *Three Negro Classics*, ed. John Hope Franklin (New York: Avon Books, 1965), 386.

[3] Ibid., 384, 380.

[4] Ernst Bloch, *Atheism in Christianity: The Religion of the Exodus and the Kingdom*, trans. J. T. Swann (New York: Herder and Herder, 1972), 88.

their wisdom and power. Thereafter, Moses went out to his people and looked on their burdens.[5]

For the enslaved Africans, the first blows of liberation from bondage could only have been brought about by those liberated from a slave mentality—who, being brought up in the midst of oppressors, appropriated the power and wisdom of the gospel. Uncountable were those like Moses, who looked on their people's burdens and when seeing an overseer beating an African, looked this way and that, and seeing no one, killed the overseer. Not everyone was or had to be a Moses in order to initiate the process of liberation; too many of his kind would have resulted in revolution rather than exodus. But with the first blows of liberation dealt, it was God's time to compel the oppressors by a mighty hand.

With reference to Exod. 3:19, "I know that the King of Egypt will not let you go unless compelled by a mighty hand," Dan Cohn-Sherbok maintains that, in cases of extreme oppression, liberation is necessarily violent. "God acted violently in the Exodus account because the situation of the Hebrews admitted no other path."[6] For enslaved Africans the situation also lacked any alternative.

It would have been perilous if the Africans openly expressed their approval of Moses' manslaughter. Instead, they masked their consent by lyricizing similar biblical events in spirituals. They lauded David for his victory over Goliath:

> Little David was a shepherd boy,
> He killed Goliath and shouted for joy.

They cheered on the victorious Joshua in his leveling of Jericho:

> Up to the wall of Jericho
> He marched with spear in hand.
> "Go blow them ram horns," Joshua cried
> 'Cause the battle am in my hand.

---

[5] Martin Buber, *Moses: The Revelation and the Covenant* (New York: Harper, 1958), 35.
[6] Rabbi Dan Cohn-Sherbok, *On Earth as It Is in Heaven: Jews, Christians, and Liberation Theology* (Maryknoll, N.Y.: Orbis Books, 1987), 93.

> Then the lamb ram sheep horn begin to blow,
> Trumpets begin to sound,
> Joshua commanded the children to shout
> And the walls come tumblin' down.

And because God's mighty hand was going to compel the oppressors to let God's people go, they boasted:

> My God is a man of war (*3X*)
> And the Lord God is his name.[7]

Refusing to accept the situation of repression, judgment and condemnation of the oppressor implies to Hugo Assmann "a word of *confrontation* and *conflict.*"[8] Although "slave talk" figuratively condoned the first blows of liberation and the mighty hand of intervention, the spirituals were nonetheless fatal words of confrontation and conflict. Sure "slave talk" wears a mask, admits Ernst Bloch, but it "wears it freely," allowing liberation to be more than merely whispered. "Slave talk" is, as Bloch says, "the art of cursing while blessing," and is perilous to the oppressors[9] because it spurred the likes of Moses to look upon their people's burdens in search of that overseer beating an African. "Did [Gabriel Prosser] not apply the deeds of Samson as related in Judges 15 to himself?" prods Leo Witvliet. "Was Denmark Vesey not in turn fascinated by the story of the fall of Jericho in Joshua 6?"[10] Hence, the mask of the Christian soldier—"soldiers of the cross" and "soldiers in the army of the Lord"[11]—says John Lovell, was ideal for the kind of warfare in which the enslaved were engaged.[12] It allowed confrontation and conflict, first blows

---

[7] Respectively, "Little David Play On Your Harp," two verses of "Joshua Fit the Battle of Jericho," and "Sinner, Please Don't Let This Harvest Pass" (or "My God is a Man of War").

[8] Hugo Assmann, *Practical Theology of Liberation*, trans. Paul Burns (London: Search Press, 1975), 47.

[9] Bloch, 14–15.

[10] Leo Witvliet, *The Way of the Black Messiah: The Hermeneutical Challenge of Black Theology as a Theology of Liberation* (Oak Park, Ill.: Meyer-Stone Books, 1987), 210–11.

[11] Respectively, "We Are Climbing Jacob's Ladder" and "In the Army of the Lord."

[12] John Lovell, *Black Song: The Forge and the Flame: The Story of How the Afro-American Spiritual Was Hammered Out* (New York: Macmillan, 1972), 341.

of liberation, to be more than whispered by those actually "singing with a sword in their hands."[13]

Why Do You Strike Your Fellow?

When he [Moses] went out the next day, behold, two Hebrews were struggling together; and he said to the man that did the wrong, "Why do you strike your fellow?" (Exod. 2:13).

African slaves also struggled together, but there were always those like Moses who sang to the one who did the wrong:

You say the Lord has set you free; . . .
Why don't you let your neighbor be?

Not only were those who struggled together to let their neighbors be, that is, not to strike their fellows, they were also to walk in unity:

Walk together children, don't you get weary (2X)
Talk together children, don't you get weary,
There's a great campmeeting in the promised land.

And they were to commune together:

Let us break bread together on our knees . . . (2X)
When I fall on my knees with my face to the rising sun,
O Lord have mercy on me.[14]

The Lord Appeared to Moses

The angel of the Lord appeared to him [Moses] in a flame of fire out of the midst of a bush; and he looked, and lo, the bush was burning, yet it was not consumed. . . . God called to him out of the bush, "Moses, Moses!" And he said, "Here am I". . . . Then the Lord said, "I have seen the affliction of my people who are in Egypt, and have heard their cry because of their taskmasters; I know their suffering, and I have come

[13] "The sword may be the symbol of the need of black slaves to strike a blow for freedom even though the odds were against them." James H. Cone, "Black Spirituals: A Theological Interpretation," *Theology Today*, 29, no. 1 (Apr. 1972), 61.

[14] Respectively, "Give Me Your Hand," "Walk Together Children," and "When I Fall On My Knees."

down to deliver them out of the hand of the Egyptians"
(Exod. 3:2–8a).

"Liberation is not simply a history that breaks in from a
future totally unconnected with the present," defines José
Míguez-Bonino. "It is a project which springs from the protest
born of the suffering of the present; a protest to which God
grants a future in which man enters through his action."[15]
James Cone adds that revelation is "God's self-disclosure to
man *in a situation of liberation.*"[16] Thus the situation of liberation initiated by Moses' first blow of freedom—the time of
God's self-revelation in a flame of fire out of the midst of a
bush—included God's promise of a future land, which the
Israelites would enter by their actions behind the rod of
Moses, under the watchful eye of God.

Whether the people of Africa were engaged in actions
of insurrection, or exodus, or incessant passages into liberation, or through masked confrontation and conflict, one
thing is clearly evident in the spirituals: The enslaved
figured out why they should be free—"My Lord delivered
Daniel/*and why not every man?*"—and the figuring was
done in a situation of liberation, commencing with the
"middle passage" when some engaged in insurrection and
others leaped headlong into the sea just to be free. The
spirituals were theological reflections of a long-standing
practice of liberation and therefore songs of revelation and
liberation.

Behold the Cry of the People

Behold, the cry of the people of Israel has come to me,
and I have seen the oppression with which the Egyptians oppress them (Exod. 3:9).

Because the people of Africa cried out in anguish, it
could be argued that the spirituals reflected a theology of
survival rather than liberation; that they were paltry "sorrow

---

[15] José Míguez-Bonino, *Doing Theology in a Revolutionary Situation* (Philadelphia: Fortress Press, 1975), 76.
[16] James H. Cone, *A Black Theology of Liberation* (Philadelphia: Lippincott,
1970), 91.

songs" rather than potent pieces of *confrontation, conflict,* and *revelation.* Leo Witvliet takes up this controversy with reference to Henry Mitchell and Gayraud Wilmore. Witvliet says Mitchell asserts that in spite of its liberative aspect, "black folk theology" cannot be exclusively labeled a theology of liberation. "It is more likely a theology of existence or survival."[17] Wilmore, continues Witvliet, also postulates that slave religion is a religion of survival, and the distinction between survival and liberation is that between *making do* and having the power and audacity to *do more.* Wilmore explains that liberation comprises the determination to survive, but survival does not necessarily include the "strategies of elevation" liberation requires. Much like Mitchell, Wilmore proceeds no further than to resolve that survival and liberation are intertwined throughout black experience.[18] The Mitchell-Wilmore outline of evolutionary passage looks like this:

repression ———→ *freedom* ———→ *liberation* ———→ *salvation.*

Witvliet's ultimate model reflects a differing stance on liberation theology in black spirituals:

repression ———→ *liberation* ———→ *freedom* ———→ *salvation.*

However, Witvliet does not initially break with the Mitchell-Wilmore conspectus. He agrees that the spirituals "contain a liberating potential—survival,"[19] a notion he inversely states later by claiming that there is a "liberating dimension" that "points beyond mere survival." With "a wider vision" the black struggle for survival points to "total liberation in a world without tears."[20] In the spiritual "Didn't My Lord Deliver Daniel," Witvliet pinpoints the liberating dimension that goes beyond the desire to survive all the way to total liberation:

[17] Henry H. Mitchell, *Black Belief* (San Francisco: Harper & Row, 1975), 120. Quoted in Witvliet, 211.
[18] Gayraud S. Wilmore, *Black Religion and Black Radicalism* (Maryknoll, N.Y.: Orbis Books, 1983), 227.
[19] Witvliet, 213.
[20] Ibid., 213, 242–43.

> He delivered Daniel from the lion's den,
> Jonah from the belly of the whale,
> And the Hebrew children from the fiery furnace,
> *And why not every man?*

In response to the cadential phrase he says:

> In this struggle and expectation the prime concern is
> for one's own existence, for the continuation of one's
> own descendants, one's own people. But the universal-
> ity of the "And why not every man?" is comprised in the
> particularity of this struggle.

> More than the thesis of racial oppression is needed for
> the antithesis "we too are human beings"; . . . The an-
> tithesis of black liberation is not simply preceded by the
> thesis but also by the synthesis of the "And why not
> every man?" The synthesis which is the goal, its *telos*, is
> at the same time its presupposition.

Thus Witvliet breaks with Mitchell and Wilmore and re-
solves that "the particularity of this experience carries
within itself the synthesis of 'And why not every man?'. . .
and precisely in this involvement of the whole [of human
history] lies the difference between liberation theology and
survival theology."[21]

> You got a right, I got a right,
> *We all got a right to the tree of life.*

Go Back to Egypt

The Lord said to Moses in Midian, "Go back to Egypt;
for all the men who were seeking your life are dead"
(Exod. 4:19).

There is an additional aspect to the self-revelation of
God in situations of liberation. It is God's timeliness. Only
after all the men seeking Moses' life were dead did the Lord
say to Moses in Midian, "Go back to Egypt."
God also used timely revelation with the people of
Africa. One ex-slave called God a "time God": "He don't

---

[21] Ibid., 78, 81.

come before time; he don't come after time. He comes just on time."[22] In the words of *Moses* Harriet Tubman, "God's time is always near."[23] God's being *on time* (in Moses) and God's revelatory "nearness" *in time* (in Christ Jesus) was manifested in Tubman's accrual of physical strength and God's gift of a guiding pillar of fire in the sky by night: "He gave me my strength, and he set the North star in the heavens; he meant I should be free."[24] Upon her exodus she sang:

> Goodbye, I'm going to leave you,
> Goodbye, I'll meet you in the kingdom.[25]

You Have Made Us Offensive in the Sight of Pharaoh

The foremen of the people of Israel . . . met Moses and Aaron . . . as they came forth from Pharaoh; and they said to them, "The Lord look upon you and judge, because you have made us offensive in the sight of Pharaoh and his servants, and have put a sword in their hand to kill us" (Exod. 5:19–21).

Moses and Aaron were risking their lives for the freedom of the Hebrew slaves, and the slaves were more concerned with their survival (making do) than with their liberation (doing more). Among the enslaved Africans were those whose sorrow songs of survival droned beneath the predominant songs of liberation:

> Were you there when they crucified my Lord? *(2X)*
> O sometimes it causes me to tremble, tremble, tremble.
> Were you there when they crucified my Lord?

With the taskmasters whipping them into submission, lynching their men, raping their women, and selling their children, the murmurers also felt forsaken, left upon the cross. They did not rejoice in their death, nor were they resurrected.

---

[22] Clifton H. Johnson, ed., *God Struct Me Dead* (Boston: Pilgrim Press, 1969), 170.

[23] John W. Blassingame, ed., *Slave Testimony: Two Centuries of Letters, Speeches, Interviews, and Autobiographies* (Baton Rouge: Louisiana State University Press, 1977), 464.

[24] Ibid.

[25] Ibid., 458.

However, for the most part, the songs of the enslaved Africans were not murmurous. As DuBois aptly phrased it, "few men ever worshipped Freedom with half such unquestioning faith as did the American Negro for two centuries."[26] Throughout the corpus of spirituals the enslaved Africans are portrayed as liberated from the sorrow songs by their unquestioning faith. This is evident in the spirituals because, as Frederick Herzog explains, the liberated being always rejoices when the self is loosed through "audacious suffering."[27]

> Nobody knows the trouble I've seen,
> Nobody knows but Jesus.
> Nobody knows the trouble I've seen,
> *Glory, hallelujah!* [28]

If black spirituals had been murmurous sorrow songs of survival, then Joseph Washington would have denounced them as "inauthentic." Distinguishing between murmurous "escapism" and "the will to freedom and equality through the 'fiery furnace' of this land," Washington says:

> The authenticity of the Spirituals resides in their expression of the love of and drive for freedom and equality with and for all men. The inauthenticity of the Spirituals are those expressions of escape from this world without becoming "an offering for sin"—a life-denying rather than life-affirming motif which does not seek through fire, bloodshed, and war to be "realized eschatology."[29]

Washington's proviso for the inauthenticity of escapism in the face of needed liberationism is not left unsupported. However, for Marc Ellis, that which affirms escape from this world is not necessarily inauthentic unless it is "a false transcendence which legitimates oppression."[30] For instance, a

---

[26] DuBois, 216.

[27] Frederick Herzog, *Liberation Theology: Liberation in the Light of the Fourth Gospel* (New York: Seabury Press, 1972), 211.

[28] In lieu of "Nobody Knows" the sorrow song, which left Christ crucified, there developed a more popular version of "Nobody Knows," the song of a crucified one resurrected.

[29] Joseph R. Washington, Jr., *The Politics of God: The Future of the Black Churches* (Boston: Beacon, 1967), 157.

[30] Marc H. Ellis, *Toward a Jewish Theology of Liberation* (Maryknoll, N.Y.: Orbis Books, 1987), 90.

false transcendence to Assmann might be hope merely contemplated or believed but which neglects to motivate actual stages in struggle.[31] Spirituals, as expressions of hope (unquestioning faith) that actually motivate in stages of struggle, are life-denying through fire, bloodshed, and war. Through crucifixion and resurrection, their corpus is an offering for sin. Although spirituals wear a mask, they wear it freely; they are *authentic* and *audacious*.

The Groaning of the People

I have heard the groaning of the people of Israel whom the Egyptians hold in bondage and I have remembered my covenant. Say therefore to the people of Israel, "I am the Lord, and I will bring you out from under the burdens of the Egyptians" (Exod. 6:5–6a).

If one could have unmasked the groaning of the people of Israel while under Egyptian bondage, it would have been discovered that they cherished the idea of eventually being free. Solomon Northup, in his autobiographical narrative, *Twelve Years a Slave*, alludes that the groaning of the people of Africa, whom the Americans held in bondage, was also a transcendent utterance that penetrated history as a masked, but no less concrete, longing for freedom:

Let them know the *heart* of the poor slave—learn his secret thoughts—thoughts he dare not utter in the hearing of the white man . . . and they will find that ninety-nine out of every hundred are intelligent enough to understand their situation, and to cherish in their bosoms the love of freedom, as passionately as themselves.[32]

Behind the mask of the spirituals was authentic *confrontation* and *conflict*. In a foreign land, the Africans were demanding that the covenant God made with Abraham, with Isaac, and with Jacob also be fulfilled in their lives. "Every tone," attested Frederick Douglass, "was a testimony against slavery, and a prayer to God for deliverance from chains."[33]

---

[31] Assmann, 95.

[32] Solomon Northup, *Twelve Years a Slave*, eds. Sue Eakin and Joseph Logsdon (Baton Rouge: Louisiana State University Press, 1968), 158.

[33] Frederick Douglass, *My Bondage and My Freedom* (New York: Dover, 1969), 99.

Hmm mm-mos' done toilin' here
Hmm, Lord, I'm *mm*-mos' done toilin' here.[34]

They Did Not Listen to Moses

Moses spoke thus to the people of Israel; but they did not listen to Moses, because of their broken spirit and their cruel bondage (Exod. 6:9).

When the Moses of the people of Africa spoke they listened, for in spite of their cruel bondage they had no broken spirit. Yet, even prior to the coming of their Moses, they knew the Messiah-Liberator; and his gospel, which loosed them from the bondage of the "sorrow songs," was an affirmation of their impetus to be free.

Everybody come and see
A man's been here from Galilee;
Came down here and he talked with me,
Went away and left me free.[35]

As evidenced in James Cone's explanation of "The Old Ship of Zion," casting off the chains of slavery in the midst of bondage is evident throughout the spirituals:

The presence of Jesus as the Captain was the black people's assurance that the ship would "carry [them] all home." The "Old Ship of Zion" was a symbol that their life had meaning despite the condition of servitude. It was their guarantee that their future was in the hands of the One who died on Calvary. That is why they proclaimed: "Glory hallelujah!" It was an affirmation of the faith that black slaves would triumph over life's contradictions, because they had met the Captain of that "Old Ship of Zion" and were already on board.[36]

The spirituals lyricized an inward liberation exhibited in the conversion of Virginia ex-slave George Anderson. Long before the Confederate Army surrendered, Anderson claimed to have found the source of liberation at a camp

---

[34] "Mos' Done Toilin' Here."
[35] "Can't You Live Humble."
[36] James H. Cone, *God of the Oppressed* (New York: Seabury Press, 1975), 56.

meeting: "I did not cast off the chains of slavery at the time of the surrender," he said, "they fell of at that camp meeting."[37] Anderson's conversion into the Christian body of liberation was the consequence of anticipation. As Witvliet argues, "The emancipatory longing for liberation is included in the anticipation through faith of a new world in which the last are first."[38] Witvliet's postulate, that anticipation is hope in action, is alluded to interrogatively by Jürgen Moltmann: "Does the present determine the future in extrapolations or does the future determine the present in anticipations? Is there a third factor in which present salvation-in-faith and not-yet-present salvation in hope can be meaningfully united?"[39] Frederick Herzog assuredly answers the query, contending that Jesus Christ is the "third factor." "There can be no meaningful final eschatology without its anticipations in Jesus Christ," he says, "and there can be no meaningful embodied eschatology without the prospect of the final consummation."[40] Consequently, when Moses spoke what the Lord said regarding the promise, the people of Africa, with active hope (faith) in Christ, fervently anticipated emancipation and salvation.

> The very time I thought I was lost
> The dungeon shook and the chains fell off.
> You may hinder me here but you cannot there,
> 'Cause God in the heaven going to answer prayer.

The spirituals seem to indicate that the type of conversion Anderson had was a prerequisite to faithfully seeking freedom from bondage, that Christ was the source of *authentic* anticipation and *audacious* emancipatory longing. This is perhaps what Herzog meant when he said that liberation "antecedes and transcends our efforts at self-liberation." He says: "We are not liberated. Jesus is. Only through him can we grasp our liberation. For us liberation, in terms of realization, is an eschatological reality."[41] Because liberation is an

---

[37] Blassingame, 569.
[38] Witvliet, 37.
[39] Cited in Herzog, *Liberation Theology*, 256.
[40] Ibid.
[41] Ibid., 232, 225.

eschatological reality, it is "an eschatological favor from God."[42] In this regard, "Hush, hush, there's somebody callin' my name" refers to an anticipatory summons (a favor) from Jesus Christ to personhood and inward liberation.[43] Herzog concurs that, "Confronted with God's liberation in Jesus men can confess that Jesus encounters them not as a stranger, but as the one who gives them true identity: he calls them by name—by their true selfhood."[44]

> My Lord calls me,
> He calls me by the thunder,
> The trumpet sounds in my soul.

Pharaoh Will Not Listen to You

> The Lord said to Moses, "See I make you as God to Pharaoh; and Aaron your brother shall be your prophet. You shall speak all that I command you; and Aaron your brother shall tell Pharaoh to let the people of Israel go out of his land. But I will harden Pharaoh's heart, and though I multiply my signs and wonders in the land of Egypt, Pharaoh will not listen to you" (Exod. 7:1–4a).

The Moses portrayed in the spirituals was like a God to Pharaoh, and he spoke all that the Lord commanded him. But Pharaoh's heart was hardened even amidst the multiplicity of God's *confrontive* and *conflictive* signs and wonders. The Pharaoh's obstinacy, illustrated in the 1932 essay on black spirituals by Robert Gordon, reveals why the mask of "cursing while blessing" could be freely expressed in the spirituals:

> The entire concept of spiritual slavery, of the bonds and shackles of sin, of Pharaoh and Moses, and the Red Sea . . . is to be found expressed in minute detail in any number of hymns of demonstrable white origin, often in the identical words used by the negro in his spirituals. On the other hand, the total number of cases in all the known spirituals of the negro in which we can be certain that he refers to physical and not to spiritual

---

[42] Leonardo Boff, *Jesus Christ Liberator: A Critical Christology for Our Time* (Maryknoll, N.Y.: Orbis Books, 1978), 281.
[43] "Soon One Morning."
[44] Herzog, 145.

slavery can almost be counted on the fingers. Among them are, of course, "No More Auction Block for Me," "No Driver' Lash in de Heaben, O Lord," and a very few others.

I do not mean to imply that the negro did not often see in such white songs the possibility of a double meaning, that he did not in his own mind apply whatever he adopted from these songs to physical, as well as spiritual, slavery. But he did not himself create any body of song on his enslaved condition.

He found in white hymns, as commonly sung, fully developed ideas concerning spiritual slavery, the Last Judgment, and the joys of Heaven. These he used as a basis of song building. . . . In no case did he change greatly the basic concept, present it from any new point of view, or introduce to it any new philosophy. He reexpressed the borrowed concept in his own way.[45]

The autobiographical narratives of Frederick Douglass and Thomas Wentworth Higginson refute the claims that Africans failed to create a body of song on their enslaved condition. In his *My Bondage and My Freedom* (1855), Douglass gave this illustration:

A keen observer might have detected in our repeated singing of "O Canaan, sweet Canaan,/ I am bound for the land of Canaan," something more than a hope of reaching heaven. We meant to reach the *north* —and the north was our Canaan.

In the lips of some, it meant the expectation of a speedy summons to a world of spirits; but in the lips of *our* company, it simply meant a speedy pilgrimage toward a free state, and deliverance from all the evils and dangers of slavery.[46]

Thomas Wentworth Higginson, in his *Army Life in a Black Regiment* (1869), told about the outbreak of the civil war

---

[45] Robert W. Gordon, "The Negro Spiritual," in *The Carolina Low-Country*, ed. Augustine T. Smythe et al. (New York: Macmillan, 1932), 217.

[46] Douglass, 278–79.

when enslaved blacks of Georgetown, South Carolina, were chanting the old spiritual, "We'll soon be free/ . . . When the Lord will call us home." A little drummer boy confided in him, said Higginson, that "Dey tink *de Lord* mean for say *de Yankees.* "[47] Cone offers one last retort:

> Seeking to detract from the theological significance of the spirituals, some critics may point out that black slaves were literalists in their interpretation of the scripture. . . . But the critical point is that their very literalism supported a black gospel of earthly freedom. They were literal when they sang about Daniel in the lions' den, David and Goliath, and Samson and the Philistines.[48]

The people of Africa were literal in their interpretations of the Old Testament liberation events. However, the pharaohs of the African slave trade (and their contemporary disciples such as Gordon) projected the David and Samson types into the New Testament—interpreting the Old Testament liberation situations with a Pauline epistemology, an otherworldly rather than empirical eschatology. The scholars who examined the black spirituals with the pharaonic interpretation turned deaf ears and blind eyes to third- and fourth-generation children. These scholars did not listen to or see the solemn warnings, signs, and wonders of the Lord.

Let My People Go

> The Lord said to Moses, "Go in to Pharaoh and say to him, 'Thus says the Lord, Let my people go, that they may serve me'" (Exod. 8:1).

It is evident in the spirituals that the exodus event was the pattern of liberation—*confrontation, conflict, revelation.* The singers believed that God would do for them what was done for the Israelites. Jewish liberation theologian Marc Ellis, amenable to designating the African slave trade a

---

[47] Thomas Wentworth Higginson, *Army Life in a Black Regiment* (Boston: Beacon, 1962), 217.
[48] Cone, "Black Spirituals," 61.

holocaust, found it fitting that the people of Africa adopted the Hebrew exodus story as their own. He says,

> the paradigm of liberation that forms the heart of the Jewish experience, the dynamic of bondage confronted by the call to freedom, has been appropriated also by struggling peoples throughout the ages. The songs of African slaves in nineteenth-century America calling on God for freedom echo the lamentations of the Jews in Egypt.[49]

Cone explains why this adaptation is authentic by stating, "The resurrection-event means that God's liberating work is not only for the house of Israel but for all who are enslaved by principalities and powers."[50] Thus the enslaved Africans would sing with anticipation:

> When Israel was in Egypt's land
>   Let my people go,
> Oppressed so hard they could not stand,
>   Let my people go.

> "Thus spoke the Lord," bold Moses said,
>   Let my people go,
> If not I'll smite your first born dead,
>   Let my people go.

> REFRAIN
> Go down, Moses,
> 'Way down in Egypt land,
> Tell ole Pharaoh,
> Let my people go.[51]

All the Hosts of the Lord Went Out from Egypt

The time that the people of Israel dwelt in Egypt was four hundred and thirty years. And at the end of four hundred and thirty years, on that very day, all the hosts of the Lord went out from the land of Egypt. It was a night of watching by the Lord, to bring them out of the land of Egypt (Exod. 12:40–42a).

---

[49] Ellis, 84, 1.
[50] Cone, *A Black Theology of Liberation*, 21.
[51] "Go Down Moses."

Among the collection of black spirituals are the "train" songs. These symbolize the liberating activity of the underground railroad, which, *passage by passage,* led the hosts of the Lord out from the land of oppression. These were songs that Moses Harriet Tubman and other underground railroaders sang in conveying the promise, as well as the means of communication in preparation for, and celebration during, the activity of going out.

There were many nights of watching by the Lord; in one spiritual the Africans declare that the "same train" that carried away their mothers and sisters would "be back tomorrow." Everyone was encouraged to pack their bags in preparation; though the train was due on the morrow, it could pass through any night.

> Little black train is a-comin'
> Get all your business right;
> Go get your house in order,
> For the train may be here tonight.[52]

When the little black train (perhaps Moses Tubman, who was "little" and "black") was heard returning, potential passengers far and wide were invoked to get on board:

> The gospel train's a-comin',
> I hear it just at hand,
> I hear the car wheels movin'
> And rumblin' through the land.
>
> CHORUS
> Get on board, little children (*3X*)
> There's room for many more.[53]

---

[52] Mary Allen Grissom considered "the little black train" ("Little Black Train Is a-Comin'") to be a train of death (Mary Allen Grissom, *The Negro Sings a New Heaven* [Chapel Hill: University of North Carolina Press, 1930], 11). Even if she were correct it would have been death for the sake of life. Similarly, sometimes crossing the river meant death, other times it meant freedom. But even when the river represented the "ice-cold water of death," says Witvliet, "on the other side of the experience of death (slavery, physical death) is life" (Witvliet, 205). Hence, although the "Jordan river is chilly and cold," we hear the enslaved sing "It will chill my body, but not my soul" ("Stand Still Jordan").

[53] Respectively, "Same Train," "Little Black Train Is a-Comin'," and "Get on Board Little Children."

To Die in the Wilderness

When Pharaoh drew near, the people of Israel lifted up their eyes, and behold, the Egyptians were marching after them; and they were in great fear. And the people of Israel cried out to the Lord; and they said to Moses, "Is it because there are no graves in Egypt that you have taken us away to die in the wilderness. . . . And Moses said to the people, "Fear not, stand firm, and see the salvation of the Lord, which he will work for you today; for the Egyptians whom you see today, you shall never see again" (Exod. 14:10–13).

When pharaoh drew near, the people of Africa lifted up their eyes, and behold, the oppressors were marching after them. But the people of Africa, being unafraid, sang:

> I will die in the field (*3X*)
> I'm on my journey home.

Those who vowed in song that they would die in the field, Lovell said, "are a part of the evidence that the spiritual fully echoed this militant noncooperation in the face of increasing pressures from the well-armed enemy."[54]

The spirituals were a reflection of the militant noncooperation of the enslaved, but Joseph Washington believed that it was the "spirited songs" themselves that "aided slaves to be religiously or psychologically supported in their feats of courage—to be tenacious, resolute, and militant."[55] As militant songs of noncooperation and liberation, rather than murmurous sorrow songs of survival, the spirituals mirrored more the mentality of Moses than that of the Hebrew children. Instead of Moses reminding the people of Africa of the salvation of the Lord, they courageously urged him to lead them forth into freedom in spirited song:

> I've been travelin' all day long,
> > Ride on, Moses,
> To hear the good folks sing and pray;
> > I want to go home in the morning.

[54] Lovell, 171.
[55] Joseph R. Washington, Jr., *Black Religion: The Negro and Christianity in the United States* (Boston: Beacon, 1964), 207.

> They prayed so long I could not wait,
>   Ride on, Moses,
> I know the Lord would pass that way,
>   I want to go home in the morning.[56]

Into the Midst of the Sea

Moses stretched out his hand over the sea; and the Lord
drove the sea back by a strong east wind all night, and
made the sea dry land, and the waters were divided.
And the people of Israel went into the midst of the sea
on dry ground, the waters being a wall to them on their
right hand and on their left. The Egyptians pursued,
and went in after them into the midst of the sea, all
Pharaoh's horses, his chariots, and his horsemen (Exod.
14:21–23).

The children of Israel were awed as they headed into
the midst of the great abyss with the enemy in pursuit. Those
who fled were neither slaves nor free, those who pursued
neither captors nor victors. It was war between chaos and
creation. Chaos represented the violently oppressed life of
the enslaved Israelites as well as the people of Africa, and
creation their impending liberation (Isa. 43:1). Passing
through the midst of the sea was akin to the trans-historical
rites of passage out of the gates of hell and in through the eye
of the needle. The way being opened up was the focal point
of numerous black spirituals:

> When Moses and his soldiers
> From Egypt's land did flee,
> His enemies were in behind him
> And in front of him the sea.
> God raised the waters like a wall
> And opened up the way,
> And the God that lived in Moses' time
> Is just the same today.

Because Moses' God is the same today, the Moses of
Africa, Moses Tubman, could confidently stretch out her
hand over the sea of slavery, for the Lord would "trouble the
waters" of oppression with a strong east wind all night:

---

[56] "Ride on, Moses."

> Wade in water, children (*3X*)
> God's gonna trouble the water.[57]

Pass into the abyss of water and fire, children; there shall be war in the water!

> When you pass through the water, I will be with you;
> And through the rivers, they shall not overwhelm you;
> When you walk through fire you shall not be burned,
> And the flame shall not consume you (Isa. 43:2).

The Waters Returned and Covered the Chariots

The Lord said to Moses, "Stretch out your hand over the sea, that the water may come back upon the Egyptians, upon their chariots, and upon their horsemen. . . ." The waters returned and covered the chariots and the horsemen and all the host of Pharaoh that had followed them into the sea; not so much as one of them remained (Exod. 14:26–29).

The moment the water came back upon the Egyptians, their chariots, and their horsemen, not one of them remained. It should have been an Egyptian victory with all their military might and skill. But God fought for his helpless children. Such triumph, similar to that of the resurrected Lord, occurs when "death is swallowed up in victory" (1 Cor. 15:54). Israel rose; and the people of Africa celebrated in anticipation of their own emancipation:

> Then down came raging Pharaoh
> That you may plainly see,
> Ole Pharaoh and his host
> Got lost in the Red Sea.[58]

Passing through the Red Sea and being saved was an eschatological event of such proportion that in the Israelites' spirituals the land on the other side was often perceived as the promised land across the River Jordan. In the lyrical discourse of DuBois, "Emancipation was the key to a promised land of sweeter beauty than ever stretched before the eyes of wearied Israelites."[59] The promised land of sweeter beauty

---

[57] Respectively, "He's Just the Same Today" and "Wade in Water."
[58] "Didn't Ole Pharaoh Get Lost."
[59] DuBois, 216.

was perceived by faith as "Sweet Beuly Land" in the spirituals, the place of the gospel feast "way over in the Rock of
Ages" "where sabbaths have no end."

Lovell concurs with DuBois that the key of emancipation opened the gates of the heavenly promised land. When
the enslaved sang "when I get to heav'n," says Lovell, they
meant "when I get free."[60] Witvliet makes a strong case for
the foregoing consensus:

> That for slaves heaven is as it were a historical category
> and not an idea of a metaphysical reality is evident from
> the connection which the spirituals constantly make with
> the exodus story. For them this story is an experienced
> reality: they are the chosen people ("we are de people of
> de Lord," "we are de people of God") on the way to the
> promised land ("To the promised land I'm bound to go").

"Heaven," concludes Witvliet, "is a reality which is described
in extremely evocative terms, in which above all the stress is
on what no longer occurs."[61]

Perhaps heaven was whichever kingdom came first to
Africans engaged in life-denying feats of courage. Or as
Lovell suggests, heaven meant the land of freedom first and
the world beyond death later.[62] For instance, when Moses
Tubman had completed one of her many passages from
Maryland to Canada, or from Egypt to Canaan, as the fugi-
tives figured it,[63] she said: "only one more journey for me
now, and dat is to Hebben!"[64]

> O wasn't that a wide river, dat river of Jordan, Lord,
> Wide river! There's one more river to cross.[65]

The Lord Saved Israel

> Thus the Lord saved Israel that day from the hand of
> the Egyptians; and Israel saw the Egyptians dead upon
> the seashore (Exod. 14:30).

[60] Lovell, 343.
[61] Witvliet, 204, 203.
[62] Lovell, 343.
[63] John F. Bayliss, ed., *Black Slave Narratives* (New York: Macmillan, 1970),
117.
[64] Ibid., 122.
[65] "O Wasn't That a Wide River?"

The "heaven" portrayed in the spirituals was a reality described in such evocative terms that emancipation and salvation appeared to comprise a homogeneous whole. What seems to be the value of freedom, Cone describes as "a style of freedom that included but did not depend upon historical possibilities."[66] With reference to the spiritual "Oh Freedom," he explains:

> Oh Freedom! Oh Freedom!
> Oh Freedom, I love thee!
> And before I'll be a slave,
> I'll be buried in my grave
> And go home to my Lord and be free.

Says Cone:

> Here freedom is obviously a structure of, and a movement in, historical existence. It is black slaves accepting the risk and burden of self-affirmation, of liberation in history. That is the meaning of the phrase, "And before I'll be a slave, I'll be buried in my grave." But without negating history, the last line of this spiritual places freedom beyond the historical context. "And go home to my Lord and be free." In this context, freedom is eschatological. It is anticipation of freedom, a vision of a new heaven and a new earth. Black slaves recognized that human freedom is transcendent—that is, a constituent of the future—which made it impossible to identify humanity exclusively with meager attainment in history.[67]

In his *Twelve Years a Slave,* Solomon Northup spoke of a slave named Patsey who struggled with the physical and spiritual notions of heaven. "A thousand times she had heard that somewhere in the distant North there were no slaves—no masters. In her imagination it was an enchanted region, the Paradise of the earth."[68] Patsey's experience was that of a human being attempting but unable to transcend her real nature. What she thought was God-consciousness was essentially self-consciousness. Illustrating this principal of projection,

---

[66] Cone, "Black Spirituals," 67.
[67] Cone, *God of the Oppressed,* 11.
[68] Northup, 200–201.

Ludwig Feuerbach says, "If God were an object to a bird, he would be a winged being: the bird knows nothing higher, nothing more blissful than the winged condition."[69] Michael Walzer concurs with Feuerbach. He says that because Egypt was a land of milk and honey (Num. 16:13a), God's divine promise of milk and honey of their own was shaped to the Israelites' consciousness. Correlatively, says Walzer, "Canaan is a promised land because Egypt is a house of bondage."[70]

If Feuerbach and Walzer are well-grounded in their theory that the self can know nothing higher than itself, then to the slave God could only be an unharnessed God and heaven a wide-open freedom, inclusive of but not dependent on transcendent possibilities. To the enslaved (a liberated soul in a shackled body) God could only be a God of free will and heaven a realm of deliverance, inclusive of but not dependent on historical possibilities—a dyadic cosmos existing midway between the North and the North Star, "way in the middle of the air."

> Over my head I see freedom in the air (*3X*)
> There must be a God somewhere.[71]

The People of Israel Sang

Moses and the people of Israel sang this song to the Lord, saying. . . (Exod. 15:1–18).

Moses Tubman and the people of Africa sang this song to the Lord:

> I'm on my way to Canada,
>   That cold and dreary land;
> The sad effects of slavery,
>   I can't no longer stand.
> I've served my master all my days,
>   Widout a dime's reward;
> And now I'm forced to run away,
>   To flee the lash abroad.

[69] Ludwig Feuerbach, *The Essence of Christianity*, trans. George Eliot (New York: Harper, 1957), 11–12, 17.

[70] Michael Walzer, *Exodus and Revolution* (New York: Basic Books, 1985), 21, 39–40, 21.

[71] Respectively, "John Saw the Number" and "Over My Head."

CHORUS
Farewell, ole master
Don't think hard of me,
I'll travel on to Canada
Where all the slaves are free.

The hounds are baying on my track,
    Ole master comes behind,
Resolved that he will bring me back,
    Before I cross de line.
I'm now embarked for yonder shore,
    There a man's a man by law;
The iron horse will bear me o'er,
    To shake de lion's paw.

CHORUS
Oh, righteous Father,
Wilt thou not pity me,
And aid me on to Canada
Where all the slaves are free.

Oh, I heard Queen Victoria say,
    That if we would forsake
Our native land of slavery,
    And come across the lake;
That she was standin' on de shore,
    Wid arms extended wide,
To give us all a peaceful home
    Beyond de rolling tide.[72]

Sing to the Lord

Miriam, the prophetess, the sister of Aaron, took a timbrel in her hand; and all the women went out after her with timbrels and dancing. And Miriam sang to them: "Sing to the Lord, for he has triumphed gloriously; the horse and his rider he has thrown into the sea" (Exod. 15:20–21).

For the people of Africa *passing through* was not a singular event. Gustavo Gutiérrez explained that the many passages were "partial fulfillments through liberating events,

---

[72] Bayliss, 119–20.

which [were] in turn new promises marking the road toward total fulfillment."[73] These partial fulfillments were historical rites of passage that made the enslaved's world revolve, albeit ever so slowly.

One of the many partial fulfillments is told by a firsthand biographer of Harriet Tubman. It is Moses Tubman, a *mother,* who brought the fugitives through the womb of the sea into life, and Joe, a *son,* who goes out and dances and sings:

> Harriet knew by the rise in the center of the bridge, and the descent on the other side, that they had crossed "the line." She sprang across to Joe's seat, shook him with all her might, and shouted, "Joe, you've shook de lion's paw!" Joe did not know what she meant. "Joe, you're *free!*" shouted Harriet. Then Joe's head went up, he raised his hands on high, and his face, streaming with tears, to heaven, and broke out in loud and thrilling tones:
>
> > Glory to God and Jesus too,
> >   One more soul is safe!
> > Oh, go and carry de news,
> >   One more soul got safe. . . .
>
> Loud roared the waters of Niagra, but louder still ascended the anthem of praise from the overflowing heart of the freeman. And can we doubt that the strain was taken up by angel voices, and that through the arches of Heaven echoed and reechoed the strain:
>
> > Glory to God in the Highest,
> > Glory to God and Jesus too,
> > One more soul is safe.[74]

If You Will Obey My Voice

You have seen what I did to the Egyptians, and how I bore you on eagles' wings and brought you to myself. Now therefore, if you will obey my voice and keep my covenant, you shall be my own possession among all

---

[73] Gustavo Gutiérrez, *A Theology of Liberation: History, Politics and Salvation* (Maryknoll, N.Y.: Orbis Books, 1973), 167.
[74] Bayliss, 120–21.

peoples; for all the earth is mine, and you shall be to
me a kingdom of priests and a holy nation (Exod.
19:4–6).

If Herzog is well grounded in his position that transcendent freedom prompts human beings to manifest it in
historical freedom, and transgression is the negation of
transcendent freedom and the succumbing to oppression,[75]
then being a "holy nation" was the only way the people of
Africa could achieve unconditional emancipation. The spirituals indicated that God's promise of a land flowing with
milk and honey of their own included the condition, "*if* you
will obey my voice and keep my covenant." God would indeed bring them out of bondage on eagles' wings and they
would be free, but by teaching and admonishing one another in their spiritual songs they learned that God's full
liberation required priestliness and holiness.

> You must have that true religion,
> You must have your soul converted.
> You must have that true religion
> Or you *can't cross* there.

Before one could ride the "gospel train" to freedom, or
"cross there," one's house had to be in order and one's ticket
to ride divinely signed:

> If the Son grant my ticket, the Holy Ghost sign,
> Then there's no way to be left behind.

Prior to Paul and Silas's "crossing there," namely, being freed
from prison, they had to be "reborn again."

> Paul and Silas they in jail
>   O got to reborn again,
> One keep watch while the other one pray,
>   O got to reborn again.[76]

Rebirth through the passage of the womb of redemption allowed one to "cross there":

[75] Herzog, 84, 81.
[76] Respectively, "You Must Have that True Religion" (emphasis added), "If I
Have My Ticket," and "Reborn Again."

Paul and Silas bound in Jail (*3X*)
Nothin' but the blood of Jesus can pay their bail.[77]

The people of Africa realized that if, figuratively speaking,
the requirements of priestliness and holiness were conditions
for having their own milk and honey, then crossing the River
Jordan actually preceded the crossing of the Red Sea.[78]

Invest Him with Some of Your Authority

The Lord said to Moses, "Take Joshua the son of Nun, a
man in whom is the spirit, and lay your hand upon him;
cause him to stand before Eleazar the priest and all the
congregation, and you shall commission him in their
sight. You shall invest him with some of your authority,
that all the congregation of the people of Israel may
obey" (Num. 27:18–20).

The Lord directed Moses to lay his hand upon Joshua
and invest in him some authority in the sight of the priest and
all the congregation so that the people would obey him;
Joshua was thereby commissioned the "second Moses," the
one who would deliver the people of Israel across the River
Jordan into the land of Canaan.

For the people of Africa, Jesus was Joshua the "second
Moses" (both names mean *deliverer*). Witvliet alludes to this
by claiming that the exodus story forms the context which
allowed the appearance of Jesus as messiah and liberator to
be localized. In this framework the people of Africa viewed
Jesus Christ as a "second Moses."[79] Leonardo Boff explains
the correlation between Moses and Jesus by presenting a view
of the "first" and "new" Moses found in the spirituals:

---

[77] "Walk about Elders."

[78] If we assume that such spirituals were always masking concrete liberative
meaning, to the exclusion of any Christian literalism, then Joseph Washington
would be correct in his assumption that "when a spiritual speaks of freedom it is
outside the context of the Christian faith" (Washington, *Black Religion*, 217). If this
were so, then liberation, which is God's gift to those who keep the covenant, would
be unattainable. It is probable, however, that these spirituals were sometimes principally songs of faith and other times principally songs of escape, but in any case
they were both songs of faith and escape.

[79] Witvliet, 205.

> In New Testament times people believed that the
> Messiah-Liberator of the last days would also be a new
> Moses, performing signs and miracles just like Moses.
> They would even say that the liberator (the Messiah) is
> like unto the first (Moses). We know that Matthew in
> his Gospel presents Jesus as a new Moses, that like the
> first liberator Jesus too gave a new law.[80]

Dan Cohn-Sherbok concurs that Jesus is "the typological cor-
relate of Moses";[81] however, Herzog warns that the Jesus
figure "is not a sheer duplication of the exodus," that "it is a
new event with its own validity."[82]

The Jesus of the spirituals was not a duplication of the
exodus. He was a much greater creation. He was Christ-
Moses, the Messiah-Liberator. Because the people of Africa
adopted the exodus as their life narrative, passing through the
abyss was baptism with water into Moses; but because they
were a resurrection people, passing through was also baptism
with fire and the Spirit into Christ. Therefore, their real-life
experiences of passing through were the combined liberation
efforts of Christ-Moses. This joining of personages is speci-
fied in the lines of a spiritual: "Oh Mary, don't you weep, don't
you moan/ . . . Pharaoh's army got drownded." Mary Mag-
dalene need not murmur because Christ-Moses, even in his
crucifixion, could not be subjugated by Pharaoh's army; for he
victoriously passed through the womb of creation/Red Sea/
gates of hell/eye of the needle, leaving Pharaoh swallowed up
in the fiery abyss.[83] These four meta-historical rites of passage
converged in a single exalted moment of revelation—Christ-
Moses rose! Moses and Christ Jesus mounted up to be Christ-
Moses, whose eschatological favor of freedom constituted the
fullness of liberation. Just as in other spirituals the Red Sea
and the River Jordan comprised a holistic point of passage, the
"crossing there" of which (w)hole led to a "heaven" inclusive of
but not dependent on historical possibilities.

[80] Boff, 173–74.
[81] Cohn-Sherbok, 78.
[82] Frederick Herzog, *Justice Church: The New Function of the Church in North
American Christianity* (Maryknoll, N.Y.: Orbis Books, 1980), 4.
[83] See Gutiérrez, 154–55, for an argument for creation as a saving act of
liberation.

The religion of the enslaved African people allowed for the fullness of liberation, "freedom-in-bondage" and "freedom from bondage."[84] Those who "went out" sought freedom from bondage in God's revelation of liberation through Moses. Those who remained in bondage sought freedom-in-bondage in God's revelation of liberation through Christ Jesus. And the spirituals keenly taught that the full freedom from bondage was preceded by freedom-in-bondage—holistically the Christ-Moses passage. In the spirituals the belief was fundamentally trinitarian—Moses the human liberator; Christ the holy Spirit; Jesus, comforter and redeemer of sin; and the transcendent God revealing God's real person in situations of liberation: God the Creator-Revelator (Maker), God the Freedom-Fighter (Christ Moses), God the Redeemer-Comforter (Holy Spirit Jesus)—God the Revelator, Freedom-Fighter, Liberator. However, when the people of Africa sang "Singin' with a sword in my hand, *Lord,*" the godhead was *one*.

The Lord Commissioned Joshua

And the Lord commissioned Joshua the son of Nun and said, "Be strong and of good courage; for you shall bring the children of Israel into the land which I swore to give them; I will be with you" (Deut. 31:23).

The people of Africa projected Jesus into the exodus story fully knowing that he was commissioned to commence and consummate a process of *maturation-into-liberation* that Moses and even Joshua were unable to fulfill. Moses could lead the people of Africa through the Red Sea, past "the separatin' line," to physical freedom; but standing on the banks of the River Jordan, only through (Jesus/Joshua) the Christ-Moses could they cross. Saint Paul alludes to Christ's presence in Moses:

I want you to know . . . that our fathers were all under the cloud, and all passed through the sea, and all were baptized into Moses in the cloud and in the sea, and all

---

[84] James H. Cone, *The Spirituals and the Blues: An Interpretation* (New York: Seabury Press, 1972), 30.

ate the same supernatural food and all drank from the same supernatural drink. For they drank from the supernatural Rock which followed them, and the Rock was Christ (1 Cor. 10:1–4).

Jesus Christ, the deification of Joshua—Moses projected out into the transcendent—was, in the words of Bloch, "the new eschatological Exodus," "the *Exodus into God as man,* "[85] thus making him, as Cone says, "the eternal event of liberation."[86] Jesus is, says Boff, "the new Moses, who now, at the apex of history and at its final moment, will take the people of the exodus from Egypt to a definitive homeland."[87] But Christ-Moses of the spirituals was not only the passage, he was, using Gutiérrez's words, "the *Promise,*" that "unfolds . . . in the *promises* made by God throughout history."[88] The exodus is, as Míguez-Bonino says, "fulfilled and deepened in Jesus Christ,"[89] because "the Promise is not exhausted by these promises nor by their fulfillment; it goes beyond them, explains them, and gives them their ultimate meaning."[90]

Christ *the Promise* has promised a promised land (John 14:2–3). It is Canaan, the promised land Moses promised projected into eternity. Because it is a land that is always coming—disallowing any flesh to claim, "Alas, it is here,"— liberation is best understood as a process of maturation. It is an "ever-increasing freedom, a growth into greater freedom,"[91] which the spirituals conceive of as a train of promises and passages. Such linking together occurs in history, which is an "ongoing process" leading toward "the utopia of absolute liberation."[92] This promise (summed up in Jesus Christ) "is *already* fulfilled in historical events, but *not yet* completely; it incessantly projects itself into the future, creating permanent historical mobility."[93] For the people of Africa the ongoing process of ever-increasing

[85] Bloch, 137.
[86] Cone, *God of the Oppressed,* 34.
[87] Boff, 174.
[88] Gutiérrez, 161.
[89] Míguez-Bonino, 205.
[90] Gutiérrez, 161.
[91] Herzog, *Liberation Theology,* 126.
[92] Boff, 281, 280.
[93] Gutiérrez, 161.

freedom was distilled in the image of "climbing Jacob's ladder":

> We are climbing Jacob's ladder (*3X*)
> Soldiers of the cross.
>
> Every round goes higher, higher (*3X*)
> Soldiers of the cross.[94]

"Every round goes higher, higher."

[94] "We Are Climbing Jacob's Ladder." See also "You Go, I'll Go with You" and "To See God's Bleeding Lamb" for additional images of Jacob's ladder.

2

Songs of the Free:
Moral Abolitionism in Antislavery Hymnody

The Sacredness of Abolitionist Verse

"How natural for Music, as well as Poetry to be on the side of Humanity and the Captive."[1] "No sentiment inspires men to such exalted strains as the love of liberty."[2] "The poets are with us."[3] These lines by Nathaniel P. Rogers, founder and editor of the (New Hampshire) *Herald of Freedom*, Samuel J. May, Unitarian minister and Garrisonian, and Frederick Douglass ("the fugitive Othello"), founder and editor of the *North Star,* are glimpses into the hallowed office bestowed upon abolitionist verse and song. Not necessarily written to be sung, much of this sacred poetry was first published in antislavery newspapers, journals, tracts, and anthologies by writers who were either abolitionists or "friends

---

[1] Nathaniel Peabody Rogers, "The Hutchinson Singers" (from the *Herald of Freedom*, Dec. 9, 1842), in *A Collection from the Miscellaneous Writings of Nathaniel Peabody Rogers* (Manchester, N.H.: William H. Fisk; Boston: Benjamin B. Mussey & Co., 1849), 244.

[2] Samuel J. May, *Some Recollections of Our Anti-Slavery Conflict* (Boston: Fields, Osgood, & Co., 1869), 260.

[3] Frederick Douglass, "The Anti-Slavery Movement" (lecture given before anti-slavery organizations in the winter of 1855), in *My Bondage and My Freedom* (New York and Auburn: Miller, Orton & Mulligan, 1855), Facsimile reprint (New York: Dover, 1969), 462.

of freedom."[4] "The columns of *The Liberator,* from the beginning," said Samuel May, "were every week enriched by gems
in verse, not unfrequently the product of [William Lloyd
Garrison's] own rapt soul."[5] As an indication of scholarship in
addresses and essays, verses also graced the often brusque
language of ultra-abolitionism.

The Garrisonian Hymnbooks

Between 1834 and 1856 abolition verse, or what Garrison called "fugitive poetical effusions," were compiled
into a dozen songbooks and hymnals. The initial publication
was a pamphlet printed the year following the charter of the
American Anti-Slavery Society by the arch-elder of abolition, William Lloyd Garrison. Titled *A Selection of Anti-
Slavery Hymns, for the Use of Friends of Emancipation* (1834),[6]
classic hymn tunes by Elizabeth M. Chandler, Lydia H.

---

[4] *Poems on the Abolition of the Slave Trade; Written by James Montgomery, James
Grahame, and E. Benger* (London: Printed for R. Bowyer, 1809); Lydia H. Sigour-
ney, *Moral Pieces in Prose and Verse* (1815); William Cowper, *The Negro's Com-
plaint: A Poem. To Which is Added Pity for Poor Africans* (London: Printed for
Harvey and Darton, 1826); George Moses Horton, *Poems by a Slave* (Raleigh:
Gales & Son, 1829); William Lloyd Garrison, comp., *Juvenile Poems, for the Use of
Free American Children, of Every Complexion* (Boston: Garrison & Knapp, 1835);
*Slavery Rhymes, Addressed to the Friends of Liberty Throughout the United States. By a
Looker On* (New York: John S. Taylor, 1837); John Greenleaf Whittier, *Poems
Written During the Progress of the Abolition Question in the United States, Between the
Years 1830 and 1838* (Boston: Isaac Knapp, 1837); *Emancipation. Poem Dedicated by
the Board of the Boston Female Anti-Slavery Society, to the Women of Great Britain, in
Commemoration of their Untiring Efforts in the Cause of British West India. By a
Member of the Board* (Boston: Boston Female Anti-Slavery Society, 1839); *Star of
Emancipation* (Boston: For the Fair of the Massachusetts Female Emancipation
Society, 1841); William Lloyd Garrison, *Sonnets and Other Poems* (Boston: Oliver
Johnson, 1843), republished under the title *Sonnets* (Upper Saddle River, N.J.:
Literature House/ Gregg Press, 1970); John Pierpont, *The Anti-Slavery Poems
of John Pierpont* (Boston: Oliver Johnson, 1843), republished (Upper Saddle
River, N.J.: Literature House, 1970); John Greenleaf Whittier, *Voices of Freedom*
(Philadelphia: for Thomas S. Cavender; by Boston: Waite, Pierce & Co.; New
York: William Harned, 1846); David Woodward, *Slavery; Its Origin, Progress and
Effects. A Poem* (Boston: John M. Hewes, 1856).

Poetry was also published in such comprehensive periodicals as *The Liberty
Bell: By Friends of Freedom* (Boston: Massachusetts Anti-Slavery Fair, 1839–46;
National Anti-Slavery Bazaar, 1847–58), an annual periodical; *Freedom's Gift: Or
Sentiments of the Free* (Hartford: S. S. Cowles, 1840).

[5] May, 260–61.

[6] William Lloyd Garrison, comp., *A Selection of Anti-Slavery Hymns, for the Use
of the Friends of Emancipation* (Boston: Garrison & Knapp, 1834).

Sigourney, Hannah F. Gould, Charlotte Elizabeth, John Pierpont, Charles W. Denison, James Montgomery, William B. Tappan, James Scott, William J. Snelling, and William Lloyd Garrison were suggested for all but three of its thirty-two pieces. Several anonymous poems were attributed to the *Greensboro Patriot, Genius of Universal Emancipation, African Repository, New York Evangelist,* and *The Liberator.* In summarizing the objective of the publication, Garrison gave this introductory description:

> The rapid multiplication of Anti-Slavery Societies, in various portions of our land, and the frequency of their public convocations, seem to require a judicious selection of Hymns, descriptive of the wrongs and sufferings of our slave population, and calculated to impress upon the minds of those who read them, or commit them to memory, or hear them sung, a deep sense of their obligations to assist in undoing every burden, breaking every yoke, and setting every captive free. Hitherto, in all meetings for the delivery of anti-slavery addresses, much embarrassment has been felt, in consequence of the difficulty of finding in the Hymn Books which are in common use, appropriate pieces to be sung on those occasions: hence the earnest desire has been widely expressed that the defect might be remedied by a collection of anti-slavery hymns. I have therefore ventured to make the following collection, as an experiment, which, if it succeed, may lead to something better and more voluminous.

Garrison resolved with a barrage of moral persuasion, "May the God of the oppressed bless it to the advancement of the cause of humanity and righteousness!"

If William Lloyd Garrison was "one of God's nobility—the head of the moral aristocracy," as Harriet Martineau vouched, then Maria Weston Chapman was Garrisonian gentry, whom the women of the Boston Female Anti-Slavery Society dubbed "Captain Chapman."[7] *Songs of the Free and*

---

[7] Harriet Martineau, *The Martyr Age of the United States* (Boston: Weeks, Jordan & Co., Otis, Broaders & Co.; New York: Jogn S. Taylor, 1839), 7, 28.

Hymns of Christian Freedom (1836),[8] compiled by Chapman two years later, is probably the improved and larger work Garrison had envisioned. It was printed by the same Boston publisher, Garrison's good friend Isaac Knapp (who also published his *Liberator*). Its 188 pieces incorporate nearly half, fourteen of the thirty-two hymns in the 1834 primer. Furthermore, the preface to Chapman's volume indicated that she was a devoted draftee into the antislavery moralism and pacifism of the Garrisonian guerrilla warfare:

> Those who are laboring for the freedom of the American slave, have felt their need of aid which has ever been sought by those in all ages who have striven for the good of their race;—the encouragement, consolation and strength afforded by poetry and music. This generally expressed feeling was the origin of the present book of hymns. . . .
>
> They feel that the spiritual warfare in which they are engaged, requires the exercise of all the faculties; and they cannot allow the opponents of their principles the selection of the moral and intellectual powers with which it shall be carried on,—no, though this free use of their own souls should occasion men to call them agitators and fanatics.

Chapman's hymnbook, unlike the primer of her mentor, provided classic hymn meters rather than suggested hymn tunes. And incorporated alongside the reform poetry of Pierpont, Montgomery, Whittier, Garrison, and other abolitionists were the hymns of Watts, Wesley, Doane, Heber, Newton, and other compatriotic saints of the evangelic community. Chapman, a vanguard feminist and member of Boston's Female Anti-Slavery Society, included, in addition to seven of her own pieces, a large representation of poetry by women poets: Elizabeth M. Chandler, the Quaker poet who supervised the "Ladies Department" of the weekly *Genius,* Eliza

---

[8] Maria Weston Chapman, comp., *Songs of the Free and Hymns of Christian Freedom* (Boston: Isaac Knapp, 1836). See the facsimile reprint (Freeport, N.Y.: Books for Libraries Press, 1971).

Follen, Felecia Hemans, Harriet Martineau, Lydia Sigourney, and Anne Weston. Footnotes and extended annotations
from various writings[9] added a distinctive literary quality to
Chapman's work.[10]

Chapman explained that in adapting some of the evangelical pieces to abolitionism "slight alterations have been
made in a few of the Hymns . . . not with the idea of increasing their literary merit . . . but of increasing their use-
fulness in this book." This footnote to "The Lord is Great! Ye
Hosts of Heaven, Adore Him" substantiated her altering a
line from "O'er sin, and death, and hell, now made victorious" to "O'er fraud, and war, and slavery, made victorious."
Her comment reveals theological considerations involved in
making editorial modifications:

> These words have been used till they have lost their origi-
> nal force and depth of meaning. In these days, when
> *wrong* is denied to be sin, and death and hell are denied to
> be the natural consequence of sin—when God's laws are
> declared by salaried ministers, to be less binding than
> man's laws—when the advocates of crime profess to have
> ability to calculate consequences with such certainty as to
> stand in no need of revelation—when man's devices are
> substituted for God's commands, and all consequences
> calculated but the final consequences; it is well that our
> religious ideas should be clearly defined. The words war,
> slavery, intemperance, aristocracy, [etc.] introduced into
> a page, "like water-drops on some dim picture's hue,"
> give clearness and distinctness to the whole.

At the request of the Executive Committee of the American Anti-Slavery Society, Edwin F. Hatfield, a Presbyterian

---

[9] Such footnotes and annotations were commonly used to strengthen the anti-
slavery argument. For instance, George W. Clark closed his *The Harp of Freedom*
(1856) with "A Cloud of Witnesses," an appendix containing antislavery dictums
from the great philosophers, theologians, and politicians, as well as excerpts from
political documents condemning slavery.

[10] While explaining the placement of the hymn meters to the Index of First
Lines, Chapman's preface alludes that these pieces were meant to be read as well as
sung: "The machinery of meters, names of tunes, numerals, and characters, has
been omitted, because they are useless to those who are unable to sing, and because the spirit and the understanding are a sufficient directory to those who can."

clergyman and hymnologist,[11] compiled an antislavery hymn-book. The hymnal, published in 1840, was given the affectionate title of *Freedom's Lyre: Or, Psalms, Hymns, and Sacred Songs for the Slave and His Friends.*[12] Like Chapman's volume this work included half of the 32 pieces in Garrison's *Anti-Slavery Hymns.* The fact that *Freedom's Lyre* remained committed to "moral insurrection" and was untainted by the "divinity of politics" is the distinct Garrisonian signature. It is likely that both *Songs of the Free* and *Freedom's Lyre* were the progeny of Garrison's prophetic agenda.

Garrison and Chapman were radical abolitionists; Hatfield was probably more of a "friend of the slave." Biographical documents among his personal papers neither list antislavery organizations among his memberships nor *Freedom's Lyre* as one of his publications.[13] In his posthumous magnum opus, *The Poets of the Church* (1884), he also disregards the foremost reform poets—Pierpont, Martineau, Chapman, Chandler, and Whittier—and his biographical treatment of Montgomery and Sigourney completely neglects their antislavery verse. The implication is that the American Anti-Slavery Society commissioned Hatfield to compile *Freedom's Lyre* because of his hymnological expertise and not because of his active involvement in abolition. Nevertheless, of the complete corpus of antislavery song and hymnbooks, *Freedom's Lyre* was the most reverent and well wrought. *Freedom's Lyre* was the only authentic hymnal solely

[11] Edwin Francis Hatfield's (1807–83) later hymnological works: *The Church Hymn Book for the Worship of God* (New York: Ivison, Blakeman, Taylor & Co., 1872); an abridgement to which tunes are added: *The Chapel Hymn Book, With Tunes; for the Worship of God* (New York: Ivison, Blakeman, Taylor & Co., 1873), and a posthumous work, *The Poets of the Church: A Series of Biographical Sketches of Hymn-Writers, with Notes on Their Hymns* (New York: Anson D. F. Randolph & Co., 1884).

The two hymnals commissioned by the publisher contained songs of praise, several by Hatfield, and had no relationship to abolitionism.

[12] In 1969 an enlarged facsimile reprint of *Freedom's Lyre* was issued by the Mnemosyne Publishing Co., Miami.

[13] These premises are derived from the study of sermons, clippings, and biographical documents in the Edwin Francis Hatfield collection at the Presbyterian Historical Society, Philadelphia. Further evidence of my theory is that all of Hatfield's publications, except *Freedom's Lyre*, are available here. Neither is it listed among his works in the *Encyclopedia of the Presbyterian Church in the United States of America,* ed. Alfred Nevin (Philadelphia: Presbyterian Encyclopedic Publishing Co., 1884), 309–10.

devoted to the abolition of the African slave trade.[14] Because the volume amassed a diversity of hymns and psalms theologically categorized in a well-delineated table of contents, it is a paramount source for the theological study of American abolitionism.

The Antislavery Songbooks

The two decades following the appearance of *Freedom's Lyre* produced a variety of antislavery songbooks published in Massachusetts, New York, and Ohio, where abolitionism flourished and slavery was abolished early. In contrast to the three Garrisonian hymnbooks, these compilations comprised more secular pieces. Parodies and other popular verse sung to minstrel ditties such as "Dandy Jim" and "Dan Tucker" could hardly be considered serious liturgical music. The Garrisonian hymnbooks embodied no such frill and frolic, but an intrinsic religiosity still smoldered beneath the extrinsic secularity of these later verses; for the antislavery movement, out of which these popular songs initially evolved, was a by-product of nineteenth-century revivalism. In this regard, abolitionism was a radical testimony of conversion and sanctification, and the ecumenical holy communion of the American Anti-Slavery Society was a moral malignancy eating at the nation's impiety:

> The Anti-Slavery movement (as conducted, for twenty-three years past, by the American Anti-Slavery Society) was at its commencement, and has ever since been, thoroughly and emphatically a *religious* enterprise. The earliest official documents of that Society (its Constitution and its Declaration of Sentiments, both adopted at Philadelphia in 1833) show that its prominent and preponderating appeal was to religious considerations; that

[14] The Wesleyan Methodists published *Miriam's Timbrel: Sacred Songs, Suited to Revival Occasions; and also for Anti-Slavery, Peace, Temperance, and Reform Meetings* (1853), but as its title suggests, it was not only an antislavery hymnal. *Miriam's Timbrel*, 2d ed., comp. John P. Betker (Mansfield, Ohio: Wesleyan Methodist Church, 1853). This hymnbook best exemplifies the assimilation of the social and the spiritual, holiness and humanitarianism. Among its antislavery hymns is William Lloyd Garrison's popular "Ye Who in Bondage Pine," which was sung to the tune of "America." Timothy L. Smith, *Revivalism and Social Reform: American Protestantism on the Eve of the Civil War* (New York: Harper & Row, 1965), 212–13.

Slavery, whatever else it might be, was *first,* "a heinous
crime in the sight of God;" that immediate emancipation
was the divinely imposed "duty" of the slaveholder.[15]

The antislavery songbooks that evolved against this
backdrop of social Christianity were *Anti-Slavery Melodies,*
compiled by Jarius Lincoln (1843); *The Liberty Minstrel,* 199
pieces compiled by George W. Clark (1844); *A Collection of
Miscellaneous Songs, from the Liberty Minstrel, and Mason's Juvenile Harp; for the Use of the Cincinnati High School,* 48 pieces
compiled by H. S. Gilmore (1845); *The Anti-Slavery Harp,* 48
pieces compiled by William Wells Brown (1848);[16] *The Free
Soil Minstrel,* 140 pieces compiled by George W. Clark (1848);
Anti-Slavery Songs, an anonymous collection of 59 pieces
(1849); *Original Anti-Slavery Songs,* 13 poems by Joshua Mc-
Carter Simpson (1852); and *The Harp of Freedom,* 192 pieces
compiled by George W. Clark (1856).[17] These songbooks

[15] Charles K. Whipple, "Relations of Anti-Slavery to Religion" (Anti-Slavery
Tracts, no. 19). New York: American Anti-Slavery Society, 1856. See the facsimile
reprint (Westport, Conn.: Negro Universities Press, 1970), 1.
   The attack upon slaveholders was made on religious grounds. As early as
1816, Rev. George Bourne, a Presbyterian minister, provided William Lloyd
Garrison with the liberal theological language of "ultra-abolition." Notice Bourne
is uncompromising:
   "Very few *Men-Stealers* comparatively, are even *nominal* Christian Believers.
How can a person pretend to be a disciple of the crucified Jesus, who hinders his
worship and contravenes his commands; in whom all evangelical charity is extinct;
and who will neither enter the kingdom of heaven, nor permit those to approach
who would crave admission at the gate? The spirit of Christianity and the practices
of *Men-thieves* are a total oppugnation; and consequently they exert their energies
to counteract the progress of pure and undefiled religion." George Bourne, *The
Book and Slavery Irreconcilable* (Philadelphia: J. M. Sanderson, 1816), republished
(Wilmington, Del.: The Historical Society of Delaware; Philadelphia: The Presbyterian Historical Society, 1969, with an introduction by John W. Christie and
Dwight L. Dumond), 130.
   [16] William Wells Brown's volume was indebted to the earlier *Anti-Slavery
Melodies* and *The Liberty Minstrel.* Perhaps his prefatory comment that his volume
contains "songs of a more recent composition" is to say that, in contrast to Chap-
man and Hatfield, he excludes classic hymns. Among the selection are pieces by
Pierpont, Whittier, Lowell, Garrison, and Jesse Hutchinson, Jr., the elder brother
and organizer of The Hutchinsons.
   Closer attention to Brown's volume and its relationship to that of Lincoln and
Clark can be found in William Edward Farrison's *William Wells Brown: Author and
Reformer* (Chicago: The University of Chicago Press, 1969), 122–26. Eileen South-
ern also refers to it in her history, *The Music of Black Americans* (New York: W. W.
Norton, 1971), 126–28.
   [17] Jarius Lincoln, *Anti-Slavery Melodies: For the Friends of Freedom* (Hingham,
Mass. [Prepared for the Hingham Anti-Slavery Society], 1843); George W. Clark,

characteristically suggested "airs" (tunes) to which the verses were to be sung. Lincoln's and Clark's volumes were the only ones to incorporate written music.

George Washington Clark's contribution was primarily to political abolitionism. His seven editions of *The Liberty Minstrel* (1845–48)[18] were aligned with the platform of the Liberty Party, as evidenced in such songs as "The Liberty Party," "The Liberty Flag," "Birney and Liberty," "Ode to James G. Birney," and "The Election" (Birney being the party's candidate for the 1840 presidential election). Correspondingly, the politico-prospectus of *The Liberty Minstrel* was, as enunciated by Clark in its preface, to uplift the wrongs of slavery, the blessings of liberty, and the equality of humanity; "Until by familiarity with these sentiments, and their influence upon their *hearts, the people,* whose *duty it is,* shall 'undo the heavy burdens and let the oppressed go free.'"

The Free Soil Minstrel (1848) was essentially *The Liberty Minstrel* adapted to the Free Soil Party, the successor of the Liberty Party. Pieces like "The Free Soil Debate," "The Free Soil Gathering," "The Free Soilers' Song," and "The Free Soil Chorus" replaced most of the Liberty songs. In agreement with the party's compromise on the issue of

---

The Liberty Minstrel (New York: Leavitt, Alden, Jackson & Chaplin, 1844); William Wells Brown, comp., *The Anti-Slavery Harp: A Collection of Songs for Anti-Slavery Meetings* (Boston: Bela Marsh, 1848); H. S. Gilmore, comp., *A Collection of Miscellaneous Songs, from the Liberty Minstrel, and Mason's Juvenile Harp; for the Use of the Cincinnati High School* (Cincinnati: Sparhawk & Lytle Printers, 1845); George W. Clark, comp., *The Free Soil Minstrel* (New York: Martyn & Ely, 1848); *Anti-Slavery Songs: A Selection from the Best Anti-Slavery Authors* (Salem, Ohio: I. Trescott & Co., 1849); *Original Anti-Slavery Songs, by Joshua McCarter Simpson, a Colored Man* (Zanesville, Ohio: The Author, 1852); *Lays of Liberty; Or, Verses for the Times* (Boston: Bela Marsh, 1854); George W. Clark, comp., *The Harp of Freedom* (New York: Miller, Orton & Mulligan; Boston: J. P. Jewett & Co.; Rochester, N.Y.: The Author, 1856).

In addition is a small body of abolitionist sheet music. Intended to be sung in concert, this music is written in a classical idiom for voice and piano: Henry Russell, "The Slave Ship, A Descriptive Song" (London: Brewer & Co., n.d.); Henry Russell (music) and Angus B. Reach (text), "The Slave Chase" (London: Chappell, n.d.); Alfred Mullen (music) and R. Kitchen (text), "The Death of Uncle Tom" (London: B. Williams II, n.d.). Two other songs also based on Harriet Beecher Stowe's *Uncle Tom's Cabin* are by Stephen Glover (music) and Charles Jeffreys (text). They are "George's Song of Freedom" and "Sleep My Child, Let No One Hear You" (London: C. Jeffreys, n.d.).

[18] Actually there are two editions, both of which had several reprints. Nineteen new pieces were added to the original volume in an appendix, constituting the sixth and seventh editions.

egalitarianism, the preface of *The Free Soil Minstrel* deleted references to the Liberty party. Maintained verbatim in the preface was a more universal declaration of intent: "An ardent love of humanity—a deep consciousness of the injustice of slavery—a heart full of sympathy for the oppressed, and a due appreciation of the blessings of freedom, has given birth to the poetry comprising this volume."

Again divulging the party's "color phobia" or "negro phobia" (as it was then known), Clark prefaced *The Harp of Freedom* (1856) with an only slightly modified adjuration to reflect the platform of the Republican Party that had displaced the Free Soil Movement two years earlier. In addition to having "an ardent love of humanity" and "a heart full of sympathy," that which gave birth to this volume, wrote Clark, was a deep concern about the outrages of slavery upon "free thought, free speech, a free press, free soil and free men."

Garrison had clamored prophetically that political abolitionism would lose sight of complete racial reform, and that displacing the moral impulse with a civil thrust would cause general compromise in the charter by the fathers of abolition. George Clark retorted in behalf of his party compatriots by omitting Garrison's poems from his three songbooks. Nathaniel Rogers, joining in the dispute on behalf of the Garrisonians, complained that affiliation with politico-abolition had caused compromise in the versification of John Greenleaf Whittier:

> Where is Whittier now, that we no more see his verses streaming up like a "meteor to the troubled air?" What has palsied his muse? Why does he no longer furnish anti-slavery with the poetry for her movement? New Organization has touched his glorious genius with her torporfic wand—and he soars not above the dunghill of Third Party. He ought to be . . . abroad in the moral tempest—letting down sheets of fire—for anti-slavery to inflame her press with. . . . He has hung his bugle on the dog-wood boughs of New Organization.[19]

Frederick Douglass implicated a similar compromise in the poetry of William Cullen Bryant: "Bryant, too, is with us," he

[19] Rogers, "Poetry" (from the *Herald of Freedom*, Nov. 5, 1841), 194–95.

said, "though chained to the car of party, and dragged on amidst a whirl of political excitement."[20]

If the conversion from moral to political abolition (as the latter party movement evolved from Liberty to Free Soil to Republican) were measurable in terms of revivalistic piety, which initially generated social reform, then the political conversion represented a reversion from sanctification and holiness.

Although both popular and political music were intrinsically religious due to their pious origin and pursuit of human liberation, it is doubtful that either was ever used liturgically, particularly the latter whose sidetracked concern had become increasingly less moral. Abolition hymns were perhaps sung in "free" Northern churches formed by those who withdrew (or were forcibly withdrawn) from their denominational affiliations that were unwilling to condemn slavery. The hymns may also have been sung in Northern Wesleyan Methodist churches whose hymnbook, *Miriam's Timbrel* (1853), incorporated antislavery hymns alongside other reform verse.

Antislavery songs were sung by children in schools of the Northern free states, as evidenced in the title of H. S. Gilmore's Ohio primer, *A Collection of Miscellaneous Songs, from the Liberty Minstrel, and Mason's Juvenile Harp; for the Use of the Cincinnati High School.*[21] In the foreword to *The Harp of Freedom*, George Clark recommended his songs be used in "the domestic circle, the social gathering, the school, the club-room, the mass-meeting, and in short, wherever music is loved and appreciated—Slavery abhorred, and Liberty held sacred." Similarly, in the preface to *The Liberty Minstrel*, he called for "associations of singers, having the love of liberty

[20] Douglass, "The Anti-Slavery Movement," 462.

[21] Although William Lloyd Garrison's *Juvenile Poems, for the Use of Free American Children of Every Complexion* contains poems apparently meant to be read rather than sung, its purpose, explained in the preface, reveals the importance of "juvenile Harps": "All missionary labors, expended upon the manhood of heathenism or oppression, have been of little service to the cause of righteousness or freedom. The only rational, and certainly the most comprehensive plan of redeeming the world *speedily* from its pollution, is to begin with the infancy of mankind. If, therefore, we desire to see our land delivered from the curse of prejudice and slavery, we must direct our efforts chiefly to the rising generation, whose minds are untainted, whose opinions are unfashioned, and whose sympathies are true to nature and its purity."

in their hearts, [to] be immediately formed in every community." However, there is no evidence that these recommenda-
tions were any more than Clark's attempt to promote his
songbooks, for the number of places where slavery was abhorred and liberty held sacred were sparse. These "songs of
the free" were primarily sung at religious and political anti-
slavery conventions, fairs, picnics, and freedom rallies either
congregationally or by choirs "composed partly of colored
singers." They were even sung by soloists such as William
Wells Brown[22] and George Clark, "the well-known liberty
singer," and by The Hutchinsons, "the matchless anti-slavery
songsters."[23]

Although Garrison addressed his *Juvenile Poems* to "free
American children of every complexion" and commented in
his preface to *Selection of Anti-Slavery Hymns*, "Some of the
pieces . . . are intended specially for the use of our colored
brethren," antislavery songbooks basically comprised pieces
written by whites to be sung by whites. For example, the only
identifiable ethnicity in William Wells Brown's *Anti-Slavery
Harp* is one selection credited to Frederick Douglass's *North
Star* and Brown's poem, "Fling Out the Anti-Slavery Flag."[24]
Clark's *Harp of Freedom* has a single piece attributed to "Fred
Douglass's Paper," and *Freedom's Lyre* has two poems by
James Moses Horton, the North Carolina slave. *Original
Anti-Slavery Songs* (1852), the privately published pamphlet
of thirteen original poems by Joshua McCarter Simpson, "a
colored man," is the only collection of original abolition
songs by a black writer.

The miscellaneous songs of William Wells Brown, James
Moses Horton, and Joshua McCarter Simpson were insufficient to constitute a corpus of black abolition song. Furthermore, "songs of the free" were not intended to be sung by
those in bondage; the slave's abolition hymns were spirituals

[22] William Edward Farrison, *William Wells Brown: Author & Reformer* (Chicago:
University of Chicago Press, 1969), 122.
[23] Nathaniel Peabody Rogers, "The Hutchinsons" (from the *Herald of Freedom*,
June 14, 1844) in *A Collection from the Miscellaneous Writings of Nathaniel Peabody
Rogers*, 272.
[24] William Farrison says that this piece by Brown (which is listed anonymously)
was apparently his first attempt at publishing verse; Farrison, 125.

with invisible strains of militancy that petitioned the Lord for immediate and unconditional emancipation. It is likely that the only blacks who sang these songs were Northern freemen, specifically abolitionists like William Wells Brown, Frederick Douglass, Richard Allen, Harriet Tubman, and Sojourner Truth, as well as black Presbyterian clergymen like Henry Highland Garnet, Samuel Cornish, Theodore S. Wright, J. W. C. Pennington, Francis Grimke, and Elymas P. Rogers, whose education earned them respect and entrance into the white male-dominated antislavery aristocracy. There is no evidence that these white abolition songs were ever sung at the Negro conventions that addressed such issues as abolition and temperance. Their antislavery songs, as evidenced in the black denominational hymnals of that time, were select Wesley and especially Watts hymns to which they brought a relevant social interpretation.

The Composition of Freedom's Lyre

"A work of this character has, for a long time, been called for, by those who have been accustomed to meet and pray for the Emancipation of the Slave," Hatfield said in the preface to *Freedom's Lyre*. "No volume of a similar kind has heretofore been given to the American public." Notwithstanding Garrison's *Selection of Anti-Slavery Hymns* (1834) and Chapman's *Songs of the Free and Hymns of Christian Freedom* (1836), *Freedom's Lyre* was comparatively the only genuine hymnal. Its pocket size, meter signatures, author's italicized titles, and inclusion of page and hymn numbers, as well as both psalms and hymns were evidently modeled after Isaac Watts's 1819 volume of *Psalms, Carefully Suited to the Christian Worship in the United States.*[25] That Hatfield was a Wattsian hymnist is further confirmed in the preface to his later hymnological project, *The Church Hymn Book for the Worship of God.* "Five generations of Christian Worshipers have fully tested the value of his sacred songs, and proved their worth," avouched Hatfield. "No collection, that is not largely

---

[25] Isaac Watts, *Psalms, Carefully Suited to the Christian Worship in the United States* (Geneva, N.Y.: James Bogert, 1819).

composed of his inimitable productions, can meet the de-
mands of the churches of Christ."[26]

The pocket-size (3" × 4 1/2") hardbound volume with
Freedom's Lyre etched on its spine encloses 209 hymns, 64
metricized psalms, and 18 doxologies—a total of 291 pieces
with over 70 known writers represented. The selection of
nearly 300 hymns addressing the subject of abolitionism was
no simple task. "In consequence," complained Hatfield, "the
compiler has admitted some hymns—more than he desired—which cannot be regarded as very poetical; but have
been retained, because better, on the subject, were not to be
found." Because antislavery was, in the words of Nathaniel
Rogers, still "young and rude, and as yet unfertile in bards
who [could] stand fire as well as emit it,"[27] Hatfield, like
Chapman, had to intermix the classic hymns of Wesley,
Fawcett, Heber, and other evangelicals with current reform
poetry.

The largest number of pieces by a single writer in *Freedom's Lyre* are the 35 psalms and 14 hymns of Isaac Watts.
This is followed by the 22 psalms and one hymn of Hatfield,
the 10 hymns each of Elizabeth Margaret Chandler and
James Montgomery, the six of Lydia Huntley Sigourney, and
the four each of Maria Weston Chapman, William Cowper,
and John Newton. Such revered reformers as John Greenleaf
Whittier, William Lloyd Garrison, and Harriet Martineau
are also represented.[28]

Hatfield selected some of the poetry in *Freedom's
Lyre* from works written by English abolitionists involved in

---

[26] Hatfield, *The Church Hymn Book for the Worship of God*, 5.

[27] Nathaniel Peabody Rogers, "Poetry" (from the *Herald of Freedom*, Dec. 10,
1841), in *A Collection from the Miscellaneous Writings of Nathaniel Peabody Rogers*,
212.

[28] One of Cowper's hymns, minus two stanzas with slight word changes, Hatfield took from *The Negro's Complaint: A Poem* (1826), a pamphlet with color illus-
trations.

Whittier was one of the 62 charter abolitionists of the American Anti-Slavery
Society, founded in 1833, and one of the 21 Quakers (three of whom were women).

George Moses Horton was the slave of a Mr. James Horton of Chatham County,
North Carolina. Some of his poems had been published in the *Raleigh Register*. At
least one of his two poems in *Freedom's Lyre* was taken by Hatfield from Horton's
Poems by a Slave (1829), which contains several antislavery pieces. The poem is titled
"On Liberty and Slavery" and has the first line "Alas! and am I born for this."
Hatfield omits four of the ten stanzas and makes only minor punctuation changes.

terminating slavery, first in their own colonial West Indies and then in North America. Three of these are attributed to *Wrongs of Africa* (1787), an extended poem published in "liberty's chief town"—London.[29] Eight pieces were attributed to Pratt's, Dublin['s], Salisbury['s], Hawkin's [Hawker's], and Alex[ander's] collections, and one piece to Kenyon College.[30] An additional twenty-eight poems were credited to such antislavery periodicals as the (New York) *Slave's Friend,* the (New York-Boston) *Emancipator and Republican,* and the (New York) *Human Rights,* all three of which were publications of the American Anti-Slavery Society's national pamphlet campaign, chaired by Lewis Tappan. A single piece is ascribed to the (New York) *Zion's Watchman,* a journal founded by the Wesleyan Conference Society, which was the Methodist sector of the American Anti-Slavery Society. Other contributors included the *New York Evangelist,* the (New York) *Churchman,* the *New York Baptist Register,* the (Worchester) *Massachusetts Spy,* the (Boston) *Liberator,* and the (Mountpleasant) *Philanthropist,* a weekly journal of the Ohio Anti-Slavery Society that contained essays on moral and religious subjects.

The diverse sources used to compile *Freedom's Lyre* are partial proof that the American Anti-Slavery Society had selected the most capable scholar for the task. Hatfield, a learned Presbyterian pastor,[31] was a meticulous hymnologist

[29] The first part was published in 1787, the second in 1788. The third part was probably published in sequence the following year. The preface to this pamphlet (published in three parts over a period of several years) explains the significance of the poem: "Feeling for the honour of his country, and for the suffering of the friendless and injured negroes, the author has attempted to attract public notice to the slave trade, by committing his thoughts to the press in the form of a poem." William Roscoe, *The Wrongs of Africa, A Poem,* Part One (London: Printed for R. Faulder, 1787), viii.

[30] In the preface of *Church Psalmody: A Collection of Psalms and Hymns Adapted to Public Worship* (Boston: Perkins, Marvin & Co.; Philadelphia: Henry Perkins, 1834) or the later enlarged reprint (Boston: T. R. Marvin, 1848), the compilers, Lowell Mason and David Greene, stated: "In selecting the hymns, in addition to the hymnbooks used by the various denominations of Christians in the United States, the compilers have examined eight or ten extensive general collections of hymns, besides a large number of smaller collections published in England, and which have never been republished, or for sale, in this country" (p. viii). Pratt's, Dublin, Salisbury, and Hawker's (except Alex. Coll. and Kenyon Coll.), to which hymns are attributed in the above volume, are apparently among the obscure "smaller collections published in England."

[31] Hatfield was educated at Middlebury College in Vermont and Andover Seminary in Massachusetts.

"able to trace to the original source many lines falsely supposed to be alterations and imitations," one to whom "hymn-
tinkerers were an abomination."[32] Liberal editing of hymns
was the accustomed practice of the day; however, Hatfield
believed that great care should always be taken to maintain
the purity of the text. "Even in cases where the phraseology
might possibly be improved," he wrote in a later work, "it has
been thought best to overlook slight variations from the laws
of good taste, in deference to the author's peculiar idioms
and shades of thought."[33] Yet, Hatfield exercised even
greater editorial liberty than Chapman by altering the
hymns of *Freedom's Lyre* "wherever it appeared that the piece
could thereby be improved, or adapted to the holy cause of
Emancipation." That the "holy cause of emancipation" took
precedence over Hatfield's own hymnological convictions is
further indication that he was "a friend of the slave."[34]

The verse of the reform poets was specifically composed for the "holy cause of emancipation," so only minor
modifications in punctuation were required. But the free
treatment of evangelical hymnody was needed to enlarge the
hymnal, and quite necessary for the sake of relevancy. The
fact that only two of Charles Wesley's poems were included is
either indicative of the impracticality of inverting them inside out from evangelical to the liberal, or of Hatfield's hesi-
tancy to tamper with "the author's peculiar idioms and shades
of thought." A glance at Wesley's "Come on, My Partners in
Distress" (No. 44) reveals the "hymn-tinkering" necessary to
socialize evangelical hymns. Hatfield omits the three closing
stanzas of the original seven. Below are stanzas one and four
with changes in the altered version italicized:

SUFFERING SAINTS

Come on, my partners in distress,
My comrades through the wilderness,
    Who still your bodies feel:
Awhile forget your griefs and fears,

[32] "Dr. Hatfield's Library," *New York Observer*, Aug. 18, 1883, n.p.

[33] Hatfield, *The Church Hymn Book for the Worship of God*, 4.

[34] On the other hand, the compromises Hatfield had to make may be the
reason *Freedom's Lyre* is always surreptitiously absent from his list of publications.

And look beyond this vale of tears,
To that celestial hill.

Thrice blessed, bliss-inspiring hope!
It lifts the fainting spirits up,
    It brings to life the dead:
Our conflicts here shall soon be past,
And you and I ascend at last
    Triumphant with our Head.

THERE REMAINETH A REST

Come on, my partners in distress,
My comrades *in* the wilderness,
    Who *groan beneath your chains!*
Awhile forget your griefs and fears,
And look beyond this vale of tears
    To *yon* celestial *plains.*

Thrice bless'd, *exalted, blissful* hope!
It lifts *our* fainting spirits up,
    It brings to life the dead;
Our *bondage* here *will* soon be past,
Then we shall rise and reign at last,
    Triumphant with our Head.

Stanza three/line three and stanza four/lines four and
five are all significant syntactic modifications—changes that
would have made John Wesley's editing of brother Charles's
poems seem sparing. By substituting words like "chains" and
"bondage" Hatfield adapted the hymn to the subject at hand.
In stanza four/line two the almost imperceptible modification of "the" to "our" and in stanza four/line five from "you
and I" to "we" is evidence of the value given to pluralizing or
socializing these once private evangelical pieces. Wesley's
hymns, no matter what social concern they initially addressed, have a heavenward polarity that is most magnetic in
the closing stanza(s). By omitting the concluding stanzas five
through seven, Hatfield (intentionally or unintentionally) in-
terrupts the predictable heavenward digression. Conversely,
Wesley's "Soldiers of Christ, Arise" (No. 192), has relevance
without modifications, first because of its intrinsic element
of militaristic imagery, and second because of Hatfield's

interruption of the predictable heavenward polarity by concluding the twelve-stanza hymn after stanza four.

Hatfield treated Watts's Calvinistic hymns similarly.
Some required substantial editing while others managed to
evade his theological tailoring due to his daring interruption
of their final emotional transcendence. For instance, Watts's
"Judges, Who Rule the World By Laws" (No. 82) reflects intensive editing. Hatfield omits the fourth stanza from the
original six. In stanzas one and six below, changes in the original are italicized in the succeeding Hatfield version:

WARNING TO MAGISTRATES

Judges, who rule the world by laws,
Will ye despise the righteous cause,
    When th' injured poor before you stands?
Dare ye condemn the righteous poor,
And let rich sinners 'scape secure,
    While gold and greatness bribe your hands?

Thus shall the vengeance of the Lord
Safety and joy to saints afford;
    And all that hear shall join and say,
"Sure there's a God that rules on high,
A God that hears his children cry,
    And will their suffering well repay."

WARNING TO MAGISTRATES

Judges, who rule the world by laws!
Will ye despise the righteous cause,
    When *vile oppression wastes the land?*
Dare ye condemn the righteous poor,
And let rich *despots live* secure,
    While gold and greatness bribe your hands?

Thus shall the vengeance of the Lord
Safety *to all th'oppress'd* afford;
    And *they who* hear shall join and say,
"Sure there's a God that rules on high,
A God that hears *the bondmen* cry,
    And will their sufferings well repay."

Theology and History in Freedom's Lyre

While the ideological growth of political abolitionism is traceable in the three songbooks of George Washington Clark, the theology of moral abolitionism is most carefully delineated in *Freedom's Lyre*. The masterful organization of this hymnal, as seen in the table of contents, is the compiler's momentous musicological contribution to the understanding of abolitionist theology. While black spirituals reveal the inside of slavery looking out, the "songs of the free" in *Freedom's Lyre* reveal the outside of slavery looking in.

Chronologically ordered according to theological events, the categories of the table of contents comprise an "eschatologizing of the contemporary"—a prophetic flowing together of a quarter-century commencing in roughly 1840 with the slave's petition for freedom and proceeding through emancipation to rapturous celebration:

Section I, "The Cries of the Slave," contains 37 hymns. Thirty of the latter are addressed "to God" (Part 1). It is fitting that over two-thirds of the thirty (21) are psalms, for the pre-trinitarian foreparents of this psalmody had customarily cried "to God" out of their oppression and anguish. Of Watts's 35 and Hatfield's 22 psalms in *Freedom's Lyre,* herein are nine each (together one-third of their combined psalms in the hymnal). The two poems by North Carolina slave George Moses Horton are appropriately placed. Yet the authenticity of a slave petitioning for freedom for himself and his people questions the white reformers' ability to capture the bleeding tears of slaves hidden from them behind the *veil.* However, a close reading of Hatfield's tear-filled psalms "to God" discloses devoutly impassioned sensibility. The abolitionists themselves were oppressed—mobbed, murdered, despised, and scorned—so they could genuinely commingle their poetic sighs with "the cries of the slave to God."

Although hymn number one, "Pleading That God Would Help, as of Old" (from *The Wrongs of Africa*) is not a psalm, it is thoroughly entrenched in Old Testament theology. The poet adapted the biblical exodus to the plight of the African slave and rekindled the ethos that centuries earlier had raised the psalmists' plaintive entreaty, "How long?"

> How long, Most Holy, Just, and True!
>   Dost Thou our blood behold?
> Nor rise th'oppressor to subdue,
>   As in the days of old?

There is further imploring in the opening couplets of stanzas two and three. "Where is the Pow'r, that led thy seed/ From Egypt's blighted plains," and then "Where is the Mighty Arm, that clave/ The waters of the sea[?]" Finally, in the closing couplets of the fourth and fifth quatrains reassurance is granted: "Soon for the crush'd and bleeding Slave/ Jehovah will appear" and then "Our iron bondage he will brake/ And ev'ry slave set free."

Sections II and III, "The Slave Comforted with the Consolations of Religion [and] the Hope of Deliverance" and "The Slave Exhorted to Patience and Hope" indicate the pacifism that typified Garrisonian abolition, particularly its verse. The Garrisonian poets stressed that warfare was being waged on "parchman, scroll, and creed," "not with martial steel grasped with murderous zeal," and that vengeance was neither the slave's, nor the abolitionist's, nor the Union Army's, but the Lord's.

Section IV, "The Rights of the Slave," is comprised of only four hymns. The brevity of the section might be contrasted with the contention of Henry Highland Garnet who enunciated the criticism shared by all abolitionists. Garnet accused that the friends of the slave assembled at conventions merely to sympathize with one another and to weep over the slaves' unhappy condition while neglecting to send them sound advice. Garnet's advice: "forget not that you are native-born American citizens, and as such you are justly entitled to all the rights that are granted to the freest."[35] It seems that "The Rights of the Slave" rather than "The Friends of the Slave Assembled" (Section VIII) should have been the major division. In light of Garnet's point, Sigourney's and Martineau's tasteful poeticizing of egalitarianism in two of

---

[35] Henry Highland Garnet, "An Address to the Slaves of the United States of America," *Slavery Attacked: The Abolitionist Crusade*, ed. John L. Thomas (Englewood Cliffs, N. J.: Prentice-Hall, 1965), 99, 101. Emphasis added.

the four hymns goes relatively unnoticed. In Section V, the polite persuasion and pacifist "appeals in behalf of the slave" to masters, rulers, freemen, women, and Christians seem to lack real impact. Correspondingly, in Section VII, "The Friends of the Slave Encouraged to Act [and] Pray," is also homologous with the pervading pacifism. Here, to act was to engage in what Nathaniel Rogers termed "moral insurrection," and to pray what Lydia Sigourney called "prayerful toil"—clearly nonrevolutionary action according to the Garnetian prototype.

However, according to Nathaniel Rogers, pacifism did not necessitate compassionate condolence in poetry. We want no "laments of the lacerated slave," he declared, no "whining wail about our *blotted 'scutcheon,* or our *stained flag.*" With Garnetian tone he swelled: "We want a battery of thunder against the slaveholding North, and the 'peculiar institutions' here. We want a broad-side for the hulk of the gory old church. She is bloody as a butcher."[36] Frederick Douglass, on the other hand, seemed complacent about the moderation in abolitionist verse. Perhaps momentarily tranquilized by the ambrosia of his own beauteous language, the "white-haired lion" purred like a pussycat:

> Your own Longfellow whispers, in every hour of trial and disappointment, "labor and wait." James Russell Lowell is reminding us that "men are more than institutions." Pierpont cheers the heart of the pilgrim in search of liberty, by singing the praises of "the north star." Bryant, too, is with us; . . . he snatches a moment for letting drop a smiling verse of sympathy for the man in chains. The poets are with us.[37]

The poets' consensus was that by nature the language of verse is that of moderate moral agitation.

The verse of Section VI, "Slaveholders Admonished," came closest to broadsiding the hulk of the proslavery church.

---

[36] Rogers, "Poetry" (from the *Herald of Freedom,* Dec. 10, 1841), 212.

[37] Frederick Douglass, "The Anti-Slavery Movement" (lecture given before anti-slavery organizations in the winter of 1855), in *My Bondage and My Freedom,* 462.

Douglass's reference to the poem by Pierpont is published in William Wells Brown's *The Anti-Slavery Harp* under the title "The Slave-Holder's Address to the North Star."

Nine of the fourteen pieces in this Garnetian fleet are psalms (seven by Watts and two by Hatfield). Exhibiting the theology of Old Testament psalmody, these poems predicate the Lord's judgment and vengeance upon the bloodguilty "flesh-merchants." In the language of biblical psalmody, and more specifically the Wattsian brand, the Calvinistic verse of Watts expresses disdain for the depravity and corruption of humankind due to original sin.[38] The theological vocabulary, which was not at all foreign to Presbyterians such as Hatfield, made his pieces easily adaptable to admonishing the "men-stealers." Note Watts's psalm, "The Lord, the Judge, His Churches Warns" (No. 118):

> To heav'n they lift their hands unclean;
> Defil'd with lust, defil'd with blood;
> By night they practice ev'ry sin,
> By day their mouths draw near to God.

The preface foretold that Section VIII, "The Friends of the Slave Assembled," would comprise the largest division (72 hymns). Hatfield explained that *Freedom's Lyre* was compiled for those who gathered to pray for emancipation. According to the table of contents, the slaves' friends also gathered for consultation, on the Fourth of July, the first of August, and on a fast-day.

The hymns of Part 3, "The Friends of the Slave Assembled on the Fourth of July," figuratively answered the question raised by Frederick Douglass in his Rochester oration of July 5, 1852: "What to the American slave is your Fourth of July?" In his poem "Seeking Independence for the Captives" (No. 203), John Greenleaf Whittier came close to versifying Douglass's own response, "I answer, a day that reveals to him, more than all other days in the year, the gross injustice and cruelty to which he is the constant victim."[39] Whittier wrote:

---

[38] Watts says: "And not only must we be sensible of our being expos'd to Divine Anger by reason of Sins actually committed, but we must also be acquainted with the Corruption of our Natures, the Body of Sin which dwells within us." Isaac Watts, *A Caveat Against Infidelity: Or, the Danger of Apostasy from the Christian Faith* (London: Clark, Hett, Matthew & Ford, 1729), 10.

[39] Frederick Douglass, "What to the Slave is the Fourth of July?" in *My Bondage and My Freedom*, 445. Douglass's autobiography was first published in New York by Miller, Orton & Mulligan in 1855.

We thank thee, Father!—hill and plain
  Around us wave their fruits once more,
And cluster'd vine, and blossom'd grain,
  Are bending round each cottage door;—
But Oh! for those this day can bring,
  Not, as to us, the joyful thrill;—
For those, who, under freedom's wing,
  Are bound in slavery's fetters still:—

The hymns in Part 4, "On the First of August," were sung in celebration of the August 1, 1838, emancipation of African slaves in the British West Indies. Pieces like "The West Indies Emancipated" (No. 209) and "Britannia Hath Triumphed" (No. 210) were first of all reminders to the American abolitionists that they could indeed succeed. Secondly, they were retorts to skeptics as to the feasibility of immediate emancipation. For instance, hymn No. 209 turns its attention from celebrating the West Indies emancipation to criticizing the continuance of slavery in North America. Stanza three embraces the transition. It commences with the celebrative cheer, "Joy to the Islands! the cloud has pass'd o'er them." Exactly halfway through the hymn begins questioning, "When will our land thus arouse from its slumber,/ And be deliver'd from tyranny's stain?"

The hymns of Part 5, "The Friends of the Slave Assembled on a Fast-day," are prayerful intercessions on behalf of a sinful nation. Poems like "Mourning for National Sins" (No. 215) and "Mourning and Pleading That God Would Spare" (No. 217) contain seeds of Walter Rauschenbusch's Social Gospel theology that states not one but all, slaveholders and nonslaveholders alike, share in the transgression of the evil institution. The moral abolitionists, whose parish was their country, pleaded on behalf of their national flock: "Long has thy presence blest our lands,—/ Forsake us not, O God!"

The "Dismissions" and "Doxologies" of Sections XI and XII closed these various gatherings of the friends of the slaves and were relegated to the back of the hymnal as was hymnologically customary. The compiler made no effort to adapt the dismissions to "the holy cause of emancipation." Herein, Rippon, Hart, Cennick, Fawcett, and Newton were able to stretch their evangelic wings unclipped. The doxologies are also traditional, comprising such classics as "Praise God from Whom All Blessings Flow," "From All That Dwell Below the Skies," and Hatfield's oft-used piece, "To God—the Father, Son." The dismissions and doxologies only close the hymnal for the sake of format.

Sections IX and X, "Emancipation at Hand [and] Accomplished" and "Thanksgiving and Praise," comprise the finishing theological categories. The sixteen pieces of Section X, half of which are thanksgiving and praise psalms adapted by Watts and Hatfield, represent the eschaton of abolition—the Jubilee. The last hymn (No. 291) is a fitting doxology:

> We'll praise thee, Lord! forever;
>   Thou reignest, King of kings;
> Thy wondrous love and favor,
>   Each ransom'd captive sings:
> We'll celebrate thy glory
>   With all thy saints above,
> And tell the joyful story,
>   Of thy redeeming love.

3

Thy Kingdom Come:
Hymns for the Social Awakening

SOCIAL GOSPEL HYMNODY

Social Awakening via "Kingdom" Hymnody

For the average churchman the hymn book is more a book of religion than his Bible. More religious interest is brought him by song than by the scriptures. In fact much of scriptural truth is conveyed to him through hymns.

The growth, development and future of all our religious ideals rests largely with our hymnology. The songs of a nation will in the long run make the nation.[1]

If this measurement of hymnody's role in the religious life of laity is accurate, then Social Gospel hymnody was a prerequisite for America to become Christianized and the kingdom of God to be ushered in.

As early as 1909 Walter Rauschenbusch began thinking about hymnody's place in the proclamation of progressive orthodoxy. "[The] Church has developed hymns, prayers and sacraments connected with private redemption," he noted. "[There is] Very little about social redemption. Now that this is on us, we need these social expressions of emotion and

---

[1] Benjamin F. Crawford, *Religious Trends in a Century of Hymns* (Carnegie, Pa.: Carnegie Church Press, 1938), 24.

purpose. If [we] cannot find them, [we] must create them."[2]
The following year his complaint was distilled and publicized
in the preface to his *Prayers of the Social Awakening* (1910).
"The ordinary church hymnal," he sighed, "rarely contains
more than two or three hymns in which the triumphant
chords of the social hope are struck."[3]

Rauschenbusch deplored the dearth of the "kingdom" hymnody and disparaged the preponderance of the
orthodox:

> The hymns of the Church are like an auriferous sand-bed
> in which the intenser religious feelings of past genera-
> tions have been deposited. They perpetuate what would
> otherwise be most fugitive: the religious emotions. If any
> one will look over either the standard church hymnals or
> the popular revival collections, he will find very few
> hymns expressing the desire for a purer and diviner life
> of humanity on earth. . . . On the other hand, the
> hymns expressing the yearning of the soul for the blessed
> life in the world to come are beyond computation.[4]

In a five-page typescript, "Comments," he continued developing his theological examination of evangelical hymnody,
objecting most to its individualism:

> The hymns are mainly individualistic, with the idea of
> coming to God, of recognizing one's own guilt; they call
> us from personal sins to a personal cross; they persuade
> us to give to and serve Christ, without, however, con-
> necting such service with service to our fellowmen.
> Many songs have a partial message of service, but this
> service is too often for personal gains of bliss or heav-
> enly reward, or in order to secure special blessing.

Rauschenbusch, a social pietist and postmillennial optimist,
further chided that "where hymn subjects deal with social
problems or strife, they teach resignation or defer all hope of

[2] Walter Rauschenbusch, untitled MS, Walter Rauschenbusch papers, American Baptist Society, Colgate Rochester Divinity School, Rochester, New York.
[3] Walter Rauschenbusch, *Prayers of the Social Awakening* (Boston: Pilgrim
Press, 1910), 10.
[4] Walter Rauschenbusch, *Christianity and the Social Crisis* (New York: Macmillan, 1912), 163.

correction to the future life."[5] He carefully examined seven hymnbooks that attempted to highlight the social aspect of the gospel. Yet, in 1914, he still complained that he had been calling for the composition of social hymns because standard hymnbooks contained little, and that when he needed such hymns to back up his preaching he found himself "forsaken."[6]

"If we cannot find them," Rauschenbusch stated, "we must create them." Yet, there is no evidence that he ever attempted "creating" hymns, whereas he was quite successful in publishing his original social prayers. However, he had planned to edit a volume—a project revealed in a December 14, 1910, letter from A. D. Watson, General Treasurer of the Executive Counsel of the Methodist Church Department of Temperance and Reform, in Toronto. Watson's motion that a collection of reform songs be published was carried unanimously at one of the counsel meetings. "The purpose," he wrote to Rauschenbusch, "is to sing the Gospel of Social Christianity into the minds and hearts of the people of America." Watson continued, "You told me . . . that you were making such a work a specialty and I should be glad to know if you can help us in any way to realize our purpose."[7] Rauschenbusch received another letter within the week from T. Albert Moore, general secretary of the organization, saying, "In conversation with Dr. A. D. Watson of this City, I learned that you have in contemplation the preparation of a Hymn Book, containing hymns with regard to social questions. . . . We are sure you could help us by suggestion of certain hymns that would be applicable to our great work."[8] Nearly a year later, Rauschenbusch again shared his idea, now with Rev. C. S. Macfarland, in response to a circular letter soliciting suggestions for a forthcoming social service conference in Chicago:

> We need hymns that will voice the new social enthusiasms. As you know the old fashioned hymnals are almost

[5] Walter Rauschenbusch, "Comments," MS, 3, Rauschenbusch papers.
[6] Rauschenbusch, untitled MS, 4.
[7] A. D. Watson to Walter Rauschenbusch, MS, Dec. 14, 1910, Rauschenbusch papers.
[8] T. Albert Moore to Walter Rauschenbusch, MS, Dec. 19, 1910, Rauschenbusch papers.

bare of any such material. Some of the more recent are
beginning to enrich the supply. But if we had some small
collection, perhaps of twenty-four pages, which would
contain the most beautiful and dependable hymns of
that character, that could be brought cheaply, that might
serve for special assemblies. At the same time such a
collection would furnish the necessary material from
which others could draw. I think this is really of great
deal more importance than other more scientific under-
takings that we might contemplate.[9]

In addition to being the first national figure to seriously espouse the dissemination of a Social Gospel hymnody,
it is likely that Rauschenbusch's articles and books served as
the inspiration and undergirding theology that led to the
building of the "kingdom" repertoire. One of the finest
hymns inspired by his work is "God Save America," by
William G. Ballantine. Ballantine wrote to him expressing
his appreciation:

> I doubt whether anyone welcomed your little volume of
> *Prayers for the Social Awakening* more warmly than I did,
> for the need of such an enrichment of our liturgy has
> long pressed upon me.
>   But we need hymns as well as prayers. An attempt at
> such a hymn from my pen appeared in this morning's
> *Springfield [Massachusetts] Republican.* . . . You will
> observe that I could not resist the temptation to "dedi-
> cate" it to you, since I wanted to call attention to the fact
> that the thoughts are the same as in your prayers.[10]

The fact that Rauschenbusch immediately expressed his grat-
itude is reflected in Ballantine's next letter: "My dear Dr.
Rauschenbusch, I thank you most heartily for the kind words
with which you have received my hymn and the dedication of
it to yourself."[11]

[9] Walter Rauschenbusch to Rev. C. S. Macfarland, Ph.D., MS, Oct. 27, 1911,
Rauschenbusch papers.
    [10] William G. Ballantine to Walter Rauschenbusch, MS, Jan. 21, 1912,
Rauschenbusch papers. Italics added.
    [11] William G. Ballantine to Walter Rauschenbusch, MS, Jan. 26, 1912,
Rauschenbusch papers.

The Premier "Kingdom" Hymnals

"I am told," wrote theologian Charles Clayton Morrison, "that Rauschenbusch had made a very large collection of hymns of the social awakening and was to put them in form for publication and use by the churches."[12] It actually appears that his hymnological project never proceeded beyond the planning stage. However, it is conceivable that cumulatively the publication of such volumes as Henry Sloane Coffin and Ambrose White Vernon's *Hymns of the Kingdom of God* (1911), Mabel Mussey's *Social Hymns of Brotherhood and Aspiration* (1914), and Mornay Williams's *Hymns of the Kingdom of God* (n.d.) fulfilled the need that had been gnawing at his priestly conscience. Following the appearance of Mussey's hymnbook Rauschenbusch began instead to consider the idea of forming a liturgy for the Social Gospel, in which the "awakened" hymnody would assume an integral part. A preliminary study of the new "kingdom" hymnbooks gives a clue as to why he abandoned his hymnological project in favor of a liturgical one.

In an overview of these three "kingdom" hymnals there are at least three points that can be made. First, some of the newer hymns in these volumes were probably casually written by various persons interested in American reform, while others were written at the request of modern hymnbook editors. Therefore, one of the complaints of Simon N. Patten, whose idea it was that *The Survey* publish social hymns, was that each poet tended to follow his own style, that the old theology was intermixed with the new, and that the language for the new expression had yet to be coined and gain symbolic power. For instance, griped Patten: "The devil is no longer as Luther thought the greatest power on earth. We are now looking for a jail in which to confine him, instead of a fortress to which we may flee from his power."[13]

This brings about point two. In the hymns of the Social Gospel Satan is portrayed (to use Rauschenbusch's phrase) as

---

[12] Charles Clayton Morrison, *The Social Gospel and the Christian Cultus* (New York: Harper, 1933), 103.

[13] Simon N. Patten, "Hymn Writing," *The Survey*, 31, no. 14 (Jan. 3, 1914), 403.

a "theological devil," while in the gospel hymns of evangelical revivalism Satan's portrayal is medieval. For this reason gospel hymns are excluded from among the "kingdom" repertoire. Furthermore, Rauschenbusch reasoned:

> In all these (Gospel) Hymns, mankind are sharply divided into two classes, saints and sinners. The sentiment of brotherhood is confined to the saints. There is pity for the sinners (e.g. "Rescue the perishing," etc.), but no sense of unity or solidarity with them. The very essence of the Christian life is separation from sinners. . . . Brotherhood, in the strict sense, is impossible until they repent.[14]

Third, although gospel hymns are included, the "kingdom" hymnals are nevertheless dependent on pieces that not only commingle orthodox and liberal theologies, but which predate the Social Gospel. Preeminent among these are hymns of social Christianity dating back to 1820. Among these are the works of the evangelical reformers James Montgomery, John Pierpont, John Greenleaf Whittier, Samuel Longfellow, and Alfred Tennyson.

Hymns of the Kingdom of God (1911) is a perfect example of the comprehensiveness of the "kingdom" repertoire. A large compilation of 508 hymns, Coffin and Vernon's volume was "an attempt to furnish the Church with a hymnal in which Christian communion with God is viewed as fellowship with the Father and the Son in the establishment of the Kingdom."[15] The compilers mention the prevailing kingdom idea up front, but they make no clear explanation of its social meaning. Moreover, in their effort to avoid "divisive theology," most of the hymnody is socially irresolute. The contemporary hymns of social Christianity, more specifically the hymns of the Social Gospel, are included, but so are a large number of orthodox classics by Luther, Wesley, and Watts. In drawing the distinction between the evangelical and the social, hymnologist Henry Wilder Foote comments that, "It is true that Latin hymnody, and still more Anglo-American

---

[14] Rauschenbusch, "Comments," MS, 5.
[15] Henry Sloane Coffin and Ambrose White Vernon, eds., *Hymns of the Kingdom of God* (New York: A. S. Barnes, 1911), iii.

hymnody of the early nineteenth century, did inculcate certain humanitarian virtues, especially charity, but it was an individualistic virtue rather than the idealism of a regenerate social order."[16] Similarly, Rauschenbusch claims that many of Charles Wesley's hymns "express pretty definitely the hope of a social redemption. In most of these, however, it seemed . . . that earthly fraternity was recommended merely as a prelude to [the] celestial, and not for its own sake."[17]

"Kingdom" hymnbooks did not immediately embrace the more radical verse of reform writers, but Rauschenbusch admitted that "There could not have been a rapid transition, . . . so we must take the improvements as the fruit of a tree whose roots are some where in the 19th century." Perhaps his sentimental justification of the social nature of his favorite classics gives partial credence to Coffin and Vernon's respect for "the sacred canon of Christian experience," and their inclusion of "the older and more widely used" hymns:

> My own favorite hymns are largely individualistic. E.g. "Lead, kindly light"; "Abide with me"; "O Love that will not let me go"; "Crossing the bar," etc. But, after all this is not so self-centered as it appears, for these grand old hymns are but the individual expression of soul states common to the whole brotherhood of man; and I do not doubt when they are sung by the congregation, each person, recalling the Gethsemanes of his own life, feels more compassionate toward the rest of the race.[18]

Mornay Williams's privately published volume, also titled *Hymns of the Kingdom of God* (n.d.), is a typical Social Gospel hymnal in its inclusion of hymns of social Christianity that predate the movement (e.g., Longfellow and Whittier), its emphasis on the "kingdom" and "brotherhood," and its neglect of pieces relevant to the "race problem." Except for including Washington Gladden's "O Master, Let Me Walk with Thee," it is atypical in excluding all of the other well-known Social Gospel hymns and in heavily depending upon

[16] Henry Wilder Foote, *Three Centuries of American Hymnody* (Hamden, Conn.: Shoe String Press, 1940), 307.
[17] Rauschenbusch, "Comments," MS, 3.
[18] Ibid., 3–4.

pieces by the more obscure but excellent poets of the era:
J. B. S. Monsell, John Ellerton, Ebenezer Elliott, Charles
Kingsley, Mary A. Lathbury, and Gerald Massey.

Although Rauschenbusch had been calling for a small
collection of songs similar to what Williams compiled, it is
unlikely that Williams's forty-four piece pamphlet (texts only)
was the result of this petition. Williams was a Social Gospeler,
but less liberal than Rauschenbusch in many respects. "I do
not go, as you know, as far as you do in your leanings toward
socialism," he told Rauschenbusch in a letter. Sounding more
like a nineteenth-century evangelical social reformer than a
progressive member of the Brotherhood of the Kingdom,
Williams also commented:

> Personally, of course, I believe . . . in individual re-
> generation, but that that is exclusive of social regenera-
> tion, and that all the good deeds that our Lord
> personally did were simply illustrations of His power to
> support his claims as the Messiah, and were not in-
> tended to be imitated, and that he was left untouched
> by all the sorrow and suffering of the world, and was
> content that it should rot out to its final dissolution, is a
> conception of our Lord's character that . . . [for me]
> would be blasphemous.[19]

In an earlier letter Williams thanked Rauschenbusch for the
complimentary copies of his "little book of prayers" and for
the inscription in one of them, but told him that he greatly
regretted Rauschenbusch's concept of prayer as set forth in
the book's preface.[20]

Williams may not have been as liberal as Rauschenbusch, but he was a serious proponent of the gospel of labor,
as alluded to in his inclusion of hymns by labor poets Elliott,
Kingsley, and Massey. In fact, the largest number of hymns by
a single writer are the seven pieces of Massey, himself a la-
borer.[21] A characteristic of Massey's writing is found in his

---

[19] Mornay Williams (Esq.) to Walter Rauschenbusch, MS, Nov. 23, 1911,
Rauschenbusch papers.

[20] Mornay Williams to Walter Rauschenbusch, MS, Nov. 23, 1910, Rauschenbusch papers.

[21] See Elizabeth Balck, "Songs of Labor," *The Survey*, 31, no. 14 (Jan. 3, 1914),
422.

poem "We Thank Thee, Lord, for One Day," in which he designates Sunday the heaven of the "weary pilgrim." The closing octrain concludes with this couplet:

> 'Tis open Heaven one day in seven,
> The Poor Man's holiday.

Another fine piece is the closing half of the seventh stanza to Massey's "High Hopes That Burned Like Stars Sublime":

> Triumph and Toil are twins, though they
>   Be singly born of Sorrow;
> And 'tis the Martyrdom To-day
>   Brings victory To-Morrow.

The Paradigm of "Kingdom" Hymnals

Mabel Mussey's collection, *Social Hymns of Brotherhood and Aspiration* (1914), contains one-fifth the number of pieces in Coffin and Vernon's *Hymns of the Kingdom of God*, but it is more progressive in its christocentric liberalism. Compared to Williams's volume its social selection is much more comprehensive. Its hymns are also of a higher ecumenism that looks beyond the denomination to the nation. To use the words of hymnologist Henry Wilder Foote, they are "increasingly songs of human brotherhood; of redemption of the social order rather than the salvation of the individual soul; and of the higher patriotism which looks beyond the nation to mankind."[22]

"The first object," wrote Mussey, "was to find hymns that could be sung by all people in all places, whether in churches, in halls, in schools, in the open, . . . hymns which Jew and Gentile, Protestant and Catholic might sing with equal fervor."[23] This ecumenism was partially attainable via the denominational cross-section of jurors Mussey chose for selecting the hymns. Representatives from the Baptists, Methodists, Presbyterians, Congregationalists, Episcopalians, Unitarians, Jews, Socialists, and ethical culture were among the twelve professionals[24]—Mussey being

---

[22] Foote, 307.

[23] Mabel Hay Borrows Mussey, "How the Hundred Hymns Were Brought Together," *The Survey*, 31, no. 14 (Jan. 3, 1914), 383.

[24] Ibid., 384.

one of the Unitarians. The hymnbook was accurately characterized by New Jersey Unitarian Rev. Edgar S. Wiers (not among the jurists) as one that would "help us to take all trace of denominationalism away from the Forum." *Christian Work and Evangelist* believed *Social Hymns* would constitute progress toward erasing denominationalism from the forum if it supplemented denominational hymnbooks in the pews of churches supportive of the Social Gospel.[25] By obliterating the lesser loyalty to denomination, the higher devotion to the nation could be nurtured, for it was the nation that ultimately received judgment.

Social Hymns contains 111 pieces (with music) based on a compilation of one hundred hymns (ten with music and the remaining with suggested tunes) that first appeared in the January 3, 1914, issue of *The Survey.*[26] Following Rauschenbusch's meticulous study of *Social Hymns* against the *The Survey,* he corresponded with the publisher regarding the alterations made: "I write chiefly to inquire why so many changes have been made from the collection published in *The Survey.* In checking them up I find nearly twenty substitutions. . . . Did . . . single hymns seem too radical? I found one or two myself that I thought were a little sharp."[27] The publisher's response:

> Answering your inquiries in regard to the changes and substitutions from the original collection in *The Survey,* we may say that the publication of the hymns in *The Survey* stirred up many people to send in their contributions, some of which appeared to be better than those originally printed. Then too some of the hymns were not singable, and no satisfactory tune could be found.

[25] The two foregoing endorsements were compiled onto a sheet that was attached to the correspondence of Samuel C. Fairley to Walter Rauschenbusch, MS, July 30, 1914, Rauschenbusch papers.

[26] Hymns were borrowed from these recently published hymnals: *Hymns for the Church* (Century), *Hymns of the Kingdom of God* (A. S. Barnes), *Hymns for the Centuries* (A. S. Barnes), *Service Songs* (Christian Endeavor Hymn Book), *Fellowship Songs* (Ralph Albertson, New York), *Fellowship Hymnal* (Association Press), *Moyer's Songs of Socialism, Socialist Songs, Ethical Culture Hymn Book, Unity Hymns and Chorals,* as well as from recent Methodist, Presbyterian, and Catholic hymnals, and the forthcoming Unitarian hymnal. *The Survey,* 31, no. 14 (Jan. 3, 1914), 421.

[27] Walter Rauschenbusch to A. S. Barnes Company, MS, July 22, 1914, Rauschenbusch papers.

Possibly also the reason that you suggest had its weight,
that some of the hymns seemed too radical.[28]

The selections in *Social Hymns* fall into six categories
(original with *The Survey*): (1) Aspiration and Faith, (2) Liberty and Justice, (3) Peace, (4) Labor and Conflict, (5) Brotherhood, and (6) Patriotism. A number of Social Gospel
hymns are included that eventually became classics in denominational hymnals of both white and black congregations:[29] Washington Gladden's "O Master, Let Me Walk with
Thee" (1879), a hymn of labor and conflict; William DeWitt
Hyde's "Creation's Lord, We Give Thee Thanks" (1903) and
Walter Russell Bowie's "O Holy City, Seen of God" (1910),
hymns of liberty and justice; Katherine L. Bates' "O Beautiful for Spacious Skies" (1904) and William G. Ballantine's
"God Save America" (1912), hymns of patriotism; Frank
Mason North's "Where Cross the Crowded Ways of Life"
(1905), a hymn of aspiration and faith; and William Merrill's
"Rise Up, O Men of God" (1911), a hymn of brotherhood.

Social Hymns and other "kingdom" hymnals were incomplete without "O Master, Let Me Walk with Thee" (1879),
credited as the earliest piece specifically written for the
Social Gospel, and by the "father" of the movement—
Washington Gladden. Verses one, two, and four read:

---

[28] Samuel C. Fairley to Walter Rauschenbusch, MS, July 20, 1914, Rauschenbusch papers. Concerning the anachronism of these letters as dated, the latter is clearly a response to the former.

[29] For instance, observe the results of a study of African Methodist Church hymnals of 1897, 1941, 1954, and 1984 (excluding the 1801, 1818, 1837, and 1876 hymnals that predate the Social Gospel). Out of a total of 760 pieces, the 1897 hymnal, *The African Methodist Episcopal Church Hymn and Tune Book,* has 23 social gospel hymns (hymns whose language and evangelization is social). The 1941 *A.M.E. Hymnal* (also known as *The Richard Allen A.M.E. Hymnal*) shows an increase of 12 such hymns, so out of 461 pieces, 35 have substantive social strains. (It is in this 1941 hymnal that we first see the inclusion of some of the great hymns of the movement—Ballantine's "God Save America," Bates's "O Beautiful for Spacious Skies," Gladden's "O Master, Let Me Walk with Thee," William Merrill's "Rise Up, O Men of God," and North's "Where Cross the Crowded Ways of Life.") The 1954 *A.M.E.C. Hymnal* has an increase of seven such pieces, so that out of 673 hymns, 42 are social ones. In summary, in a span of a half century, the number of social hymns in the 1954 hymnal nearly doubles that in the 1897 volume. The 1984 *AMEC Bicentennial Hymnal* has an increase of 19 social hymns, so that out of a total of 670 hymns, 54 are social. Hence, the 54 social hymns in the 1984 hymnal more than double the number found in the 1897 volume.

O Master, let me walk with Thee
In lowly paths of service free;
Tell me Thy secret; help me bear
The strain of toil, the fret of care.

Help me the slow of heart to move
By some clear winning word of love,
Teach me the wayward feet to stay,
And guide them in the homeward way.

In hope that sends a shining ray
Far down the future's broadening way;
In peace that only Thou canst give,
With Thee, O Master, let me live.

Commenting on the early hymn Horton Davies replied, "It is hardly a fully matured expression of the social gospel, for though it is a commitment to the service of men and points to an optimistic earthly future, the concept of the Kingdom is missing."[30] Rauschenbusch, portrayed as a religious romantic by later neoorthodox theologians, displays stark realism and commitment to social activism in his comment on verse three of the hymn:

> Even the beautiful hymn, "O Master let me walk with thee, In lowly paths of service free," has this verse—
>
> > Teach me thy patience, still with thee
> > In closer, dearer company,
> > In work that keeps faith sweet and strong,
> > In trust that triumphs over wrong.
>
> The I. W. W. [Industrial Workers of the World] and many others cannot say that their work "keeps faith sweet and strong." It is often a bitter and weakening ingredient. Further, they don't want "a trust that triumphs over wrong," but a religion of action which will annihilate the wrong.[31]

Of the two hymns each by former abolitionists John Greenleaf Whittier, James Russell Lowell, and Thomas

---

[30] Horton Davies, "The Expression of the Social Gospel in Worship," *Studia Liturgica*, 2, no. 3 (Sept. 1963), 188.
[31] Rauschenbusch, "Comments," MS, 3.

Wentworth Higginson, three of them appear to have been written as an expression of antislavery sentiment. What Horton Davies says about Lowell's and Whittier's hymns, which "urged men to a social crusade against the war," seems more applicable to their hymns that prompted men and women to crusade against slavery:

> It was left to the hymnodists of the social gospel only to clothe their social aspirations in the category of the Kingdom of God, and to substitute for the generalities of their predecessors the specific abuses from which industrial man was to be delivered by God and the awakened people. The opportunity was avidly and widely seized.[32]

The new hymns of Social Gospelism were essentially the old hymns of moral abolitionism, minus black Americans, plus European immigrants, minus the "exodus," plus the "kingdom."

The opening piece in *Social Hymns* lyricizes the Hebrew exodus but the Social Gospel did not encompass a systematic theology based on the liberation motif. The evidence is that this opening hymn is listed under the heading of Aspiration and Faith rather than Liberty and Justice. However, no hymnbook of any reform movement would be complete without a piece expositing the exodus. Stanzas two and three of the opening hymn, W. Russell Bowie's "God of the Nations," read:

> Thine ancient might did break the Pharaoh's boast,
> Thou wast the shield for Israel's marching host,
> And, all the ages through, past crumbling throne
> And broken fetter, Thou hast brought Thine own.
>
> Thy hand has led across the hungry sea
> The eager peoples flocking to be free,
> And from the breeds of earth, Thy silent sway
> Fashions the Nation of the broadening day.

Lowell's "Men, Whose Boast It Is," listed as a hymn of liberty and justice, uses the classic antislavery imagery of "chains," "fetters," and "slaves." Yet, the opening verse illustrates that the questions it raises were just as applicable to the Social Gospel:

[32] Davies, 188.

> Men, whose boast it is that ye
> Come of fathers brave and free,
> If there breathe on earth a slave,
> Are ye truly free and brave?
> If ye do not feel the chain
> When it works a brother's pain,
> Are ye not base slaves indeed,
> Slaves unworthy to be free?

"Once to Every Man and Nation," Lowell's hymn of social Christianity, was also being adapted for the Social Gospel. Hymnologist Homer Rodeheaver recounts the story of its composition:

> The American poet, James Russell Lowell, in December, 1845, wrote a poem, "The Present Crisis," against the war with Mexico, in which he argued that annexation to the United States of any considerable portion of Mexico would only add to the American territory in which slavery was permitted. . . . From this poem a cento was taken which forms our own stirring hymn of social justice, "Once to every man and nation."[33]

The first half of the opening octrain informs that, not either-or, but the individual and the nation collectively were required to choose between the good and evil side—an idea elaborated on by the Social Gospel:

> Once to every man and nation
>   Comes the moment to decide,
> In the strife of truth with falsehood,
>   For the good or evil side; . . .

The concluding quatrain of the third stanza prophetically foresaw another doctrine of the Social Gospel: that the transmission of "ancient good" down through the generations may be the wrongful perpetuation of evil under the guise of social tradition:

> New occasions teach new duties,
>   Time makes ancient good uncouth;
> They must upward still and onward,
>   Who would keep abreast of truth.

[33] Homer A. Rodeheaver, *Hymnal Handbook for Standard Hymns and Gospel Songs* (Chicago: Rodeheaver Company, 1931), 83.

One of Colonel Thomas Wentworth Higginson's two pieces in *Social Hymns* sounds reminiscent of his years in command of a regiment of slaves recruited for service in the Union Army.[34] Stanzas one and three contain military imagery and signal prophecy:

> From street and square, from hill and glen,
>   Of this vast world beyond my door,
> I hear the tread of marching men,
>   The patient armies of the poor.
>
> The peasant brain shall yet be wise,
>   The untamed pulse grow calm and still;
> The blind shall see, the lowly rise,
>   The work in peace Time's wondrous will.

It is likely that the Social Gospel interpreted the word "race" to mean the various races of European immigrants (and more symbolically—and ambiguously—"Jews and Gentiles"); however, there is one famous hymn of the movement so sympathetic to the ideas of brotherhood, equality, and liberty that it seems to speak inclusively of the single race being neglected amid all of this "progress."[35] Verse two of

---

[34] Thomas Wentworth Higginson, *Army Life in a Black Regiment* (1869; republished, Boston: Beacon, 1962), xiii (biographical introduction by John Hope Franklin).

[35] Rauschenbusch was opposed to slavery and lynching, considering them to be manifestations of the kingdom of evil (Rauschenbusch, *Christianity and the Social Crisis*, 79, 81), and he contested all efforts white Southerners made to exclude blacks from the protection of moral law (Rauschenbusch, *A Theology for the Social Gospel* [New York: Macmillan, 1917], 186). However, in an Apr. 30, 1916, "Address to a Negro Baptist Church," he disclosed his racial posture (which was suspected all along to be Darwinian): "[The] White man decides only his own future," he exhorted, "so should Negroes work for their race"—"not by playing politics and getting offices," he prodded. Rauschenbusch was comfortable injecting into the aorta of the black church such heavy doses of religious opium because he believed blacks were a "belated race climbing up, surrounded by the antagonism of another race," which had a "long [head] start" (Walter Rauschenbusch, "Address to a Negro Baptist Church," MS, Apr. 30, 1916, Rauschenbusch papers). Although he did not go as far as Josiah Strong in wanting to impose on blacks partial blame for the race problem (Josiah Strong, "The Race Question," *Homiletic Review* 58 [Aug. 1909], 122–29), implicit in his sermon (in a Darwinian distortion of Booker T. Washington pragmatism) was the implication that whites were morally superior to blacks and that the latter would have to "evolve" by means of "self-help" in order to eventually earn admittance into the messianic brotherhood of the kingdom.

Having bypassed the race that had been beaten and robbed by the thievery of slavery and left for dead on the side of the Jericho Road, mainline Social Gospelers

William Ballantine's hymn of patriotism, "God Save America," expresses concern not for "our race" but "all races":

> God save America! Here may all races
> Mingle together as children of God,
> Founding an empire on brotherly kindness,
> Equal in liberty, made of one blood.[36]

Of all the "kingdom" hymnals published during the Social Gospel, Mussey's *Social Hymns* surfaces as the paradigm
with its comprehensive yet potent theological emphasis on
christocentric liberalism.[37] Moreover, it is the one "kingdom" hymnal we know Rauschenbusch clearly approved of,
as revealed in his correspondence with one of the A. S.
Barnes executives. Seeking endorsement of *Social Hymns,*
publisher Samuel Fairley wrote to Rauschenbusch, "It would
interest us particularly to know how the collection pleases
you." Fairley continued, "I may add that it is being received
with considerable enthusiasm, and Churches, Forums, Open
Air Meetings, Social Settlements, Bible Study Classes, etc.
are taking to it kindly as an expression of the modern Social
Gospel."[38] "These Social Hymns represent the collective

concerned themselves with the labor problems of European immigrants, women,
and children, to the exclusion of black Americans; so that when Christ was hungry,
naked, and discriminated against, they neither found him food, clothing, nor
equality. Because the corollary hymnic corpus evolved from this prevalent
"evolutionary ethic," neither christocentric liberals nor their hymnody were the
Good Samaritans of race.

[36] Veritably, one of Mabel Mussey's twelve jurists suggested that in their compilation of social hymns the idea of "brotherhood" be broadened to include pieces
expressing "international and inter-racial sympathies" (Mussey, "How the Hundred Hymns Were Brought Together," 384), and Ballantine's "God Save America"
may in fact have been a manifestation of that ideal. However, typically the word
"race" was a symbolic reference to "Jews and Gentiles" and any strains conjuring
up images of the antebellum past interpreted in terms of industrial "slavery."
H. Richard Niebuhr unintentionally pinpointed this premise when he said, "The
kingdom of Christ faced the additional problem of liberating the new slaves of the
northern victors, the growing army in factories and cities of those who, coming
from Europe or our own land, became the serfs of a new order of masters" (H.
Richard Niebuhr, *The Kingdom of God in America* [1935; Hamden, Conn.: Shoe
String Press, 1956], 122).

[37] "In last year's hymn books," read an editorial, "the space given to social
hymns was as follows": *The Hymnal of Praise* (A. S. Barnes), 20%; *Songs of Worship
and Service* (Century), 18%; *The Pilgrim Hymnal* (A. S. Barnes), 14%; *The American
Hymnal* (Century), 12%; *Service Songs* (Christian Endeavor Society), 7%; *Songs of
the Christian Life* (Charles E. Merrill Co.), 6%. *The Survey,* Jan. 3, 1914, 421.

[38] Samuel C. Fairley to Walter Rauschenbusch, MS, July 24, 1914, Rauschenbusch papers.

knowledge and spiritual taste of many," responded Rauschenbusch, "and offer a real basis for a study of social redemption
expressed in song."[39] Further endorsement came from a
cross-section of liberals, including Josiah Strong, who commented that, "It will serve not only to express, but to culti-
vate both the deepest religious feelings and the noblest social
aspiration." Henry Atkinson, Secretary of the Social Service
Commission of the Congregational Church, stated: "The Social Service movement in the churches, as well as the movement on the outside, needs just such an expression as these
hymns give it. When the churches begin to sing the social
faith, things will be accomplished."

"Kingdom" Hymnody in Church Liturgy

Following the publication of *Social Hymns* Rauschenbusch wrote to the A. S. Barnes Company concerning his
next project. Concerned to clear possible copyright viola-
tions in his use of Mussey's volume, he said:

> In a new book which I hope to publish this Fall I am in-
> serting a chapter on the Hymns and Prayers of Social
> Redemption. I have quoted a number of the hymns, usu-
> ally one or two stanzas that seemed to me significant, in
> order to illustrate the characteristics of these hymns. Pro-
> fessor Ballantine's hymn "God Save America" is the only
> one which I have inserted entire. He dedicated the hymn
> to me, and I should like to help in making it known.[40]

A few days later (nearly four years following their initial
correspondence), he wrote back to T. Albert Moore inquir-
ing whether the Methodist Church Department of Temperance and Reform had ever published their proposed edition
of "reform songs." If so, Rauschenbusch wanted to know if it
contained any hymns "voicing social feeling and aspiration,"
in order that he might make reference to it in the book he
was writing.[41] Three months earlier, Rauschenbusch had
said this about the book itself:

[39] This and the following endorsements were compiled onto a sheet that was
attached to Fairley's correspondence to Rauschenbusch, MS, July 30, 1914.
    [40] Rauschenbusch to the A. S. Barnes Company, MS, July 22, 1914.
    [41] Walter Rauschenbusch to T. Albert Moore, MS, July 25, 1914, Rauschen-
busch papers.
    During his January 19, 1910, visit to Oberlin Theological Seminary for a

> The book will cover a similar field as "Christianity and the Social Crisis" and "Christianizing the Social Order," but will be fresh material and will raise new questions. It will deal less with the economic side and more with the problem [of] how to get the new social convictions practically embodied in the life and thought of the churches. . . . Again, how can the religious feelings called out by the new social vision be expressed and satisfied in the prayers, the hymns, and the liturgy of the churches?[42]

It became increasingly evident to Rauschenbusch that these social songs would not "save" or Christianize the nation by themselves, and that when churches sang the social faith without hearing it preached and prayed, the Social Gospel would not make the impact that it wished. However, if the new social convictions could be embodied in the churches with an integrated liturgy of social awakening, then those with "the new social vision" would turn their faces toward the Great Social Worker asking what casework they must do to save America.

Spreading this new social vision was indeed a high calling, but in a stroke of time, World War I; and Rauschenbusch, facing his Gethsemane, wrote in his "instructions in case of my death": "Since 1914 the world is full of hate, and I cannot expect to be happy again in my lifetime. I had hoped to write several books which have been on my mind, but doubtless others can do the work better."[43]

lecture (G. Walter Fiske to Walter Rauschenbusch, MS, Dec. 13, 1909), he apparently engaged in a workshop with Oberlin seminarians on the subject of Social Gospel hymnody, for among his papers are two pages of handwritten notes titled "Comments on the Papers of Oberlin Students on Hymns." One of his six Grinnell lectures at Grinnell College in Iowa (February 23–27, 1914) was to be on the subject "Hymns, Prayers, and Sacraments." Walter Rauschenbusch to J. H. Main (President of Grinnell College), MS, Oct. 6, 1913. The dates of the lecture are given in Walter Rauschenbusch to (Prof.) O. H. Cessna, MS, Nov. 22, 1913. In Walter Rauschenbusch to Ms. Hollister, MS, Jan. 19, 1914, he plans to lecture to a woman's organization on the topic "Social Prayers, Hymns, and Sacraments." All of the above correspondences are located in the Rauschenbusch papers.

[42] Walter Rauschenbusch to the Macmillan Company, MS, Apr. 16, 1914, Rauschenbusch papers.

[43] Quoted in Vernon P. Bodein, "Walter Rauschenbusch," *Religion in Life,* 6, no. 3 (Summer 1937), 431. The excerpt from Rauschenbusch's "instructions" was sent to Bodein by Mrs. Rauschenbusch in March 1935.

Because the book was left unwritten,[44] theologian Horton Davies, in his investigation into the Social Gospel, nearly a half-century after Rauschenbusch's death in 1918, could claim that a pertinent question remained unanswered: "Did the protagonists of the Social Gospel actually compose any new forms of worship for its expression?" In 1933, Charles Clayton Morrison, not as far removed from the movement, answered no; arguing that the Social Gospel never produced the required liturgy to make it applicable to "the labor movement, . . . and the scientific movement, and the peace movement, and the civic conscience, and the community spirit, and the family life, and every great human aspiration of [the] time."[45] Davies countered Morrison's statement with a yes, pointing to his failure to consider any liturgical means other than the preaching of the Social Gospel, and concluded that, "far from the social gospel having failed because it did not create suitable expressions for its prophetic concerns in worship, it tried valiantly both in its intercessory prayers and in its stirring social hymns to awaken the social conscience of Protestantism."[46]

In *A Theology for the Social Gospel* (1917) Rauschenbusch provided a theological theory for the social significance of the great doctrines, sacraments, and narratives of the church, but the book that would have conceivably precluded Davies's question altogether was never written by another who would "do the work better." Yet, the great social prophet left hidden among his papers a partial answer to the question his book would have addressed—an answer bequeathed to posterity in the form of a special liturgy apparently composed by him for the Industrial Workers of the World (I.W.W.). Morrison may have felt this work inadequate; however Davies would have endorsed this concise liturgy for the I.W.W. as one that aspired to the "civic conscience" and the "community spirit":

[44] In a five-page typescript titled "Comments" (whose data is dispersed about this paper) apparently written between 1913 and 1914, it appears that Rauschenbusch began formulating the details of the chapter segment on hymns of the social awakening.

[45] Morrison, 67–68.

[46] Davies, 175, 183, 191.

Hymns: (Brotherhood Hymns) 28 "Our Brotherhood";
13 "The Elder Brother"; 10 "Hymn of the New Crusade."
Adapted prayer from Dr. Rauschenbusch: Volume on
Social Prayers. Sermon: "Ideals in Common" (Between
I. W. W. and Christianity).

And the outline for the evening service was:

Prelude—"Day is dying in the west." Tune, Chautauqua.
Reading—"A House by the Side of the Road."
Hymn—"Somebody did a golden deed."
Scripture—Ps. 1—Read by a representative of Labor
Union.
Reading—Kipling's "If."
Address—"This is the Gospel of Labor, Ring it, ye bells
of the kirk."
Hymn—"We've a story to tell to the nations."
Prayer—By Chaplain of Central Labor Union.
Postlude—"The King of Love my Shepherd is." Tune
"Dominus regit me."[47]

Implicit in Rauschenbusch's effort to make the Social
Gospel orthodox via an integrated liturgy comprised of social preaching, prayer, and hymnody was that the movement's ideals of love and "brotherhood" only needed to be
declared persuasively in order to evangelize society, redeem
history, Christianize the social order, and corporately propel
the Christian community toward messianic theocracy, when
heaven and earth would comprise a homogeneous realm. Not
so, answers Reinhold Niebuhr, who congratulated the movement for "assigning an immediate relevance for politics and
economics to the law of love and the ideal of brotherhood,"
but who also castigated it for "assum[ing] that the law of love
needed only to be stated persuasively to overcome the selfishness of the human heart."[48] According to the neoorthodox
theologians, a political strategy incorporating some form of

[47] Walter Rauschenbusch, "A Special Service for the Industrial Workers of the
World," MS, Rauschenbusch papers.

[48] Reinhold Niebuhr, *An Interpretation of Christian Ethics* (New York: Seabury,
1979), 104. See also H. Richard Niebuhr, "The Attack Upon the Social Gospel,"
Religion in Life, 5, no. 2 (Spring 1936), 176–81; and Reinhold Niebuhr, "Walter
Rauschenbusch in Historical Perspective," *Religion in Life,* 27, no. 4 (Autumn
1958), 527–36.

coercion aimed at obtaining power equilibrium was needed and not a social liturgy comprised of what Niebuhr would have called "sentimental moralism."

It is certain that the protagonists of the Social Gospel composed new liturgical themes for its expression. But the uncertainty regarding the extent to which these new themes were defused leaves the ensuing question unanswered: If by some liturgical calculation Rauschenbusch had solved the problem of how to disseminate the new social convictions throughout America, could there have been a continuum in ushering in the kingdom starting from the abolitionist movement and progressing to the Social Gospel movement and then to the civil rights movement, at which point America would have been ready to address the "race question?"

4

We Shall Overcome:

Freedom Songs of the Civil Rights Movement

Adaptation of Traditional Spirituals

Freedom songs divide into two basic categories: (1) *group participation songs,* often extemporaneously adapted from existing material by a group involved in civil rights activities, and (2) professionally composed *topical songs,* which comment on protest events from the sideline.[1] Many freedom songs were adaptations from traditional spirituals and gospel songs. Typically these forms, especially gospel songs, were brought down to the mundane by textual modifications. For example, "If You Miss Me from Praying Down Here" was changed to "If You Miss Me from the Back of the Bus," "This Little Light of Mine" to "This Little Light of Freedom," "Woke Up This Morning with My Mind on Jesus" to "Woke Up This Morning with My Mind on Freedom," "When I'm in Trouble, Lord, Walk with Me" to "Down in the Jailhouse, Lord, Walk with Me," and "If You Want to Get to Heaven, Do What Jesus Says" to "If You Want to Get Your Freedom, Register and Vote."

[1] Bernice Johnson Reagon, "Songs of the Civil Rights Movement, 1955–65: A Study in Cultural History," Dissertation, Howard University, 1975, 25. This second category includes the music of white folk singers like Bob Dylan, Joan Baez, Pete Seeger, and Peter, Paul and Mary.

83

The "anthem" of the civil rights movement, "We Shall Overcome," is a combination of the tune to the old Baptist hymn "I'll Be Alright" and the text of C. A. Tindley's gospel hymn "I'll Overcome Someday" (1901). A side-by-side comparison reveals how the oral tradition adapts its cultural classics to meet new needs:

I'll overcome some day.	We shall overcome
I'll overcome some day,	We shall overcome
I'll overcome some day;	We shall overcome someday.
If in my heart I do not yield	If in our hearts we do believe
I'll overcome some day.	We shall overcome someday.

The anthem, customarily used as a benediction to the liturgy of mass meetings, was a baptismal dramatization of inward allegiance and mass initiation to a new socio-religious order characterized by nonviolence.

The singing of a particular song during a mass meeting, prayer vigil, sit-in, protest march, freedom ride, as well as in paddy wagons and prisons, usually lasted an extended period of time. This necessitated composing new verses, not for artistic variety, but out of the need blacks had to express the complexity of complaints and rebuttals regarding their oppression.[2] For example, additional verses to "We shall Overcome" include "The truth shall make us free/ . . . someday," "We are not afraid/We shall overcome someday," "We'll walk hand in hand/ . . . someday," and "The Lord will see us through . . . someday."[3] Sometimes such new verses were composed by an individual. Other times they spontaneously evolved out of a group experience, or were given impromptu at a mass meeting by a song leader inspired by an event or testimony. The resulting reciprocation of song energizing protest and protest energizing song generated a reservoir of courage, energy capable of propelling the group toward the mountaintop.

---

[2] An example is the spiritual "Ain't Gonna Let Nobody Turn Me Round." In a sequence of verses the word "nobody" was replaced with "injunction," "jail house," "Chief Pritchett," "Major Kelly," and so on.

[3] Sung as a protest song by segregated and integrated labor unions in the forties, the song was first introduced to the civil rights movement by Guy Carawan, a white songwriter who learned it at the Highlander Folk School in Mount Eagle, Tennessee, when he became its director in 1959.

A common textual alteration in existing songs was changing personal pronouns from first-person singular to first-person plural: "I shall overcome" became "We shall overcome,"[4] "I shall not be moved" became "We shall not be moved," and so on. Traditionally "I" has had a communal aspect in black musical culture; but "we" also had personal bearing, for when the group overcame, so did the individual. Correspondingly, when first-person singular was used it was often the songwriter's effort to personalize her or his social commentary. The collective language of the freedom songs, a trait of abolitionist and Social Gospel hymnody as well, fostered the needed sense of community.

Not all existing church songs required textual revisions to meet the protesters' needs. For instance, the spiritual "Wade in Water" was sometimes sung in wade-in demonstrations aimed at integrating public swimming pools and beaches. Spirituals like "Over My Head I See Freedom in the Air," "Free At Last," "Oh, Freedom," and "I Been 'Buked and I Been Scorned" were interpreted with obvious liberative meaning without modification. These songs, which had equipped black people with a system of "folk wisdom," were reaffirmed in the sermons at mass meetings. One writer documented that "Thundering applause had nearly drowned out King's rising, falling oratory when he told a meeting of Albany Negroes: 'Get on your walking shoes; walk together, children, and don'tcha get weary!'"[5] The original meaning of old spirituals was applicable in the new context. The ancestral messages of justice and liberation were related to the present pursuit of civil rights.

Original Freedom Songs

One of the early songs of the civil rights movement was written by Martin Luther King, Jr.,[6] soon after the movement

---

[4] The change to "we" in "We shall overcome" occurred on the picket lines during the union strike in Charleston in 1945. Reagon, 132.

[5] Reese Cleghorn, "Crowned with Crises" in *Martin Luther King, Jr.*, ed. C. Eric Lincoln (New York: Hill and Wang, 1984), 124.

The lines "free at last" in King's famous sermon on the steps of the Lincoln Memorial during the 1963 March on Washington were taken from the spiritual with the same title.

[6] Reagon, 95–96. Reagon cites Alfred Maund, "Around the U.S.A.," *The Nation*, Mar. 3, 1956, n.p.

officially commenced with the Montgomery Bus Boycott on December 5, 1955. In February 1960, five years before the Nashville sit-in movement had begun, during which "We Shall Overcome" was first introduced by Guy Carawan, King made this early effort to make song a component of civil rights activism. In Bayard Rustin's "Montgomery Diary," February 22, 1956, was the day the song became adopted as the movement's theme:

> They [the black leaders] gathered at the Dexter Avenue Baptist Church for a prayer meeting and sang for the first time a song which had been adopted that morning as the theme song for the movement. The four stanzas proclaim the essential elements of a passive struggle— protest, unity, nonviolence, and equality. Sung to the tune of the spiritual, "Give Me That Old-Time Religion," the text is:
>
> > We are moving on to vict'ry (3X)
> > With hope and dignity.
> >
> > We shall all stand together (3X)
> > Till every one is free.
> >
> > We know love is the watchword (3X)
> > For peace and liberty.
> >
> > Black and white, all are brothers (3X)
> > To live in harmony.
> >
> > We are moving on to vict'ry (3X)
> > With hope and dignity.[7]

There are striking thematic similarities between King's song and the anthem that eventually replaced it. His use of collective language reminiscent of Social Gospel hymnody is also evident.

Typically each community movement had its own freedom songs, the verses varied according to the events occurring in that area. And each community had its own talented songwriters. Albany, Georgia, had SNCC workers Rev. Charles Sherrod and Bertha Gober. Nashville, Tennessee,

---

[7] Bayard Rustin, "Montgomery Diary," *Down the Line: The Collected Writings of Bayard Rustin* (Chicago: Quadrangle Books, 1971), 56.

had collaborators Rev. Bernard LaFayette and Rev. James Bevel. Atlanta, Georgia, lauded Bayard Rustin.[8] And, in 1962, 23-year-old SNCC voter registration worker Sam Block came to Greenwood from nearby Cleveland, Mississippi. Block's song, "Freedom Is a Constant Dying," is a personal reflection of the "redemptive suffering" endured during the freedom struggle. How touching it must have been to hear the song of this "tall, black, gaunt, silent" son of a construction worker "who sings in a deep voice and looks at you with eyes large and sad."[9] Someone raised a verse of it at a 1964 Mississippi mass meeting in response to Bob Moses's announcement that James Chaney, Andrew Goodman, and Michael Schwerner, three young civil rights workers in the Summer Project, had been mercilessly executed:

> They say that freedom is a constant struggle (*3X*)
> Oh, Lord, we've struggled so long,
> We must be free.
> We must be free.

"It was a new song to me and to others," said one witness. "But I knew it, and all the voices in the room joined in as though the song came from the deepest part of themselves, and they had always known it."[10] They knew the song's truth, for shortly before they had lost Medgar Evers, who had struggled that they might be free.

Songleaders and Freedom Singers

Mrs. Fannie Lou Hamer knew the sorrow songs of the freedom struggle and the sorrow songs her mother used to

---

[8] Bertha Gober was expelled from Albany State College for her involvement in the Albany Movement. Rev. Bevel was a student at the American Baptist Theological Seminary and later became a senior staff member of SCLC.

While a student at the City College of New York in the thirties, Bayard Rustin sang with Josh White and Leadbelly. Rustin, *Down the Line*, ix.

Rustin stated, "I was a singer and I wrote songs and they were topical about what was happening, and Abernathy would usually introduce them." Howell Raines, *My Soul is Rested: Movement Days in the Deep South Remembered* (Baltimore: Penguin, 1983), 52.

Other songwriters include Len Chandler from New York and Matthew Jones from Knoxville, Tennessee.

[9] Howard Zinn, *SNCC: The New Abolitionists* (Boston: Beacon, 1965), 82.

[10] Sally Belfrage, "Freedom Summer," *Black Protest: History, Documents, and Analyses*, ed. Joanne Grant (Greenwich, Conn.: Fawcett, 1968), 402.

sing when she was a child. She was greatly influenced by
them:

> I began to see the suffering that she had gone through.
> At night she would sing . . . songs that would really
> sink down in me, . . . like, "I would not be a white man,
> I'll tell you the reason why, I'm afraid my Lord might
> would call me and I wouldn't be ready to die. . . ." [S]he
> would say in songs what was really happening to us.[11]

Fannie's mother used such songs to encourage her daughter
to be proud of her race and to reinforce her repeated exhortation: "You respect yourself as a black child, and when you
get grown, if I'm dead and gone, you respect yourself as a
black woman, and other people will respect you."[12] The
songs and their messages sank deep, establishing a core belief
system that instilled in her the "courage to be." As a courageous SNCC field secretary (1963–67) and cofounder of the
Mississippi Freedom Democratic Party (April 26, 1964),
"Her words of wisdom somehow sustained all those around
her with faith in God."[13] One participant confirmed, "When
Mrs. Hamer finishes singing a few freedom songs one is
aware that he has truly heard a fine political speech, stripped
of the usual rhetoric and filled with the anger and determination of the civil rights movement."[14]

The litanies of the original and adapted protest songs
were not only sung congregationally in the liturgy of mass
meetings and during demonstrations, they were also professionally performed by freedom choirs. Just as there evolved
professional groups like the Almanac Singers, who wrote,

[11] Fannie Lou Hamer, Aug. 9, 1968, 3–4, Ralph J. Bunche Oral History Collection, Moorland-Spingarn Research Center, Howard University.
[12] Ibid., 2–3.
[13] ReJohnna Brown, "Fannie Lou Hamer: My Personal Memoir," *Jackson [Mis-
sissippi] Advocate*, Feb. 25, 1982.
Mrs. Hamer's favorite song was "This Little Light of Mine, I'm Gonna Let It
Shine" and her famous saying "I'm sick and tired of being sick and tired."
According to Mrs. Hamer, Harry Belafonte had planned to produce an album
of her singing gospel songs. If a profit was to be made, she said, it would go toward
the campaign. "Marked for Murder," *Sepia*, Apr. 1965, 33.
These and other clippings are found in the Fannie Lou Collection, Tougaloo
College.
[14] Bob Cohen, "Mississippi Caravan of Music," *Broadside Magazine*, Oct. 1964,
n.p.

sang, and recorded union songs at protest rallies and on the picket lines,[15] and The Hutchinsons, who performed abolition songs during the antislavery movement, so did similar groups arise during the civil rights movement. Among them were the Nashville Quartet, the Selma Freedom Choir, Guy Carawan and the Freedom Singers, Carlton Reese's Gospel Freedom Choir of the Alabama Christian Movement for Civil Rights (known as the Birmingham Choir), the Montgomery Gospel Trio, and the Freedom Singers of SNCC.[16]

Of these groups the Freedom Singers gained national reputation. Organized in 1962 out of the Albany Movement by SNCC's Executive Director, James Forman, the group consisted of SNCC field secretaries Rev. Charles Sherrod, Cordell Reagon, Bernice Reagon, and Bertha Gober. They adopted a repertoire of group and topical songs first published on the picket lines, in prisons, and during sit-ins of community protest movements. Bernice Reagon, a member of the group from 1962 to 1966, explained that "With the need to gather supporters and disseminate information on the Civil Rights Movement, the music gained increased importance as a means of conveying the nature and intensity of the struggle to audiences outside the geography of Movement activity."[17] The group promoted the purpose and message of SNCC primarily by performing on black college campuses throughout the country. They also had the opportunity to sing in Carnegie Hall in July 1963 with the renowned Mahalia Jackson[18] and the following month on the steps of the Lincoln Memorial alongside Marian Anderson, Camilla Williams, Mahalia Jackson, and Odetta.[19] Part of the

---

[15] Among black singers who performed with the Almanac Singers were Sonny Terry, Brownie McGhee, Huddie "Leadbelly" Ledbetter, and Josh White. Reagon, 59.

[16] While Reese's group sang freedom songs in a gospel idiom, it is paradoxical that the Nashville Quartet, consisting of students of the American Baptist Theological Seminary, sang freedom songs in a rhythm and blues idiom. The latter used popular song tunes by such artists as Ray Charles.

[17] Reagon, 146.

[18] See "Freedom Songs at Carnegie Hall," *New York Times,* July 23, 1963, L28.

[19] The Freedom Singers sang "This Little Light of Mine" and "I Woke Up This Morning with My Mind on Freedom." Marian Anderson sang "The Lord's Prayer" and "He's Got the Whole World in His Hands." Camilla Williams sang the "Star-Spangled Banner." And Mahalia Jackson, at Martin Luther King's suggestion, sang

money the group raised was used to pay the bail of imprisoned freedom fighters throughout the South.[20] The Freedom Singers helped move the movement by being liaisons
between the movement and its audience—cavaliers courting
those who were agape-lovers of things of "ultimate concern."

While the Freedom Singers were engaged in the performance facet, the Mississippi Caravan of Music embarked
on the teaching aspect. This group of musicians, under the
direction of Bob Cohen, traveled to various Freedom Schools
in the Mississippi Summer Project of 1964 giving workshops
on the history of black song and the liberative role it assumed
since slavery. Also instrumental in spreading freedom songs
throughout the country were such publications as *We Shall
Overcome,* the SNCC songbook (1963), plus the *Broadside* and
Sing Out! magazines.[21]

Why Singing Was Essential to the Movement

"Without these songs, you know we wouldn't be any-
where. We'd still be down on Mister Charley's plantation,
chopping cotton for 30 cents a day,"[22] Cordell Reagon told a
meeting of Greenwood, Mississippi, blacks as he implored
them to sing and to be encouraged. Another SNCC field
secretary, Phyllis Martin, explained to a journalist why song
was essential in the South:

"I Been 'Buked and I Been Scorned" and led the mass in "We Shall Overcome."
Jackson tells her story in Mahalia Jackson, "Singing of Good Tidings and Freedom" [excerpt from *Movin' On Up*], *Afro-American Religious History: A Documentary Witness,* ed. Milton C. Sernett (Durham, N.C.: Duke University Press, 1985),
456.

    Others who performed are Joan Baez, Bob Dylan, Pete Seeger, and Peter, Paul
and Mary. Among Baez's repertoire were such songs as "Oh Freedom," "We Shall
Overcome," which she recorded as a single, and "Birmingham Sunday," which is
about the 1963 murder of the four Sunday school children in Sixteenth Street
Baptist Church.

[20] They were assisted in this task by entertainers who gave benefits, such as
Harry Belafonte, Sammy Davis, Jr., Mahalia Jackson, and Nat King Cole, and by
substantial contributions given by the NAACP Legal Defense Fund and black
churches.

    Belafonte and Davis were the principal contributors. Wyatt T. Walker said
that to his knowledge Belafonte contributed more to the movement than any other
entertainer. Wyatt T. Walker, Ralph J. Bunche Oral History Collection, Oct. 11,
1967, 23–24.

[21] Song sheets used at mass meetings sometimes consisted of selections copied
from the SNCC songbook.

[22] "Without These Songs," *Newsweek,* Aug. 31, 1964, 74.

> The fear down here is tremendous. I didn't know whether I'd be shot at, or stoned, or what. But when the singing started, I forgot all that. I felt good within myself. We sang "Oh Freedom" and "We Shall Not Be Moved," and after that you just don't want to sit around any more. You want the world to hear you, to know what you're fighting for![23]

Referring to Hart County, Georgia, Vernon Jordan said: "The people were cold with fear until music did what prayer and speeches could not do in breaking the ice."[24]

Singing was not only a source of courage, it was a means of responding to events and audaciously "talking back" to the establishment. It was also a form of rebellious self-assertion because it was customarily disallowed in prison. For example, in Parchman Penitentiary the guards took Stokely Carmichael's mattress (with him grasping onto it) because he was singing. He responded by singing, "I'm gonna tell God how you treat me," and his fellow prison mates joined in.[25] Dion T. Diamond, who was James Farmer's cell mate during their forty-nine day incarceration in Parchman in the summer of 1961, said that they had song fests nightly and sang songs like "Poor Silas Died in Jail."[26] In February 1960, in Orangeburg, South Carolina, 1,000 students marched through the downtown area. Hundreds were imprisoned in open-air stockades during which time they sang the "Star-Spangled Banner."[27] Singing the national anthem was perhaps the proverbial insult to America in its present state as well as a statement of intent to assimilate.[28]

---

[23] Robert Sherman, "Sing a Song of Freedom," *SR*, Sept. 28, 1963, 65.

[24] Ibid.

[25] Zinn, 57.

[26] Dion T. Diamond, Ralph J. Bunche Oral History Collection, Nov. 11, 1967, 50.

[27] Grant, *Black Protest*, 225.

[28] Singing patriotic songs was a constant reminder to the oppressive overculture of its moral error and an intolerable thorn in the flesh, for the most fervent emotions come from the powerful when the oppressed lay claim to the cardinal symbols of the ruling class. A parallel incident, which drives this point home, was observed by Rev. Edwin King in Jackson, Mississippi. Blacks had just left a mass meeting at Pearl Street A.M.E. Church and were marching to the city hall protesting the slaying of Medgar Evers the day before. Upon the occasion, American flags were jerked from the protesters' hands by the city officials: "We watched as the police met the silent flag bearing demonstrators . . . [and] soon police began

Black song was an irreplaceable survival tool for the oppressed. It equipped those raised in black communities with a system of core beliefs regarding the providence of God.[29] When Rosa Parks sat down at the front of the bus despite the threat of arrest, she was making a statement as to whether or not God could be trusted. Walter Fauntroy said the public accommodations victories of the sixties were won "because when a black woman who had been singing every Sunday 'I'm a child of the King' decided that she was going to act like a child of the King from Monday to Saturday, she sat down."[30] Roy Morrison confirmed, "Human rights must be achieved through constructive self-assertion. If a woman seeks freedom she must first be free in her own mind and in her own guts."[31] Music was the spiritual and intellectual channel to that "body wisdom"—the guts—and so it is likely that the oppressed intentionally and instinctively selected songs to encourage self-assertiveness.

Martin Luther King, Jr., at the forefront of innumerable freedom marches and mass meetings, confirmed this when he said that music was the "soul of the movement": "An important part of the mass meeting was the freedom songs. In a sense the freedom songs are the soul of the movement." Then King identified two active musical ingredients that informed the "body wisdom": "I have heard people talk of their beat and rhythm, but we in the movement are as inspired by their words."[32] Psychologist Carl Seashore would have taken issue

jerking American flags from the hands of demonstrators. I saw at least one boy holding on to his little American flag as police moved in around him. A policeman raised a club in the air and brought it down, striking the youth who then released his flag. . . . As demonstrators sang freedom songs and cheered, we on the porch shouted encouragement to them as they were loaded in trucks." Edwin King to Mrs. Margaret Myles, Mar. 20, 1964, 3–4. Edwin King Collection, The Lillian Pierce Benbow Room of Special Collections, Tougaloo College.

[29] Henry H. Mitchell and Nicholas Cooper-Lewter, *Soul Theology: The Heart of American Black Culture* (San Francisco: Harper & Row, 1986), 2.

[30] Walter Fauntroy, "The Social Action Mission of the Church." Paper delivered at Duke University Divinity School, Nov. 22, 1981.

[31] Roy M. Morrison II, "Theological Understanding of Human Rights from a Black Perspective." Paper read at Duke University Divinity School, Oct. 8, 1979.

[32] Martin Luther King, Jr., *Why We Can't Wait* (New York: Mentor, 1964), 61.

with King's emphasis of the importance of text over rhythm. Seashore said it is rhythm that "gives us a feeling of power," which "carries":

> The pattern once grasped, there is an assurance of ability to cope with the future. This results in . . . a motor attitude, or a projection of the self in action; for rhythm is never rhythm unless one feels that he himself is acting it, or, what may seem contradictory, that he is even carried by his own action.[33]

The points of Seashore's analysis join in the actual act of marching. Rhythm manifested in marching controls and inspires the activity of a large group of people, causing them to act together and to nurture solidarity. King alluded to this when he said the songs "bind us together" and "help us march together."[34]

A rebuttal to this argument might be that Christian soldiers did not really "march," that is, with the rhythmic precision of a militia. However, their courageous mass movement dramatized injustice and symbolized liberation. The resulting self-perception caused the same dynamic that rhythmically carried them. Envision the illustration of Walter Fauntroy:

> And since we could not take our issues to the polling places and the politicians who sought our votes to be elected, under King's leadership we took our issues to the street, and our instruments were not our ballots but our marching feet. . . .

> And they marched until the patter of their feet became the thunder of the marching men of Joshua, and the world rocked beneath their tread, because they took seriously their appointment to declare good news to the poor. And so, the decade of the sixties, I think, will go down as a classic example of the church of God "marching as to war with the cross of Jesus marching on before."[35]

---

[33] Carl E. Seashore, *Psychology of Music* (New York: McGraw-Hill, 1938), 142.
[34] King, 61.
[35] Fauntroy, "The Social Action Mission of the Church."

Onward Christian Soldiers

"A body of civil resisters is, therefore, like an army subject to all the discipline of a soldier, only harder."[36] This saying of Mahatma Gandhi was extracted from his essay
"Democracy and the People," in which he argued that effective civil disobedience in the pursuit of "true democracy" rests
in the discipline of its "soldiers" to endure violent provocation.
This is the reason why being a "Christian soldier" required
immense courage—the only weapon these civil resisters held
on to was the "freedom banner." In the hymn "We Are Soldiers in the Army," the "freedom banner" was taken up as an
offensive replacing the "blood-stained banner":

> We are soldiers in the army
> We've got to fight although we have to cry
> We've got to hold up the freedom banner,
> We've got to hold it up until we die.

"We did not hesitate to call our movement an army,"
said King. "But it was a special army . . . that would sing
but not slay."[37] Essentially King was explaining that had there
not been *nonviolent singing* there would have been *violent
slaying*. Singing not only occupied the tongue to control violent outbursts of profanity, but it also diffused some of the
hostility of the oppressors. For example, during the Nashville
sit-ins of 1963, seven students were picketing hamburger
joints at Christmastime. They were being slandered and bat-
tered while singing carols like "God Rest Ye Merry Gentle-
men" as the police looked on. One of the seven, Michele
Allen, said, "but we kept singing . . . like we were going to
hold them off with this one song about brotherhood, and
they didn't come and get us."[38] Singing was both a defensive

---

[36] Mahatma Gandhi, *Readings from Gandhi: Life and Thoughts of Mahatma Gandhi as
Told in His Own Words,* eds. Krishna Kripalani and Mahendra Meghani (Bhavnagar,
India: Lok-Milap Trust, 1969), 76. This writing makes reference to Thoreau's 1849
essay, "Civil Disobedience."

[37] King, 62.

[38] Michele P. Allen, Ralph J. Bunche Oral History Collection, Nov. 16, 1968,
4–5.
    The fact that students were able to respond nonviolently is perhaps due in part
to the nonviolent workshops given by Rev. Kelly Miller Smith through the
Nashville Christian Leadership Council, which he organized on January 18, 1958,
as an affiliate of SCLC, of which he was a founding member.

weapon of mitigation as well as an offensive banner of courageous self-assertion.

In this context, hymns like "Onward Christian Soldiers" and the "Battle Hymn of the Republic" are not remnants of biblical militarism. They are classics of empirical realism—reminders of the war on the streets of the South. They are Purple Hearts for those whose homes, churches, cars, and chartered freedom buses had been bombed; for the many prisoners of war who lived to tell about the torture at such camps as Parchman Penitentiary (how they were beaten, how their mattresses, sheets, towels, and toothbrushes were taken from them for singing, how the heat was turned on during the hot summer days and cool air blown in the damp cells at night, how the slop they had to eat surreptitiously missed their plates and fell to the floor); for James Meredith who, two miles outside of Hernando, Mississippi, in 1965 was felled by a shotgun blast to the back as he began his solo march against fear;[39] and to those backup troops who returned to the place Meredith had fallen to demonstrate to blacks, immobilized by fright, that they could indeed "walk through the valley of the shadow of death and fear no evil."

Meredith, only wounded, was released from the hospital two days later; but today countless others are unable to savor the singing of the battle hymns: Rev. Herbert Lee, the young SNCC worker shot to death in Amite County, Mississippi, in 1961; Medgar Evers, state head of the NAACP, "the man in Mississippi," assassinated on the driveway of his home in Jackson, in June 1963 as he returned from a mass meeting;[40] and Jimmy Lee Jackson shot to death during the Selma Campaign in February 1964. Death was such a constant threat in "the valley of fear" that the soldiers sang:

[39] An excerpt from the two-page "Manifesto of the Meredith Mississippi Freedom March," June 9, 1966 (signed by Martin Luther King, Floyd McKissick, Stokely Carmichael, Charles Evers, Mississippi Freedom Democratic Party, Delta Ministry, and the Madison County Movement), puts it this way: "James Meredith returned to Mississippi to confront the problem of fear and political disenfranchisement that have plagued black Americans of this state. Mississippi's reply to Meredith was a blast from a 16 gauge shotgun. Decent Americans will not allow this march for freedom and justice to end here."

[40] For a detailed account of the days leading up to the death of Medgar Evers, as told by his wife, see Myrlie Evers, Ralph J. Bunche Oral History Collection, 1969.

If you ever miss me from the freedom fight,
You can't find me nowhere,
Come on over to the graveyard,
I'll be buried over there.

The Unimportant Role of Song to the Militant

The day following James Meredith's shooting in Mississippi, Martin Luther King, Jr., and Kelly Miller Smith of
SCLC, Stokely Carmichael of SNCC, Floyd McKissick of
CORE, Robert Wright (an Episcopal priest) of Delta Ministry, and others arrived at the sight to continue Meredith's
march against fear. Along the way King halted the company
to sing "We Shall Overcome," but upon the verse "black and
white together" some of the marchers stopped singing. They
later explained to King that they had embarked on a new day
and no longer sang those words. "In fact," they continued,
"the whole song should be discarded. Not 'We Shall Overcome,' but 'We Shall Overrun.'"[41] Perhaps King was re-
calling Alvin F. Poussaint's speech delivered at a Meredith
March rally. Poussaint said:

> For many years we have been singing "We Shall Over-
> come" and this song is almost obsolete and too passive.
> A new day is here, brothers, and we should begin to
> think, act, and feel that "we shall overthrow." "We shall
> overthrow" the vicious system of segregation, discrimi-
> nation, and white supremacy. Deep in my heart, I do
> believe that, non-violently, "we shall overthrow."[42]

What we shall do becomes an indicator of what ideology one
espoused. There were the "we" who shall *overcome* versus the
"we" who shall *overrun* and *overthrow*. H. Rap Brown's stance
is clear in his February 21, 1968, letter from the Parrish
Prison in New Orleans. He concludes with a postscript "Note
to America," which he signs "We Shall Conquer Without a
Doubt."[43]

[41] King, *Where Do We Go from Here* (Boston: Beacon, 1967), 26–27.
[42] "Speech to be Delivered at Meredith March Rally by Alvin F. Poussaint,
M.D., Southern Field Director Medical Committee for Human Rights." Edwin
King Collection, Tougaloo College.
[43] "A Letter From Rap Brown," *The Movement*, Apr. 1968, 11.

"We" shall *overrun, overthrow,* and *conquer* was more than a flippant parody. This was reflective of a growing corpus of left-wing lyrics being written by young SNCCs. Representative of this new victory song is Len Chandler's "Move on Over or We'll Move on Over You," which (in verse two) makes "We Shall Overcome" antithetical to that for which John Brown stood:

> You conspire to keep us silent in the field and in the
> slum
> You promise us the vote and sing us, "We Shall
> Overcome"
> But John Brown knew what freedom was and died to
> win us some
> That's why we keep marching on.
>
> CHORUS
>
> Move on over or we'll move on over you (*3X*)
> And the movement's moving on.[44]

As long as SCLC, SNCC, CORE, NAACP, and the National Urban League sang together there existed a common chord. When they could no longer sing together, because the radical youth were neither in step with the drum major nor in tune with his theology, then the dissonance of their silence became more audible to those who listened on. The incessant discord between King and SNCC, caused by what Roy Wilkins termed a "generation schism,"[45] was also being heard by the media. In a CBS News Special Report on the Mississippi march, Harry Reasoner made this disparaging comment to the television audience: "From the moment the civil rights leaders rushed in to continue James Meredith's march there's been a struggle to see whose philosophy would guide the steps, the moderates or the militants."[46]

---

[44] Guy Carawan and Candie Carawan, *Freedom Is a Constant Struggle: Songs of the Freedom Movement* (New York: Oak, 1968), 223.

[45] Roy Wilkins, Oral History Interview, May 5, 1970, 78.

[46] Harry Reasoner, correspondent, "CBS News Special Report," "The March on Mississippi," June 26, 1966, 18 (transcript), Ralph J. Bunche Oral History Collection.

"We Shall Overcome" became representative of the non-violent movement and the symbolic partition between the moderates and the militants. To the right were the moderates who favored nonviolence, saying:

> Negroes are not joking when they sing "We Shall Overcome." With nonviolence and love for all mankind as watchwords, we certainly shall overcome. With our willingness to go to jail and be struck and not to strike back, we have already overcome our past role of subservience.[47]

To the left were the militants, like Malcolm X who, in his speech "Black Revolution," said "revolutions are never waged singing, 'We Shall Overcome.' Revolutions are based upon bloodshed."[48] In his speech "The Ballot or the Bullet," Malcolm also criticized the "someday" schedule posed in "We Shall Overcome," saying: "We want freedom *now,* but we're not going to get it saying 'We Shall Overcome.' We've got to fight until we overcome."[49] Albert Cleage, in his volume of sermons, *The Black Messiah* (1968), venomously verbalized the nationalistic sentiment of the SNCC and CORE members who had informed King that the era of singing "black and white together" had ended:

> Black people marching every day felt more and more that they were a people. As they marched they felt "I'm not a part of these white people." Every day as they marched and sang "We shall overcome," they were saying deep down in their hearts, "I have got to separate myself from these people. I have got to recognize the realities of my existence."[50]

[47] Robert Bradkins Gore, "Nonviolence," in *The Angry Black South,* eds. Glenford E. Mitchell and William H. Peace III (New York: Corinth Books, 1962), 149.
    [48] Malcolm X, "Black Revolution," in *The Voice of Black Rhetoric: Selections,* eds. Arthur L. Smith and Stephen Robb (Boston: Allyn and Bacon, 1971), 241.
    [49] Malcolm X, "The Ballot or the Bullet," *The Voice of Black Rhetoric: Selections,* 229.
    [50] Albert B. Cleage, Jr., *The Black Messiah* (Kansas City: Sheed Andrews and McMeel, 1968), 209.

In another sermon Cleage preached, "You can sing 'We shall overcome,' and you can talk about redemptive suffering, but neither of these will change your earthly condition."[51]

"We Shall Overcome" was not actually a *symbol;* however, it was a *sign.* It was a sign that pointed to singing, which was the symbol of nonviolence because it both pointed to and participated in that for which it stood. It was both a defensive weapon of mitigation and an offensive banner of self-assertion. But to the clear-cut militant, the element of pathos that deemed singing a defensive weapon left it an impotent offensive one. Thus, those who did not sing, like the Black Muslims and the Black Panthers, were by no means Christian soldiers, and their decree not to sing was a monotonic manifesto to those who operated under the "someday" timetable.

For a while singing was acceptable to those who had not been fully converted to Black Power. But singing ceased as violence and murder against blacks escalated and blacks became more enraged. Angered at the noxious shotgun murder of Tuskegee Institute student activist Sammy Younge on January 3, 1966, James Forman said:

> People were just filling the streets, and they weren't singing no freedom songs. They were mad. People would try and strike up a freedom song, but it wouldn't work. All of a sudden you heard this, "Black Power, Black Power." People felt what was going on. They were tired of this whole nonviolent bit.[52]

The inevitable confrontation had occurred. Nonviolence, which singing symbolized, and violence, which supremacy symbolized, had come face to face. The battlefront was mainly in the South, but it was a racial confrontation involving the entire nation, which the South symbolized. *Faith* and

---

[51] Cleage, 96.

In the film "A Time for Burning" Ernest W. Chambers, a barber in Omaha, Nebraska, said, "We've studied your history. And you did not take over this country by singing 'We shall overcome.'" Cited in *Black and White: Six Stories from a Troubled Time* (Handbook for Students). Education Development Center, 1968, 23.

[52] James Forman, *Sammy Younge, Jr.* (New York: Grove Press, 1968), 252–53. Quoted in Jerome H. Skolnick, *The Politics of Protest* (New York: Ballantine Books, 1969), 132.

faith had come face to face, no longer eclipsed by a "window darkly." The supremacists would not be converted under the exhortation of nonviolent ethicality that singing represented. Singing, which had been very much alive and nonviolent, had come to an untimely end, and not even President Johnson's March 1965 speech "We Shall Overcome" would change that. Late the following year, in an essay titled "The Angry Children of Malcolm X," came Julius Lester's mortuary pronouncement, "Now it is over":

> America has had chance after chance to show that it really meant "that all men are endowed with certain inalienable rights." America has had precious chances in this decade to make it come true. Now it is over. The days of singing freedom songs and the days of combating bullets and billy clubs with Love [are over]. We Shall Overcome (and we have overcome our blindness) sounds old, out-dated. . . . As one SNCC veteran put it after the Mississippi March, "Man, the people are too busy getting ready to fight to bother with singing anymore." And as for Love? . . . They used to sing "I Love Everybody" as they ducked bricks and bottles. Now they sing
>
>> Too much love,
>> Too much love,
>> Nothing kills a nigger like
>> Too much love.[53]

Pat Watters and Weldon Rougeau gave postmortem credence to the hostility that caused the unmelodious and ominous turn from nonviolent song to violent silence. In their 1968 report to the Southern Regional Council they made this comment regarding civil rights activities in Orangeburg, South Carolina:

> It seems worth noting that the record of violent resistance to Negro rights in the South spawned the black power movement and turned the very organizations and

---

[53] Julius Lester, "The Angry Children of Malcolm X," *Sing Out!* Oct./Nov. 1966, n.p. This essay was reproduced as the epilogue to Carawan, *Freedom Is a Constant Struggle,* 221. See also Julius Lester, *Look Out, Whitey! Black Power's Gon' Get Your Mama!* (New York: Grove Press, 1968), 107.

The original words to the song parodied here are: "Too much love,/ Too much love,/ Never in this world will there be/ Too much love."

individuals who did the most during direct action days to maintain nonviolence among volatile crowds of untrained student demonstrators into agencies and people whose current enunciated beliefs encourage violence.[54]

"Violent resistance to Negro rights" caused it to "be over" in 1964:[55] Stokely Carmichael had converted to Black Power (a conversion experience he enunciated two years later), Malcolm X had founded the Organization for Afro-American Unity and had given his speeches "The Ballot or the Bullet" (April 3) and "Black Revolution" (April 8), and the Black Panther Party had been founded in Oakland, California, by Huey Newton, Bobby Seale, and Eldridge Cleaver, who were ideologically indebted to Carmichael and Malcolm for refusing to sing the songs of Zion in a strange land.[56] Notwithstanding, singing as a symbol did not stop being a symbol when singing ceased. In fact, its symbolism was confirmed by the militant silence heard loud and at length in the rhetoric of the Black Muslims. Singing would remain a symbol as long as tension persisted between the philosophies of nonviolence and violence.

The Theology of Freedom Songs

A total of 145 freedom songs published in the three principal collections were surveyed: *We Shall Overcome,* the SNCC songbook (1963), *Freedom Is a Constant Struggle* (1968), and *Lift Ev'ry Voice,* the NAACP songbook (1972).[57]

[54] Pat Watters and Weldon Rougeau, *Events at Orangeburg: A Report Based on Study and Interviews in Orangeburg, South Carolina, in the Aftermath of Tragedy* (Atlanta: Southern Regional Council, 1968), 38.

[55] Rev. Edwin King, a white Methodist minister, longtime chaplain of Tougaloo College, and civil rights activist, confirmed this: "I haven't heard anyone in the movement really sing in Mississippi since 1964. . . . We don't have anything left to sing about. There isn't enough to praise." Gail Falk, "'Nothing Left to Sing About,' Chaplain Says of CR Movement," *The Southern Courier,* Dec. 3–4, 1966, 2.

[56] Bobby Seale stated: "Malcolm X was the first, really, to introduce black power. Brother Stokely Carmichael did a good job of spreading the need for the concept of this, but it's more Malcolm X who is the real predecessor of this organization." Bobby Seale, Ralph J. Bunche Oral History Collection, Nov. 14, 1968, 8.

However, Huey Newton called Carmichael the "Prime Minister of the Black Panther Party." "Huey Newton Speaks His Mind," *The Movement,* Apr. 1968, 3.

[57] The first two songbooks, compiled by Guy and Candie Carawan, include freedom songs (spirituals, hymns, patriotic songs, etc.) composed, adapted, and sung principally by members of SNCC, CORE, and to an extent SCLC. The latter includes songs sung by members of the NAACP.

Of the 145 pieces examined, a majority, 88, have texts that incorporate biblical language; the remaining 57 have no such reference. Of the 88 having biblical language, 27 use such vocabulary as "Jacob's ladder," "heaven," "faith," "cross," and "hallelujah," while making no mention of the Deity. The remaining 61 (of the 88), make reference to the Deity. In those 61 songs, God is referred to in all but two pieces (59 times): 41 times as Lord and 18 times as God. Jesus Christ is referred to 23 times: 12 times as Jesus, six times as Christ, three times as Savior, and two times as Lamb. The Holy Spirit is referred to three times: twice as Holy Ghost and once as Spirit.

The 59 songs with references to God (alone more numerous than the 57 with no explicit religious connotations) typically incorporate the interjection, "O Lord" (believed to be in reference to God). Therefore, they were not songs about the Lord; they were about social and political injustice, but they were sung in the hearing of the Lord. The "O Lord" crisis-interjection was essentially the singer pausing to say, "Do you hear me, Lord?" or "Hear me, Lord!" In petitioning the Lord to listen, the singers were imploring God to intervene in history as was previously done in behalf of those who sang the spirituals. In summary, the freedom songs are not trinitarian; petitions are neither made in the name of the Son nor of the Holy Ghost.

The fact that there are many more references to God than to Jesus Christ (and the two are rarely mentioned together) at first would appear to support Joseph Washington's supposition that the songs of the civil rights era were "sources of spirited support" rather than "songs of faith."[58] However, it is particularly evident that, when compared to those who would not sing, those who did sing had faith. The songs, culturally validated through their preservation in the oral tradition, provided the individual and the people as a whole with a system of core beliefs that verified the providence of God. Song was therefore a source of affirming God, and singing an act of religious faith.

[58] Joseph R. Washington, Jr., *Black Religion: The Negro and Christianity in the United States* (Boston: Beacon, 1964), 207.

Many of the freedom songs were written or adapted by members of SNCC and CORE, which were technically secular organizations, but the black church ought to be able to claim the remaining fifty-seven secular songs—if not the black church then black religion.[59] The majority of the 145 songs have religious texts. This provides sufficient evidence to deduce that in general, freedom songs are religious and were the music of black religion. However, a more engaging argument can be made. First, nonviolence as espoused by such ministers as Martin Luther King, Jr., Wyatt T. Walker, Frederick Reese, and Joseph Lowery was a Christian ethic. As Lowery attested, it was Jesus who "gave non-violence respectability in this country and credibility as far as theology is concerned."[60] Because singing was symbolic of nonviolence, it was also symbolic of the moral holiness and healing for which nonviolence stood. Second, most of the songs that lack explicit religious connotation highlight the theme of freedom, which is traditionally a sacred motif in black culture. Freedom was of "ultimate concern" to the protesters. It was holy and involved the presence and awareness of the divine. As Henry Mitchell put it, "Street folk may not mention God in all their references to justice, but everyone in the culture is likely to know who is behind the reality of justice."[61] Finally, the reason why the civil rights movement successfully drafted the mass of blacks to the battlefields was because it affixed itself to the most influential organization in the community—the black church. Wyatt T. Walker gives this qualified summary:

> The entire nonviolent movement was religious in tone, and the music did much to reflect and reinforce the religious base on which it stood. In the course of its development, the movement drew into its wake many people who were nonreligious, irreligious, and antireligious, but singing Freedom Songs for them and for others of

[59] In claiming these songs, the black church or black religion ought also to be able to claim SNCC, CORE, as well as the NAACP and the National Urban League.

[60] Respectively, King, *Strength to Love*, 15, 39, 51, etc.; Walker, Ralph J. Bunche Oral History Collection, 17; Frederick Reese, Ralph J. Bunche Oral History Collection, Aug. 1968, 38; Lowery, Ralph J. Bunche Oral History Collection, 9–11. Reese, the least known of these ministers at the time of his interview, was President of the Dallas County Voters League in Alabama.

[61] Mitchell and Cooper-Lewter, 32.

diverse persuasions was a means of comfortable participation. It was this development which contributed most
to minimizing the distinction between sacred and secular within the Black music tradition.[62]

For the nonreligious who were sincerely involved in the
movement, nonviolent singing and marching for the purpose
of an "ultimate concern" had to be more than just a means of
comfortable participation; it must have been a profound religious experience, perhaps even a conversional one.

The Historical Nature of Freedom Songs

Freedom songs, like the spirituals, captured the liberative aspect of God. They constituted a revolutionary liturgy
of song, which ushered religion out of the churches of the
black Protestant mainstream and onto the streets of human
history. There Christ could disengage the pharisaic system
of supremacy. Musically, the freedom songs were the
paradigm of militancy; blacks were not just singing about
freedom but were systematically seeking it.

As historic documents, the freedom songs chronicle the
history of events that transpired during the movement: the
various forms of protest, responses to injustice, as well as personal reflections and testimonials. Those songwriters involved in the movement were both history makers and
historians; they were participant historians. A song such as
Sam Block's "Freedom Is a Constant Dying" is not merely a
testimony of faith. As a song composed by one who had
marched beneath the sweltering sun of the South, faced
the attack of armed police and snarling dogs, fallen uncon-
scious under the toxin of tear gas and the pungent spray of
high-pressure hoses, felt the crack of the horse whip and the
billy club against flesh and bone, and suffered unjust and

---

[62] Wyatt T. Walker, *"Somebody's Calling My Name": Black Sacred Music and
Social Change* (Valley Forge, Pa.: Judson Press, 1979), 181.
    In regards to the nonreligious, Walker commented on another occasion that
those attracted to CORE were usually "the humanists, the intellectuals, etc., who
have no appetite for the church of God, especially Negro religion. . . ." Walker,
Ralph J. Bunche Oral History Collection, 38.
    However, CORE was not nonreligious across the board. For example, the
Baltimore chapter had a significant number of Catholic priests in its membership.

dehumanizing imprisonment, the testimony also becomes the epitome of documentary history. One approach is to study the collection of songs in order to follow the chronology of their developing theology and to glean their sense of historical identity and legitimacy, but it is another to behold the simple, private moments of prayer. Block's averment, "O Lord, we died so long/ We must be free," is evidence that such emotion-filled pieces have much in common with the sorrow songs.

A serious study of the civil rights era is contingent upon its freedom songs, just as a scholarly treatment of the slave era is incomplete without an in-depth investigation into the meaning of the spirituals. However, just as the slave songs were once ignored, the freedom songs are conspicuously absent from black histories and hymnals. Songs like "We Shall Overcome" are apparently omitted from black denominational hymnals because of shame for its passivity, and songs like "We Shall Overrun" are absent out of intolerance for its militancy. Only lukewarm gospel songs allow the desired dissociation from historical reality embodied in the freedom songs. As contemporary scholars return to the spirituals for documentation of slave life during the antebellum era they also must look to the freedom songs for eyewitness accounts of the struggle for civil rights.[63]

In summary, what the historical record of the freedom songs indicates is that the height of the civil rights movement corresponds with the height of singing as a means of expression (ca. 1960–64), and the move toward black nationalism was registered in the lyric and ultimate decline of singing as a mode of protest. From "We Shall Overcome" to "We Shall Overrun," SCLC to the Black Muslims, nonviolence to violence, singing to silence—the history of the movement is documented in the music.

[63] The four principal published sources for such research are *We Shall Overcome*, the SNCC songbook (1963); *Songs of the Spirit Movement* (Chicago: The Ecumenical Institute, 1968), the no. 6, January issue of *Image* (an occasional journal); *Freedom Is a Constant Struggle* (1968); and *Lift Ev'ry Voice*, the NAACP song book (1972).

5

Bluesman Adam and Blueswoman Eve:

A Theology for the Blues

T   H   E   B   L   U   E   S

Toward a Black Blues Theology

Blues is an expression of black theology. The theological content in blues songs and in the oral beliefs of blues people was organic to the evolution of this genre of music in the post–Civil War South. Those who lived blues life "behind the mule" and preached blues theology from behind their guitars were unable to (or did not care to) articulate their theology in scholarly language, so their religion was relegated to "invisibility." Similar to those who erroneously identified spirituals as merely otherworldly, recording agents and casual observers were unable to discern that blues was sacred music. It was not until the post–civil rights era that blues was taken somewhat seriously by journalists and that singers were interviewed about blues belief and the long-standing church-blues dialogue. The documentation of black blues theology gained headway as scholars gleaned filaments of theological thought from this journalistic data.

James Cone was the first theologian to clearly perceive that black theology could not make an adequate statement without critically reflecting on the theological content in the blues. In *The Spirituals and the Blues* (1972), Cone began filling in the gap between blues and black religion, first by explaining that blues were "secular spirituals" and secondly by denying that they were atheistic, profane, or immoral.[1] An earlier article by Rod Gruver, "The Blues as a Secular Religion" (1970), argued that the "religion of the blues" comprised the deification of men and women, "the gods of the blues," by means of lyric that mythologized their sexuality.[2] Paul Oliver, William Ferris, and Julio Finn[3] found the blues repertoire to be replete with what Ferris termed "blues conjuration" and Finn "hoodoo blues." What Cone and Gruver identify as the blues singer's attempt at self-affirmation, Oliver, Ferris, and Finn consider his conjuring of the gods in order to gain control over life's obstacles and women.

However, only Cone pressed on toward a theology for the blues, for only Cone matched its blue pigment with the blackness of black theology. Other writers, such as Charles Keil, William Ferris, and Albert Murray,[4] paralleled this so-called "profane" music with the extrinsic features of black church song and sermon. These writers, sensing something spiritual about the performance of blues, concluded that its

---

[1] See James H. Cone, *The Spirituals and the Blues: An Interpretation* (New York: Seabury Press, 1972), chap. 6.

[2] Rod Gruver, "The Blues as a Secular Religion," *Blues World*, no. 29 (Apr. 1970), 3–6; no. 30 (May 1970), 4–7; no. 31 (June 1970), 5–7; no. 32 (July 1970), 7–9; primarily July, 7–8.

[3] Paul Oliver, *The Meaning of the Blues* (New York: Collier Books, 1966), 161–68; William Ferris, *Blues from the Delta* (Garden City, N.Y.: Anchor/Doubleday, 1979), 77–78; Julio Finn, *The Bluesman: The Musical Heritage of Black Men and Women in the Americas* (London: Quartet Books, 1986), primarily 145–50, 213–20. Of these three writers Finn treats the thesis of "hoodoo blues" most thoroughly. Pointing to passing references to hoodoo in specific blues lyric as evidence, he argues that Muddy Waters, Robert Johnson, and others were "hoodoo bluesmen." He asserts that the awareness of references to hoodoo is the reason the churched referred to blues as "the devil's music."

[4] Charles Keil, *Urban Blues* (Chicago: University of Chicago Press, 1966), 143–44, 164; Ferris, chapter on "Bluesmen and Preachers," 79–89; Albert Murray, *Stomping the Blues* (New York: Vintage, 1982), chap. 3, titled "The Blue Devil and the Holy Ghost," 23–42. Murray defends blues against those who condemn the merriment of the Saturday night gathering as devilment. He asserts, church songs generate "paroxysms of ecstasy" far exceeding anything that occurs in the blues gathering (24, 27).

ritualism was pseudo-religious: that blues singers borrowed forms of religious expression that were superficial. In the discourse of Mircea Eliade, their supposition was that "the man who has made his choice in favor of a profane life never succeeds in completely doing away with religious behavior."[5] Other researchers such as Lawrence Levine and James Cone[6] perceived blues to be semireligious or idolatrous: that hypostatic human expression and moral commitment were to a temporal rather than ultimate value. My contention is that the Christian religion was the sacred history and the fate of blues people and that blues and blues life subsisted within the larger sphere of Christianity.

In the ensuing discourse two additional points are of fundamental importance. First, the subject matter is prewar (pre–World War II) blues. Prewar blues culture, which was far more segregated in corporate black communities of the South than the postwar genre, maintained an intimate dialogue with the black church. It also predated the integration of postwar blues with the secular idioms of jazz and rock and roll. Probably in defense of the religious ethic of the prewar genre, bluesman Sunnyland Slim pronounced: "If you want to do jazz, do jazz . . . . But you can't get jazzy with the blues."[7]

Second, this theology for the blues proceeds from the premise that blues tell the *truth;* and that truth, as the highest value in blues, is the heart of orthodox blues belief and the missing ethical element necessary to considering blues religious. Citing bluesman Henry Townsend's remark, "When I sing the blues I sing the truth," James Cone inferred that "The blues and Truth are one reality in the black experience." "There is," he asserted, "no attempt in blues to make philosophical distinction between divine and human truth."[8] In terms of the prewar idiom, then, we have the negation of Albert Murray's claim that in the performance of blues

[5] Mircea Eliade, *The Sacred and the Profane: The Nature of Religion* (New York: Harcourt, Brace & World, 1959), 23.

[6] Lawrence W. Levine, *Black Culture and Black Consciousness: Afro-American Folk Thought from Slavery to Freedom* (New York: Oxford University Press, 1977), 234–37. Cone, chap. 6.

[7] Paul Oliver, *Conversation with the Blues* (New York: Horizon Press, 1965), 150.

[8] Cone, 114, 119.

"emphasis is placed upon aesthetics not ethics."[9] To the contrary, "preaching the blues" was synonymous with the ethic of telling the truth. That blues singers always professed to have told the truth was perhaps the most enlightened language these singers could use to describe what they doubtless sensed to be a religious experience.

Being and Hope in Blues Life

By concluding the introduction to *The Spirituals and the Blues* with the confession "I am the blues and my life is a spiritual,"[10] James Cone is justified in his claim to the extent that he could not reasonably comprehend the blues unless he was the blues. Essentially he was testifying that he knows what it means to be black in America. He later phrased it, "To be black is to be blue";[11] or, as Memphis Slim put it, "I think all black people can sing the blues more or less."[12] It is venerable that Professor Cone has never forsaken his upbringing in the black community of Bearden, Arkansas. However, it is important to emphasize that blues is simply a legacy he inherited; blues is not his life. Declaring "I am the blues" is like avowing "I am the truth." It is distinct from proclaiming "I sing the truth" or complaining "I have the blues." It is sidestepping the *truth*fulness and the tragedy of blues life. To declare "I am"—whether it is "I am the blues," "I am God's child," or "I am successful"—is to claim selfhood among the community of *beings,* whereas blues people felt they were *nonbeings.*

Memphis-born Beale Street bluesman Booker T. Laury, like Professor Cone, also called himself "the blues": "I'm a blues artist," he proudly professed. "I am the blues—I'm the truth about the blues."[13] It was at the crossroads when blues musicians began considering themselves "artists," rather than just people who sang the blues, that this music ceased being as religious. The consciousness of success, which literally made

[9] Murray, 42.
[10] Cone, 7.
[11] Ibid., 115.
[12] Pete Chatman (Memphis Slim), oral history interview, by Ray Allen, May 16, 1987, Memphis, tape 2, p. 2. Center for Southern Folklore, Memphis.
[13] Booker T. Laury (b. 1914), oral history interview, by George McDaniel, Mar. 31, 1983, Memphis, 19, Center for Southern Folklore, Memphis.

one an "artist," raised the human being out of the entombment of abject blues. This is the story of jazz. The root of jazz, the funeral processions of New Orleans, was deeply religious; but when "artists" began to emerge, the consciousness of success partially stripped jazz of its religiosity. Aesthetics began to displace ethics. Professor Cone is indeed the blues, for to be the blues is not to be blue.

The inability of truly American "true-blues" (blues people) to confidently announce, "I am" did not preclude their ever being. Neither did it preclude the presence of hope in blues life and blues songs as early writers had supposed. According to Cone, hope in the blues was belief in black people's survival and progress despite their social condition. "The blues," he explained, "ground[ed] black hope firmly in history and [did] not plead for life after death."[14] Tennessee blueswoman Van Hunt said of the blues, "It's a sad thing and it's a rejoicing thing."[15] Conceivably, the sad thing was that blues people *were not;* that is, they experienced daily existence as inauthentic. The rejoicing thing was that during blues rituals on Saturday nights they *were* (they had authentic being), and that during those hours of blues *being* they gleaned glimmers of hope.

In summary: Blues *being,* firmly grounded in hope, was not entitlement to the ultimate claim with God that "I Am that I Am [therefore I Am]," neither to the penultimate claim with Descartes that "I think, therefore I am," or with H. R. Niebuhr[16] that "I feel, therefore I am," nor with Booker T. Laury that "I am the blues [therefore I am]"; but rather, blues *being* firmly grounded in hope was entitlement to Cone's ideal claim that "I am the blues and my life is a spiritual [therefore I am]."

The Religion of the Blues

Initial evidence of religiosity in blues is found in the words. Almost all blues make reference to God by means of such familiar interjections as "O Lord," "Good Lord,"

---

[14] Cone, 139, 141–42.

[15] Mrs. Van Zula Hunt (b. 1902), oral history interview, by George McDaniel, Jan. 5, 1983, Memphis, tape 3, p. 13, Center for Southern Folklore, Memphis.

[16] H. Richard Niebuhr, *The Responsible Self: An Essay in Christian Moral Philosophy* (San Francisco: Harper & Row, 1963), 109.

"Lordy, Lordy," "Lord have mercy," "the Good Lord above,"
"my God," "God knows," "for God's sake," "so help me God,"
and "Great God Almighty." The fact that blues was the only
nonchurch music to consistently and characteristically petition the Lord did not stop journalists from concluding that
such colloquialisms were blasphemously tongue-in-cheek.
True, not everyone who says "Lord, Lord" will enter into the
kingdom of heaven, but God was the reference source in
times of blueness, whether petitioned by the churched in
black spirituals or by the unchurched in blue spirituals. And
that the blues singer told the truth in the presence of God,
made blues-*truth* evidence of his highly developed capacity
for experiencing ultimate reality.

If bluesman Robert Curtis Smith's explanation of the
blues—"it's me as I is for what I is"[17]—is taken seriously as
the blues orthodoxy that it seems to be, then blues was sacred
for the religious and profane for the irreligious. And since
almost all blues singers would confess with Son Thomas
that "Everything in the Bible, I believe it,"[18] it can logically
be deduced that blues and blues culture were sacred. Entrenched in the sacred history of Judeo-Christian narratives
and doctrines,[19] pre–World War II blues were the spirituals
of postbellum "invisible" black religion.

The blues was a response to ultimate reality that under-
girded "lean blues life in black America" (Houston Baker).
The whole being of the singer was engaged in intense spiritual expression, a crooning, crying, and moaning confession
that left the blue soul washed clean at the blues altar. From
his common tongue poured out glossal nonarticulations and
tones whose spiritual meaning no vulgarity could demoralize.
The guttural moans and groans mixed in with the words
of blues songs revealed the deep religious experience of

[17] Oliver, *Conversation with the Blues*, 23; which is totally different than saying
"I am the blues."

[18] James "Son" Thomas, interview, by William Ferris, 1968, tape 30, p. 20,
William Ferris Collection, Archives and Special Collections Department, University of Mississippi.

[19] This is evident in such pieces as Mississippi Bracey's "I'll Overcome Some
Day" (apparently named after the C. A. Tindley hymn), Robert Johnson's "If I Had
Possession Over Judgment Day," Tommie Bradley's "Adam and Eve," and Pettie
Wheatstraw's "The First Shall Be the Last and the Last Shall Be First."

Charley Patton or Robert Johnson absorbed in the ritual of "preaching the blues." To have cried along with Skip James in "Sick Bed Blues" would have been to encounter the blues singer's religious fear and fascination.

It was the bluesman's religious demeanor that rebaptized profane space for the sake of the unchurched black blues community. Saturday night in the "juke houses"[20] was their sacred time and place for the communion of blues confession, what Albert Murray designated "a ritual of purification and affirmation."[21] This liturgy, in which barefaced blues people came face to face with the "truth of human existence" and the "truth of black experience"[22] as preached to them in the blues, was a way of rendering meaning to the cosmos by being brazenly truthful about it. Son House, a former preacher turned blues priest, expressed exigency for carrying out this prophetic calling. With an old Baptist whoop he crooned in his "Preaching the Blues":

> Oh, I got to stay on the job, I ain't got no time to lose
> I swear to God, I got to preach these gospel blues.
>
> Oh I'm going to preach these gospel blues and choose
>   my seat and sit down.
> When the spirit comes sisters, I want you to jump
>   straight up and down.[23]

The blues priest was the object of adoration and deification, as was his counterpart the black preacher, and the spirit was as present when the women jumped straight up and down in the blues ritual as when they "shouted" in church.

Son House's piece was probably titled after Bessie Smith's "Preachin' the Blues" recorded three years earlier in 1927. Consistent with the blues ethic, she ostensibly confessed in her sermonette to the "girls" that her intention was not to save their souls, but to practically advise them as to

---

[20] "You all may not know what a juke house is. That's way back out in the country, them old raggedy houses. You didn't have but one night to have a good time so we stay up all Saturday night and try to get some rest on Sunday." Thomas, interview, by William Ferris, New Haven, February 27–28, 1974, roll 1, p. 2.

[21] Murray, 38.

[22] Cone, 112.

[23] The last two of five verses to "Preachin' the Blues" (recorded in 1930).

how to preserve their "jellyrolls." She preached further in the idiom of blues biblicism, "Read on down to Chapter 10,/ Taking other women's men you are doing a sin." Sunnyland Slim also did his share of fire-and-brimstone preaching:

> You know the devil's got power and don't you think he
> ain't.
> Well if you ain't mighty careful he will lead you to
> your grave.[24]

While the preacher extolled the glories of heaven, the blues singer explored present reality with rarely any reference to Jesus Christ.[25] "This is not atheism," contends Cone, "rather it is believing that *transcendence* will only be meaningful when it is made real in and through the limits of historical experience."[26] As Blind James Brewer discerned, "You got to live down here just like you got to make preparations to go up there. You cain't go there until you get there; that is you cain't cross the bridge until you get to it."[27] Hence, rather than singing the spiritual

> Nobody knows the trouble I've seen,
> Nobody knows my sorrow.
> Nobody knows the trouble I've seen,
> Glory Hallelujah!

the blues singer was more explicit as to the troubles he had seen. For instance, Otis Spann had seen blue troubles, namely, money troubles and woman troubles, and he found nothing "glorious" about it:

> Nobody knows, nobody knows people the trouble that
> I've seen.
> Now you know I done lost all my money, and my
> woman she treated me so mean.[28]

---

[24] Oliver, *Conversation with the Blues,* 150.

[25] Jesus is rarely mentioned, but in verse seven of Joe Williams's "Mr. Devil Blues," Williams sings:

> I'm going to write a letter now, going to mail it in the air
> I'm going to ask Dr. Jesus if the devil been there.

Notice that Jesus is referred to as "*Dr.* Jesus," while the devil merely as "*Mr.* Devil."

[26] Cone, 127.

[27] Oliver, *Conversation with the Blues,* 167.

[28] Ibid., 52.

Trixie Smith, in her "Praying Blues," also knew blue troubles, namely, man troubles. She prayed about it in her blues but found glory wanting:

> Folks you don't know half the trouble I've seen
> Nobody knows but the good Lord and me.

> Lord, Lord, kindly hear my plea
> Please send me a man that wants nobody else but me.

The monumental value of laying bare the "lean blues life" is that blues alone has bequeathed to posterity a truthful historical portrayal and theological account of life among the unchurched (as well as the churched) in secluded black communities of the post–Civil War South.

Blues Religion as Radical Protest

The religion of the blues was not morally opaque as critics have claimed; it was oppugnant. Similar to other genres of black protest songs, in which the second and third persons of the godhead were circumvented, blues and its religious culture subsisted within the larger sphere of Christianity as a radical aberration on its periphery. This "peripheral religion" produced such songs as Hi Henry Brown's "Preacher Blues," Joe McCoy's "Preachers Blues," and Luke Jordan's "Church Bell Blues," in which the black preacher was disparaged for his moral hypocrisy and the churched for their self-righteousness (self-deception). "Now you take just a lots of people in church today. They'll drink more whisky than me," accused Son Thomas (alluding to the virtue of his truthfulness). "They'll drink more beer than me. And they'll do a lot more things than I'd do but still they belong to the church and I don't."[29] Blind James Brewer argued further, "I know it's right to serve God; I know it's right to go to church. But goin' to church ain't gonna save no one—I realize that. You got to live this life, and you got to obey God."[30]

But to the churched, singing "Lordy baby" was not obeying God. It was obeying the devil. It was mixing sacral oil and

---

[29] Thomas, interview, by William Ferris, Leland, Miss., 1968, tape 5, p. 18; tape 30, p. 21.
[30] Oliver, *Conversation with the Blues*, 167.

sewer water. A second means by which the bluesman was radical was his ethos of eros. In an article titled "Blues and the Church: Revolt and Resignation," Paul Garon ascertained that such overt eroticism was probably strategic covert revolt against the church's repressive convictions on sexuality.[31] Rod Gruver, in his piece "The Blues as Secular Religion," further sets blues over against Christian moralism:

> Woman had been nearly forgotten in the Christian doctrine of a male-dominated trinity. The Christian fathers blamed woman for the sensual depravity that helped wreck ancient Rome, and her infamous deed in the Garden of Eden has not been forgotten yet. Her place was taken by the Virgin Mary whose sexless pregnancy devalued not only sex but woman's proper role in child bearing. Under Christianity her sexual appeal became a pagan snare, her essential humanity, a heathen delusion. . . . Christianity seems to be the external expression of social male-female conflict. . . . What Christianity feared was her power to absorb man's attention, to turn him away from God, who alone was considered worth attending to.
>
> The Christian fear of woman is evident in a medieval couplet by Cardinal Hugues de St. Cher: "Woman pollutes the body, drains the resources, kills the soul, uproots the strength, blinds the eye, and embitters the voice." The Cardinal's hatred of woman contrasts sharply with Sonny Boy Williamson's exaltation of her and the good she does: "Every time she starts to lovin' she brings eyesight to the blind." Sonny Boy's Woman not only brings eyesight to the blind, but she makes the dumb talk, the deaf to hear and the lame to walk.[32]

This ethos of eros in blues songs could also have resulted from sexuality being the one area in blues life that was unrestrained by law, the county "law," and the lynch mob. Sex may have been a means of feeling potent in a society that was engaged in racial rape and castration that was approaching

[31] Paul Garon, "Blues and the Church: Revolt and Resignation," *Living Blues*, vol. 1, no. 1 (Spring 1970), 20.
[32] Gruver, no. 32, 7–8.

genocidal proportions. To be restrained socially and economically and then forced to live legalistically and pietistically was what Alan Lomax called "the double burden of Calvinist conflict and racial degradation."[33] It was simply more than some men could tolerate when they "got from behind the mule" at sundown Saturday.[34]

The third and most basic form of evil that blues people radically oppugned was "Jim Crow ethics." "Without oppression and without racism," Frantz Fanon figured, "you have no blues."[35] For instance, Huddie Ledbetter blues'd about a racial episode he and his wife encountered in Washington, D. C. Unable to find a room in any of the black-owned hotels, they were forced to spend the night in the apartment of a white acquaintance. The following morning "Leadbelly" overheard the landlord caustically complaining about their presence. Later he responded by composing his "Bourgeoisie Blues":

> Home of the brave, land of the free—
> I don't want to be mistreated by no bourgeoisie.
> Lord it's a bourgeois town.[36]

In satirical self-castigation, Sam Chatman covertly expressed his dislike for his oppressors. The verses of his song are followed by the refrain, "I'm bound to change my name, I have to paint my face,/ So I won't be kin to that Ethiopian race":

> Say God made us all, he made some at night,
> That's why he didn't take time to make us all white.

---

[33] Alan Lomax, *The Folk Songs of North America* (Garden City, N.Y.: Doubleday, 1975), 577.

[34] Cone adds that "most blacks only verbalized the distinction between the 'sacred' and 'profane' and found themselves unable to follow white Christianity's rejection of the body. And those who did not experience the free acceptance of sexual love on Saturday nights, expressed it indirectly on Sunday mornings through song and sermon." Cone, 131.

[35] Frantz Fanon, *Toward the African Revolution* (New York: Grove Press, 1967), 37. Quoted in Ortiz M. Walton, *Music: Black, White and Blue* (New York: Morrow, 1972), 33.

Even Julio Finn maintained that it was as a means of revolt against Jim Crow ethics that bluesmen turned to hoodoo. Finn, 213.

[36] *Sing Out!* vol. 14, no. 1 (Feb.–Mar. 1964), 29. Quoted from Alan Lomax, *The Leadbelly Songbook*, v. 3.

> Say when God made me, the moon was givin' light,
> I'm so dog-gone sorry he didn't finish me up white.

> Say now when God made people he done pretty well,
> But when he made a jet black nigger he made them
> some hell.[37]

Another blues singer protested just as rancorously:

> They say we are the Lawd's children, I don't say that
> ain't true,
> But if we are the same like each other, why do they
> treat me like they do?[38]

These three points of radical protest formed the acute enclave of blues culture, in which the religious story of blues life was lived out. Because blues was continuously whetted in controversy with the surrounding reference group (the black church) and overculture (white America), it sharply cut against the body of that dual civilization.

The Consciousness of Sin

"When the will abandons what is above itself, and turns to what is lower, it becomes evil—not because that is evil to which it turns, but because the turning itself is wicked."[39] There was nothing inherently evil about the blues. Yet, even though it was not really a music "taken up from the devil," as the churched had accused, a considerable faction of blues singers found themselves echoing the antiblues legalism of church. For instance, Little Son Jackson explained why it was a sin to sing the blues:

> Whether a man sing the blues or ballads or what have
> you, there's no way in the world that he can get around
> and not make a sin of it in some way. . . . because it's
> on the wrong side. It's a two-sided road and you on the
> wrong side all the time. A man who's singin' the blues—
> I think it's sin because it causes other people to sin. But

---

[37] Oliver, *Conversation with the Blues,* 35–36, vv. 1, 3–4.
[38] Quoted in James H. Cone, *God of the Oppressed* (New York: Seabury Press, 1975), 185.
[39] Augustine, *City of God,* XII, 6. Quoted in H. Richard Niebuhr, *Christ and Culture* (New York: Harper and Row, 1951), 211.

church music is from the Lord and I never knowed anybody to sin over that. I don't think it's sinful to sing of a wrong done to you, but it's the way you do it. I mean you could sing it in a spiritual form. . . . If a man feel hurt within side and he sing a church song then he's askin' God for help. . . . but I think if a man sing the blues it's more or less out of himself. . . . He's not askin' no one for help. . . . See that's the two different things about it; in singin' the blues you take a drink, then you sing the blues. . . . But on a spiritually kick —you never take a drink to say your prayers![40]

Son Thomas firmly believed that playing blues on Saturday night and going to church on Sunday morning was "goin' too far wrong." He warned: "Now I'd be afraid to do that cause somethin' bad can happen to ya. . . . You can't serve the Lord and the devil too."[41] Son House, who had been both preaching the gospel and singing the blues came to the decisive point of the crossroads. "I can't hold God in one hand and the Devil in the other. Them two guys don't get along together too well. I got to turn one of 'em loose. So I got out of the pulpit."[42]

It was orthodox blues belief that those who turned the Lord loose at the crossroads were gambling away their chance to reap the eternal bounty. Blueswoman Flora Molton, raised in Virginia as the daughter of a preacher, told this haunting story:

I never forget, I was just singing "I got the world in a jug, stopper in my hand, and if you want me, got to come under my command." I didn't know my husband was nowhere around, I looked around and he was standing behind me. I said "Oh, you scared me." He said, "That's the way death's going to slip up on you." And for a long time I didn't sing no blues.[43]

[40] Oliver, *Conversation with the Blues*, 165.

[41] Thomas, interview, by William Ferris, 1968, tape 30, p. 17.

[42] *Sing Out!* vol. 15, no. 3 (July 1965), 46. This comment was made by Son House as he introduced his song "Preaching the Blues" (first recorded in 1930) before a concert audience in Wabash, Ind., in 1964.

[43] Flora Molton, unpublished interview, by Eleanor Ellis, 7, *Living Blues* files, Center for the Study of Southern Culture, University of Mississippi.

Playing the blues, "Well, it's just the chance you take," confessed Son Thomas.[44] "When Gabriel sound that trumpet and
everybody rise, you gonna burn if you ain't right."[45]

The testimonies of Son House and Son Thomas reveal
that the principal religious personages in blues were God and
the devil. God was always within earshot of the blues singer's
complaints about evil and suffering and would act justly in
due time, but the devil was slick, always busy. It was readily
evident to blues people that evil was pervasive in culture, not
only in their own community of faith, but also among the
reference group and the overculture. For those reasons blues
lyrics were replete with references to sin. A frequent accusa-
tion, "It's a sin," was sometimes in reference to his friend's
wrongdoing, his girlfriend's two-timing, and the bluesman's
own deportment. However, as in the orthodox reading of
original sin, the sins of human beings were always pinned on
the devil.

The Fall of Bluesman Adam

Woman, in whom the bluesman had immense faith, was
primordial. To the bluesman, she was the ancestral conscience of the culture, grandmother of tradition, mother of
the church, deaconess, stewardess, usheress, the bearess of
blues babies, and, like Sonny Boy Williamson's woman, she
was sight for blind black blues boys. Memphis Slim confirmed, "The only people that ever really supported blues
and are still supporting blues now, the only black people that
are not ashamed of the blues is our black women. They always
supported the blues, and if it don't be for black women the
blues would have been dead a long long time ago."[46] Not only
did black women support the blues, but as Son Thomas
claimed, "It ain't very many blues made that ain't made up
about a woman."[47] New Orleans longshoreman Jack Simmons
loved his woman so much that he sang:

---

[44] Thomas, interview, by William Ferris, roll 15, p. 5.
[45] Ibid., roll 18, p. 2.
[46] Chatman, oral history interview, by Ray Allen, 7–8.
[47] Thomas, interview, by William Ferris, Leland, Miss., 1968, tape 5, p. 17.

> I'm prayin' for you baby, prayin' that you'll go to
> heaven some day.
> And when you get there baby, I'm prayin' that you'll
> stay.[48]

Woman, explained Rod Gruver, was "more than mortal female, she [had] become a god." She was "a manifestation of
pagan Woman, a symbol of those qualities in nature that have
always been felt to be feminine."[49]

It was the act of turning away from an invisible Jesus to
woman whom he could behold and hold that, as Amos Easton
alluded, comprised the *fall* of Bluesman Adam:

> Just give me one friend to keep me from feeling so
> sad,
> Lord, you know I want a friend like the one that Adam
> had.[50]

In his "Preachin' the Blues," Son House *falls* too:

> Oh I have religion this very day
> But the womens and whiskey, well they would not let
> me pray.
>
> Oh, well, I wish I had me a heaven of my own
> Well, I'd give all my women a long, long happy home.[51]

The key to comprehending the meaning of sin in blues religion is seeing blues as the demythologizing of Eden.

Justification in Blues

> Now the preacher told me that God will forgive a black
> man most anything he do,
> I ain't black but I'm dark-complexioned, look like he
> ought to forgive me too.[52]

These humorous words by none other than "Funny Paper"
Smith probably rang true to most blues people (even to

---

[48] Jack Simmons, "The Titanic Blues," in Bayles Benjamin McKinney's paper,
"The Riverfront," 3, Louisiana Collection (Louisiana Writers Program, WPA,
1935–43), Louisiana State Library, Baton Rouge.

[49] Gruver, 8.

[50] Amos Easton, "No Woman No Nickel," v. 5.

[51] "Preachin' the Blues" first recorded in 1930, vv. 4–5.

[52] J. T. "Funny Paper" Smith, "Howling Wolf Blues" (Pt. 1), v. 5.

those who believed they were gambling away the eternal
bounty), for it was widely accepted that "Blessed are those
who mourn." The source of Funny Paper's blues interpretation of the Sermon on the Mount—"God will forgive a black
man most anything he do"—probably lays in the colloquial-
ism that "God takes care of old folks and fools." However,
Funny Paper is skeptical in another song. Yet his skepticism
is not necessarily contradictory to the blues axiom if perceived as a response to some reference group assertion and
as anticipatory of further response in the ongoing church-
blues dialogue:

> Some people tell me God takes care of old folks and
> fools
> But since I been born he must a-have changed his rules.
>
> You know until six months ago I hadn't prayed a prayer
> since God knows when
> Now I'm asking God every day to please forgive me for
> my sin.
>
> You know this must be the devil I'm serving, I know it
> can't be Jesus Christ
> Because I asked him to save me and look like he's trying
> to take my life.
>
> My health is gone now and left me with the sickness
> blues
> People it don't seem like to me that God takes care of
> old folks and fools.[53]

The blues interpretation of truth was similar; it also
seemed to possess saving powers. "Some people think that
the blues is something that is evil—I don't," said Henry
Townsend. "If the blues is delivered in the truth, which most
of them are, . . . if I sing the blues and tell the truth, what
have I done? What have I committed? I haven't lied."[54]
Townsend was seemingly on the verge of giving the Sermon
on the Mount its ultimate blues interpretation by articulating
the meaning of truth connotatively; not only did God

[53] J. T. "Funny Paper" Smith, "Fools Blues," vv. 1, 4–6.
[54] Henry Townsend, in Paul Oliver, *Conversation with the Blues,* 169–70.

"forgive a black man most anything he do" and "take care of old folks and fools," but blessed are those who bear no false witness. That from behind the veil of their guitars blues singers confessed the truth appears to have provided them with a sense of justification.

The belief of a substantial number of bluesmen that blues is naturally sinful appears to have resulted from both their upbringing in the church and the continuous church-blues dialogue. No matter how much blues people were opposed to the hypocrisy and self-righteousness of the churched, they still accepted its ethical principles. Extrinsically the ethic of truth was axiomatic. But because the law was written upon their hearts the Christian ethic was their final judge.

On the other hand, the bluesman was justified because "Blues ain't nothin' but a good man feelin' bad."[55] For instance, to Mrs. Van Hunt the ability to sing blues was a gift from God.[56] Blind James Brewer similarly claimed that "God give me this talent and he knew before I came into this world what I was goin' to make out of this talent."[57] There was nothing inherently evil about the music, per se, for Thomas Dorsey's and Robert Wilkins's early gospel songs were little more than religious lyrics set to blues music. Correspondingly, Flora Molton recalled a woman bishop of the Holiness Church who gave blues songs new words. "It's Tight Like That," she exemplified, became "He Was Done Like That."[58] "Blues is so close to religious music that you can play a blues in the church now and they think's one of them good old swingin' hymns," informed bluesman Lowell Fulson. "All you have to do is just keep out 'baby,' and that other sweet stuff you put in there."[59]

Former blues guitarist Rev. Robert Wilkins confessed that when he was playing blues he never lived a fast life. Blues was just a way of earning a living; otherwise he was at

---

[55] Ibid., 170. This traditional blues maxim is stated here by Edwin Buster Pickens.

[56] Hunt, tape 3, pp. 6, 11–12.

[57] Oliver, *Conversation with the Blues*, 167.

[58] Molton, 8.

[59] "Living Blues Interview: Lowell Fulson," *Living Blues*, vol. 2, no. 5 (Summer 1971), 22.

home.[60] Although Ma Rainey joined the church just prior to her death, Clyde Bernhardt (one of her musicians) said that she never cursed or anything like that and that she was always "more like a spiritual person that was very active in church work more than she was a person in show business."[61] Blind Lemon Jefferson was also justified according to his churchly morality. Rev. Rubin Lacy recalled that Blind Lemon refused to play his guitar on Sunday, no matter how much money he was offered. Lacy said: "I seed a fellow offer him $20 to play him one song one morning. . . . Shook his head . . . he say, 'I couldn' play it if you gave me $200. I need the money, but I couldn't play it. My mother always taught me not to play on Sunday for nobody.'" Lacy, of course justified, volunteered: "I'll play it. I might as well play it on a Sunday as play it on a Monday."[62]

Conversion

The proof that blues singers were uncertain as to whether blues was good or evil is documented in the stories they have told. The ensuing narratives reveal singers whose rationale discerned nothing disapproving about the blues, but whose souls steered them back home to the church. For instance, Rev. Rubin Lacy claimed to have had the blues more since he had been preaching than he ever had when he was playing the blues.[63] "What is the blues? Who has the blues?" asked Lacy—and he answered:

> Sometimes the best Christian in the world have the blues quicker than a sinner do, 'cause the average sinner ain't got nothing to worry about. . . . But a Christian is obliged to certain things and obligated not to do certain things. That sometimes cause a Christian to take the blues. What is the blues, then? It's a worried mind.[64]

[60] "Reverend Robert Wilkins," interview by Pete Welding, *Blues Unlimited*, no. 55 (July 1968), 11.

[61] Clyde E. B. Bernhardt, oral history interview, by Sandy Lieb (Newark, Dec. 31, 1974), 34, 40, *Living Blues* Archival Collection, Mississippi Blues Archive, University of Mississippi.

[62] "The Rev. Rubin Lacy," interview by David Evans, *Blues Unlimited*, no. 42 (Mar.–Apr. 1967), 5.

[63] "The Rev. Rubin Lacy," interview by David Evans, *Blues Unlimited*, no. 44 (June–July, 1967), 7.

[64] "The Rev. Rubin Lacy," interview by David Evans, *Blues Unlimited*, no. 43 (May 1967), 13–14.

Blues singer Willie Thomas, believing blues to be in no way contradictory to the nature of God, contended that when church folk sang "Lord, have mercy, save poor me," they were actually singing the blues—in church![65] Agreeing, John Lee Hooker conceived that "when the spirituals was born it was born on the blues side." Moreover, Hooker said it is due to their kinship that he quit singing spirituals and started singing the blues.[66]

The conversion of Thomas Dorsey is another example of the conflict characteristic of the blues life. Dorsey admitted, on the one hand, that he started writing gospel songs due to "a definite spiritual change." On the other hand, he claimed never to have harbored inner discord when he sang the blues. He still considered blues to be "good music," even following his return to the church. He attested, "I'm a good church man, but I don't put the blues away." Convinced that blues had just as good a message as gospel, Dorsey remained in the gospel music profession only because of his success.[67] However, the fact that Dorsey experienced a "spiritual change" is evidence that, contrary to what he claimed, some indwelling struggle had subsisted and was resolved only by his conversion. "I know why they stop singing the blues," unriddled Little Jr. Parker; "their conscience troubles them."[68]

Dorsey's and Lacy's stories reveal that the church-blues controversy, which overtly occurred in the exhortations of black preachers and blues priests, also existed in the bluesman's subconscious. As Little Jr. Parker alluded, there probably developed a sense of guilt from encountering one's

Tennessee blueswoman Van Hunt gave this definition: "The blues is something . . . . Oh, Lord, you don't care, you get to the point, you give up and don't care for nothing. Right along in there, you got the blues. . . . The blues is a feeling that can't nobody do nothing with, it's a thing that will get on you. . . . It's a good feeling and it's a sad feeling and it's a sort of low down feeling. Now that's deep, deep inward, see, and it's got to—you can't push it or you can't shove it— it's got to die down itself for you just to feel like normal again. And it's a striking thing, it will strike you when you are not thinking of it or nothing of the kind." Mrs. Van Zula Hunt (b. 1902), oral history interview, by George McDaniel, Jan. 5, 1983, Memphis, tape 3, pp. 6, 11–12, Center for Southern Folklore, Memphis.

[65] Oliver, *Conversation with the Blues*, 168.

[66] Ibid., 160, 168.

[67] "Georgia Tom Dorsey" (interview by Jim and Amy O'Neal, Nov. 27, 1974; Jan. 17 and 24, 1975, Chicago), *Living Blues*, no. 20 (Mar.–Apr. 1975), 17–18, 29–30, 33–34.

[68] Keil, 147.

sinful reflection in the light of the Christian ethic. In addition, there was likely an awareness of the physical and mental
degeneration of the self in transient and abject blues life,
perhaps agitated by the sobering deaths or murders of others
in the blues community of faith. With the piecing together of
brief revelations of Truth, there conceivably developed an
apprehension that blues-truth alone was insufficient to give
life ultimate meaning.

It is true that blues deified woman (and to a lesser degree manhood and eros); however, the principal loyalty and
value center in blues was truth. All true blues singers could
maintain with Fred McDowell that "songs should tell the
truth."[69] Blues-truth, the ethic of blues religion, was higher
than woman in the pantheon of values because it qualified
woman. That is to say that it was man's relationship with
woman—love, loneliness, jealousy, infidelity—that blues
singers told the truth about. The dissonant church-blues dialogue was largely the dynamism in this deification of truth;
for without the hypocrisy and self-righteousness of the reference group (agitated at the fundamental level by the repression of the overculture) there would have been no radical
protest and no premium placed on truth. Professor Cone's
statement "I am the blues and my life is a spiritual" embodies
the paradox that the argumentative church-blues dialogue
actually comprised the interdependence and unity of church
and blues. However, because the goal of truth was grounded
in finite protest rather than in infinite homogeneity, there
was no salvation in it.

The "spiritual change" of blues people can be understood as a transferral of values from *truth,* which is historical,
relative, subjective, and finite, to what church folk call "the
Way, the Light, and the *Truth,"* which is trans-historical,
fixed, objective, and infinite. The conversion, then, was not
from truth to a lie (as seen from the penultimate blues side),
but from truth (truth for truth's sake) to Truth's truth (as
seen from the ultimate church side). Whereas they once told
the truth, now they sought the Truth. Conversion from truth

[69] "Fred McDowell Talking to Pete Welding," *Blues Unlimited,* no. 24 (July–
Aug. 1965), 5.

to Truth enabled one to claim being and hope with Professor Cone: "I am the blues and my life is a spiritual."

Parable of the Prodigal Son—Part 1

If there remains a single contention to persist with that blues lay beyond religious faith, it would probably be the assertion that its "religion" lacked a moral basis. James Baldwin would have argued to the contrary, Rod Gruver said in agreement:

> It [blues] is an attempt to replace the immature dependence that organized religion has all too often tended to foster. As James Baldwin has said: "It is not too much to say that whoever wishes to become a truly moral human being . . . must first divorce himself from all the prohibitions, crimes, and hypocrisies of the Christian church."[70]

The prodigal sons of blues, brought up in the church and having divorced themselves from it (later to return), were on a moral sojourn during which they carried on their own form of church recollective of their religious upbringing. Unfaithful to the gospel narrative momentarily (yet never beyond reach of the Father's outstretched hand), these "little children" in Christ would one day return home "young men."

The goal-oriented ethic of blues life (an ethic of survival turned ethic of redemption) was narrative in nature. This was quite natural, for blacks of Africa and of the African diaspora have always been a storied people. Enslaved Africans in America identified their emancipation with the biblical exodus. It was a story they told in spirituals and retold in preaching and testifying. During the reconstruction era of "invisible" blues religion, the principal narrative lived out within Southern black communities was that of the prodigal son. As preachers and gospel singers, former bluesmen undoubtedly turned to their "inner histories" to tell the story of repentance and redemption. Blues people basically remained faithful to the narrative, for the story almost always ends happily with the return home of the prodigal son.

[70] Gruver, 9.

Charles Keil also recognized that "there [was] a strong prodigal-son pattern here: a set of related concepts or common understandings that allow[ed] a man to move from a most decidedly secular role to the sacred role without a strain or hitch."[71] However, it appears that the conversion of blues singers to a sacred role was not as clear-cut as Keil claims. In considering conversion as a sort of evolution from sect-type to church-type, the blues singer's shift to spirituals and gospel was not a moral judgment that blues was profane. It was the testimony of a man putting away the toys of blues life and rising from the fall.

One such narrative was lived out by Charley "Papa" Patton. Raised in a church where his father was a minister, Patton remained marginally involved in the church during his entire blues life. Yet, even though he occasionally preached, performed spirituals in the church, and recorded religious songs alongside the blues, he made a decisive turn to the church when he sensed his encroaching death in 1934. According to his niece he began preaching all week and died not long afterwards.[72]

As the story was lived out in black culture, the blues singer often returned home to become a preacher. For instance, Robert Wilkins left for Memphis in 1915 where he played blues with Patton and Son House. Wilkins never lived a fast life, but he chose not to raise his children in a blues environment. So he returned to the church and in 1950 was ordained a minister in the Church of God in Christ.[73] Following Rev. Wilkins's conversion, his blues, "That's No Way to Get Along" (recorded in Memphis in 1928), was reworded and recorded in 1964 under the title "The Prodigal Son."

Nehemiah "Skip" James, son of a Baptist preacher, eventually returned to the church to become an ordained minister in 1942. He put down his blues guitar and started singing

---

[71] Keil, 147.

[72] David Evans, "Charley Patton: The Conscience of the Delta" in *The Voice of the Delta: Charley Patton and the Mississippi Blues Traditions, Influences and Comparisons, An International Symposium,* ed. Robert Sacre (De Liege: Presses Universitaires, 1987), 136–37, 139, 142, 171.

[73] Wilkins, interview by Pete Welding, 11.

gospel and playing the piano.[74] South Carolinian Rev. Gary Davis, who returned to the church an ordained minister in 1933, sang religious songs up until his death in 1972.[75] And blueswoman Flora Molton, raised the daughter of a Virginia preacher, later gave up the blues to preach in the Holiness Church.[76]

In black religious tradition the prodigal son who returned home was not only expected to tell the story, but to authenticate his conversion by telling the story within the story. In the biblical parable (Luke 15:11–24), Jesus told his disciples that life had reached a low ebb for the prodigal son when he was forced to take a job feeding swine. This crisis at the crossroads finally sent him home repenting. In the real-life narratives of former blues people the correlative story within the story was a dramatic conversion experience that typically transpired on the brink of personal tragedy. For instance, when former blues musician Gatemouth Moore returned to the church as a preacher in 1949, he could tell the story within the story of his conversion. Moore, a longtime featured attraction at a Chicago nightclub, stood on the stage to sing. As he opened his mouth—silence! Again, he storied, he went to the stage—nothing! A third time—this time to his own surprise there issued from his lips a church song. "I was converted in a nightclub," he confessed.[77]

Raised the son of an African Methodist Episcopal minister, Rev. Rubin Lacy storied about his return to the church following a life of blues. In 1932 he was seriously injured while working at a sawmill in Mississippi. Upon striking the ground he heard a voice warning him that the next time it would be death. When he recovered he went to the Missionary Baptist Church and professed his calling to preach. He traded his guitar for pastoring and preaching throughout Mississippi.[78]

[74] The twist to this story is that James (1902–69) was rediscovered and returned to performing blues in 1964. Often it was the wife who talked her husband out of playing the blues. Sometimes after the wife died the husband went back to the blues.

[75] Joan Fenton, "Rev. Gary Davis 1896–1972," *Sing Out!* vol. 21, no. 5 (1972), 4.

[76] Molton, 8.

[77] Gatemouth Moore, oral history interview by George McDaniel, Jan. 25, 1983, Memphis, tape 2, pp. 40–41, Center for Southern Folklore, Memphis.

[78] Lacy, interview, *Blues Unlimited*, no. 42, 5–6.

The Reverend Jack Harp relinquished his blues life to return to the church around 1958. For him, conversion commenced with giving up cigarettes (which he evidently believed were killing him). Harp went out onto the porch for a smoke several times a day, until one day he heard a voice decreeing, "You smoked your last cigarette." From then on, he and his wife held prayer services and eventually he was "saved." He testified as to having seen the Holy Ghost descending from atop their Christmas tree. He received the Spirit's baptism then and there. He could no longer sing the blues. "If I'm saved and sanctified and sing the blues," he explained, "I'm not clean."[79]

Most blues people who had not returned home to "testify" their stories and the stories within their stories eventually would, for the church was their sacred history and fate. For instance, Shaky Jake had promised that he would retire from singing the blues in a couple of years to become a preacher.[80] And Son Thomas hinted as to his eventual return:

> Well I hadn't made up my mind to join a church. I always say when I join the church, I would lay all them blues aside. Probably quit playing the guitar period because if you playing spirituals and used to play blues, the next thing you know the devil git in you and you gonna start right back playing the blues. I always say if I ever join the church, I'm gonna let all that go.[81]

Son Thomas also claimed to have known a forty-year-old bluesman who said he was going to "juke" for forty more years and then he was going to join the church.[82]

The Prodigal Sons—Part 2

If it was difficult for the black preacher to behold the beam in his own eye while pointing to the mote in his blues brother's eye, it was doubly difficult for the church

---

[79] "Reverend Jack Harp," interview by Jeff Godrich, *Blues Unlimited*, no. 26 (Oct. 1965), 4–5. See also Rev. Walter Davis's story in Oliver, *Conversation with the Blues*, 167.

[80] Oliver, *Conversation with the Blues*, 160.

[81] Thomas, interview by William Ferris, Leland, Miss., 1968, tape 5, p. 18; tape 30, p. 21.

[82] Thomas, interview by William Ferris, New Haven, 1974, roll 15, p. 5.

collectively to behold the beam in its own single eye in the sky. The churched, probably identifying themselves with the merciful father waiting to welcome the younger son back home, neglected to recognize themselves in the narrative as the self-righteous older brother. The older prodigal son, about whom part two of the parable speaks (Luke 5:25–32), had remained home maintaining the land and fulfilling the law. So busy chiding the sinners who sang the blues, he failed to realize that the spirituals he sang were also blue, and that both the unchurched and the churched equally needed the Father's grace (the former for their sensuousness and the latter for their selfishness).

Consequently the former blues singer acquiesced the vantage point of privity into the process of moral maturity, for his discovery of blues-truth realistically taught him to come to grips with being and hope in his black-and-blue cosmos. Now privy to Truth's truth, none other than the former bluesman could "tell the story" and reveal the prodigalness of the self-righteous. "I used to be a famous blues singer," Rev. Lacy would exhort his people, "and I told more truth in my blues than the average person tells in his church songs."[83] Only by means of falling could bluesman Adam redemptively rise and resurrect with himself the churched by telling them his story and revealing theirs.

[83] "The Rev. Rubin Lacy," interview by David Evans, *Blues Unlimited*, no. 43 (May 1967), 13.

PART TWO

PRAISE SONG

6

The Drum Deferred:
Rhythm in Black Religion of the African Diaspora

T H E   R I N G - S H O U T

An Overview of Rhythm in the Diaspora

To the African the drum was a sacred instrument possessing supernatural power that enabled it to summon the gods into communion with the people. However, to outside observers it was the drum alone that symbolized the "heathenism" of the "danced religion" practiced by these so-called "cursed sons of Ham." This disapproving attitude of missionaries, slave catchers, and slave masters significantly contributed to the drum being deferred in the diaspora. However, what they failed to realize was that the drum was not the cause of this so-called "paganism." It was actually rhythm that was largely responsible, for percussiveness produced the power that helped move Africans to dance and into trance possession. Had missionaries, slave traders, and slave masters calculated this, they would have attempted to remove rhythm from the blood and bones of the African. But rhythm endured the slave factories and the middle passage and was sold right along with the Africans on the auction blocks of North America. It sat languishingly in the galleries of white Protestant and Catholic churches until it could "steal away" and release itself without reproach among those who possessed it.

The diaspora "de-drummed" Africans, but it did not "de-rhythmize" them. With the drum banned, rhythm, which was both its progenitor and its progeny, became the essential African remnant of black religion in North America. In the ring-shouts of the South and the South Carolina and Georgia Sea Islands, rhythm rocked the praise houses and could be heard for miles around all night long. It empowered those who possessed it to endure slavery by temporarily elevating them out of the valley of oppression up to a spiritual summit.

The Sacred Instrument of African Religion

From its inception, the construction of a drum transcended the mere skill of the artisan and was circumscribed by a pervasive spirituality. Chief Fela Sowande explains the process:

> African musical materials and styles . . . have mythological origins. . . . Among the Yorubas of Nigeria (and presumably in other areas of Africa also), the very first step in the making of a drum is the ceremony which placates the spirit inhabiting the tree that is to be cut down for the wood from which the drum-frame will be subsequently carved. Furthermore, the Yorubas say that the tree must be one that has grown near the village, and is accustomed to hearing human voices. Only then will its wood "speak well" as a drum-frame. A tree in the forest, on the other hand, that has not been accustomed to hearing human voices will be unsatisfactory, for its wood will be "dumb" as a drum-frame. Moreover, every drum has its "altar" carved on the drum-frame. Here is the actual spot at which the drummer communes with the patron deity of drumming. The drummer who neglects his regular communion with his patron deity of drumming will find either that his drum goes to pieces or he will be constantly out of employment.[1]

The religiously constructed drum was sacred to the degree that Africans attributed to it an exclusive value and symbolic

---

[1] Fela Sowande, "The Role of Music in Traditional African Society," in *African Music* (Meeting in Yaounde, Cameroon, Feb. 23–27, 1970), ed. UNESCO (Paris: La Revue Musicale, 1972), 64.

status. In some African societies certain drums were even set aside as symbolic of royalty,[2] while others were regarded as deities.[3] Such drums were sometimes kept in hallowed dwelling places and removed only for special rituals.[4]

Ceremonies honoring gods and ancestors and rituals celebrating birth, puberty, marriage, and death filled traditional African culture. Music was essential to these rituals, not only because it brought a community to a central location and fostered the necessary social community, but because it also summoned the spirits to the communion grounds. The sound of music, often identified with the voices of deities,[5] had mystical properties that activated and energized the spiritual links between human mediums and the spirits of which they were vessels.[6] As a result, music was the medium for the personal and communal expression of religion as well as the principal instrument in African religious ritual.[7]

In most traditional African societies it was specifically the drum that assembled a community and its gods and that performed the necessary part in the music accompanying ritualistic song and dance. The drummers sought to mobilize the spirits into possessive action and to seduce the dancers into a state of ready fervor. Then, according to Evan Zuesse, there followed a transitional point at which the drummers relinquished their control to the power of the spirit:

> The external aids to trance induction are important. The beat becomes a focus, and then finally a replacement, for the ego's will. As the rhythm is internalized, it becomes the coordinating center—and when even this is taken away in the "break," nothing is left. One becomes the plaything of the drummer, entirely submitted to the arbitrary, external order he creates, tossing

---

[2] J. H. Kwabena Nketia, "The Musical Languages of Subsaharan Africa," in *African Music*, 37.

[3] Bruno Nettl, *Music in Primitive Culture* (Cambridge: Harvard University Press, 1956), 104.

[4] Francis Bebey, *African Music: A People's Art* (New York: Lawrence Hill, 1975), 102.

[5] Nettl, 104.

[6] Sowande, 64.

[7] Alain Danielou, "The Musical Language of Black Africa," in *African Music*, 56.

about under his beat. The center is now physically entirely outside the self.[8]

In short, the supernatural quality of the drum's powerful
percussiveness produced the fervent rhythmic monotony
prerequisite to the prompting of spirit possession.

Spirit possession was both intentional and essential. It
was intentional because it was a cultural expectation and a
learned or "acquired" aesthetic response to the music. It was
essential because it was a source of emotional catharsis for
the oppressed and impoverished and because without it there
would be no revelation, prophesying, healing, and spiritual
purgation, essential elements to African and slave theology.
The drum was a crucial aspect of African theology, as the
acoustical seducer of the spirits and the stimulator of spirit
possession.

The Drum Deferred

The drum had considerable difficulty in surviving the
African diaspora. In the West Indies and South America its
use basically continued in spite of restrictions.[9] For example,
in Haiti, the sacredness and supernatural quality of the Assotor Drum did not diminish by the removal of the African
community from its holy homeland. The Assotor, the most
revered of Haitian drums, is still used to summon to one
location all gods of every rite in Haiti and in Africa during a
religious service held once every three to seven years.[10] Like
its sacred African predecessors, the Assotor is made from
the trunk of a tree that has been ritualistically chosen and
consecrated.[11] The rhythm produced on these sacred
Haitian drums induces trance possession wherein a particular god "rides" his human medium. Filled with a god's divinity, the possessed prophesy and heal bystanders by the laying
on of hands.[12]

---

[8] Evan M. Zuesse, *Ritual Cosmos* (Athens, Ohio: Ohio University Press, 1979),
196.

[9] Harold Courlander, *Negro Folk Music, U.S.A.* (New York: Columbia University Press, 1963), 210.

[10] Harold Courlander, *The Drum and the Hoe: Life and Lore of the Haitian People*
(Berkeley: University of California Press, 1960), 63–64.

[11] Ibid., 64.

[12] Carole DeVillers, "Haiti's Voodoo Pilgrimages of Spirits and Saints," *National Geographic* 167, no. 3 (Mar. 1985), 404.

In contrast to its continued use in the West Indies and South America, the drum was abandoned in North America. Legal restrictions were so stringently enforced that its occasional unauthorized use by slaves was, for the most part, forced underground. Among the rare accounts of its use is one cited in a 1836 essay, "On the Moral Discipline and Treatment of Slaves," wherein the author wrote of a South Carolina planter who provided his slaves with drums and fiddles in order to pacify them.[13] The reminiscent narrative of a Mississippi ex-slave also records unusual occasions when drums were used. In this instance the instruments were made by the slaves to accompany fiddling for the purpose of social dancing.[14] Because the drum is almost always mentioned in conjunction with the fiddle, a secular instrument considered by Christian slaves to be of the devil,[15] it appears to have been used only to accompany secular dance, never religious ritual. Consequently, although not completely abandoned in North America, the drum was denuded of its religious symbolism.[16]

The previous accounts indicate that the use of the drum in secular functions was allowed by some permissive slave owners as a method of pacification. However, its use in religious ritual was probably puritanically forbidden even by the most liberal of Protestants. John Pobee explains the white Protestant ethnocentric perception of the drum at the point of its inception:

> One last example of the negative attitude to African culture is drumming. . . . Since drumming accompanied most, if not all, religious occasions in traditional society, the earliest missionaries assumed that drumming per se had heathen associations, and therefore, was un-Christian per se, if not sinful. Accordingly, the standing order No. 548, Section 2, of the Methodist Conference of Ghana (1st edition, 1964) has the

---

[13] Cited in Richard M. Raichelson, "Black Religious Folksong," Ph.D. dissertation, University of Pennsylvania, 1975, 350.

[14] George P. Rawick, ed., *The American Slave: A Composite Autobiography*, vol. 6, supplement, series 1 (Westport, Conn.: Greenwood Press, 1977), 124.

[15] Howard W. Odum and Guy B. Johnson, *The Negro and His Songs* (Hatboro, Pa.: Folklore Associates, 1964), 34.

[16] Exceptions are found in the Georgia Sea Islands where the drum occasionally accompanied the shout, and in Louisiana where it was used in Voodun rituals.

following line: "There shall be no drumming at a member's wake-keeping." And in recent years indeed as recent as 1972, disciplinary action has been taken by individual clergymen against families of a deceased at whose funeral there had been drumming.[17]

No serious claim can be made that drumming was heathenish or evil, claims Pobee.[18] Yet the prejudiced perception of the drum became so ingrained in the religion of the enslaved that the instrument soon lost its sacredness. The drum's religious symbolism was deferred in the diaspora.

There are a few additional factors that might explain the de-deification of the drum in North America. Since African tribes were disbanded, tribal ceremonies where trees were ritualistically chosen and consecrated prior to drum construction lost significance. When slaves did construct drums they were indiscriminately fabricated of discarded materials. A Mississippi ex-slave recalled that they made drums by stretching a coon's skin over a sawed-off keg.[19] The slaves did not have the leisure time required to carve drums to their aesthetic liking and religious requirements, so the sacred African art of drum making was almost lost. These are some reasons why the drum was deferred and de-apotheosized soon after the Africans arrived in North America.

The Essential African Remnant

The drum was a sacred instrument theologically important to African religious ritual, but it was not a required instrument. The sacred drum was no more essential to African ritual than the slave preacher was to black worship. Without the preacher there was always the deacon to line the hymns and sing the prayers, the women to lead in the testimonies, and the congregation to spontaneously create spirituals. It was the same with the Africans even in their homeland: Without the drum they could still produce rhythm with handy substitutes. African ethnomusicologist Kwabena Nketia explains:

---

[17] John S. Pobee, *Toward an African Theology* (Nashville: Abingdon, 1979), 66.
[18] Ibid.
[19] Rawick, vol. 6, supplement, series 1, 124.

> The general concept of a musical sound prevalent in Subsaharan Africa is a very broad one and includes not only sounds of definite pitches but also a large variety of sounds of indefinite pitches. Indeed such is the functional view of musical sounds that the absence of regular musical instruments hardly prevents people from making music in situations in which they can improvise with handy substitutes. Axe blades, blades of hoes, oars, sticks, dry seed pods and so forth are known to be used in certain situations.[20]

Substitute instruments were also capable of drumming the spirit into worshipers, so that such theological imperatives as prophesying, revelation, and healing could occur. The manifestation of these charisms overshadowed the importance of the drum so unconventional instruments could be substituted without really disturbing the essential traditions of dance and spirit possession.

The drum is perhaps the ideal acoustical instrument to accompany religious dance; however, rhythm is the "chief energizer" and "chief organizer" that inspires and controls the activity of a community, causing it to act together and thereby nurture a community.[21] Rhythm could confidently perform the orchestral part the drum traditionally played in African religious ritual, for when its percussive voice spoke, the people and their gods listened and were mobilized to converge in the medium of dance. Rhythm, not the drum, was the theological imperative in African religions.

Rhythm and the ability to adapt musically were aspects of the ingenious cultural attire enslaved Africans wore beneath their flesh to North America. So the denial of the drum (though a culture shock) did not cause the loss of African religiosity. Instead they drummed upon any number of unconventional instruments. Florence Dymond, who spent her childhood years among ex-slaves on her parent's Belair sugar plantation in Plaquemines Parish, Louisiana, noted in her memoirs that "when no instrument was available then

[20] Nketia, 8.
[21] E. Thayer Gaston, "Man and Music," in *Music in Therapy*, ed. E. Thayer Gaston (New York: Macmillan, 1968), 18–20.

whatever was at hand was made use of." She recalled an old gray-haired ex-slave called Pa Louis who "would take two good sized kitchen spoons, hold them together, back to back, in one hand and rattle them on his knees so that they were as rhythmic as 'bones' and mellower, as he muted them with the other hand." Some of the black boys on the plantation formed a group called "The Belair Band," which used, in addition to several other substitute instruments, a discarded lard can for a drum. Dymond admitted she was quite surprised at the music produced by all of that "junk."[22] A Georgia ex-slave also noted that after supper they all used to gather around and beat on tin buckets and pans either with their fingers or with sticks.[23]

Although the enslaved and ex-slaves made use of numerous odds and ends as instruments to accompany their secular music, their sacred music was embellished percussively by the bodily rhythms of hand-clapping, foot-stomping, body-slapping, and ring-shouting. Since response to rhythmic stimuli is instinctive and as certain as the physical reflexes,[24] these bodily modes of percussive response to the rhythms in black music are intrinsic and immediate, for the bodily instrument is always at hand.[25]

The Ring-Shout

Like rhythm, dance was also more essential to African religious ritual than the drum. Wherever dancing was disallowed in the diaspora, as in Venezuela and Colombia, for instance, African religious traditions soon dissipated.[26] It is logical that this would occur, for without dance how could there be spirit possession? How could the gods "ride" motionless vehicles? And without spirit possession, how could there

[22] Florence Dymond, Memoirs, "The Belair Band," MS, 1, Special Collections, Tulane University, New Orleans.

[23] Rawick, vol. 3, supplement, series 1, 84.

[24] Halbert H. Britan, *The Philosophy of Music* (New York: Longmans, Green, 1911), 62.

[25] This is not to attribute the rhythmic tendencies of blacks to instinct alone. It would be erroneous to say that rhythm is in the genes; a more rational explanation may lie in the process of culturization. John Booth Davies, *The Psychology of Music* (Stanford: Stanford University Press, 1978), 191. It could be said that the responses to rhythmic stimuli are culturally instinctive.

[26] George E. Simpson, *Black Religions in the New World* (New York: Columbia University Press, 1978), 176.

be prophesying, revelation, and healing?—the means by which Africans traditionally defined their place in the cosmos and felt comfortable in that place. In short, without dance these theological imperatives would cease to exist and so would African religions.

While the drum, the one material instrument denied the North American slave, was nonessential to the continuance of African religions, rhythm and dance, the two nonmaterial elements essential to African religions, endured the diaspora. This is the reason the ring-shout, which was based upon the remnants of rhythm and dance, has been recognized as an African survival.[27] As a remnant of African ritual (and African rhythm), the ring-shout was by all means dance. It was intense worshipful praise of singing bodies.[28] It was "danced religion," the choreographed steps varied according to tune[29] and geographic location. However, whereas in Haitian Voodun the rhythmic behavior of the possessed identified the god doing the "riding,"[30] in the various choreographies of the ring-shout there was manifested only one God, the Holy Spirit. Rhythm provided the pulse and the Holy Spirit the impulse.

The following accounts of the ring-shout give detailed descriptions of its choreography. The first is given by Laura M. Townes, the missionary-teacher who cofounded the Penn School on St. Helena Island, South Carolina, in 1862. That same year she witnessed a shout and wrote in her diary:

> [W]e went to the "shout," a savage, heathenish dance out in Rina's house. Three men stood and sang, clapping and gesticulating. The others shuffled along on their heels

---

[27] The factors causing the dissipation of African religions in North America stood outside the boundaries of music, but were sociological and political. One might argue that in Haiti traditional African religions survived in the form of Voodun partly because the African drum survived; however, sociological and political factors override this. Black Haitians were able to worship their gods under the guise of Catholic saints primarily due to the nature and prominence of Catholicism. The nature and prominence of Protestantism forbade this in North America. In order to verify that Catholicism was the principal factor in the survival of African religions, Courlander points to their survival in the form of Voodun cults in the Catholic province of Louisiana up to 1900. Courlander, *The Drum and the Hoe*, 6.

[28] Courlander, *Negro Folk Music, U.S.A.*, 196.

[29] William Francis Allen, C. P. Ware, and L. M. Garrison, *Slave Songs of the United States* (New York: Peter Smith, 1951), xv.

[30] DeVillers, 403.

following one another in a circle and occasionally bending the knees in a kind of curtsey. They began slowly, a
few going around a[nd] more gradually joining in, the
song getting faster and faster till at last only the most
marked part of the refrain is sung and the shuffling,
stamping, and clapping gets furious. The floor shook so
that it seemed dangerous. It swayed regularly to the time
of the song. As they danced they, of course, got out of
breath, and the singing was principally kept up by the
three apart, but it was astonishing how long they kept up
and how soon after a rest they were ready to begin
again. They kept it up till very late.[31]

The second account is also of a shout on St. Helena Island. Its
description was written by William Francis Allen in his book
Slave Songs of the United States (1867). Allen says:

The true "shout" takes place on Sundays or on "praise"-
nights through the week, and either in the praise-house
or in some cabin in which a regular religious meeting has
been held. Very likely more than half the population of
the plantation is gathered together. . . . But the
benches are pushed back to the wall when the formal
meeting is over, and old and young, men and women,
. . . all stand up in the middle of the floor, and when
the "sperichil" is struck up, begin first walking and by-
and-by shuffling round, one after the other, in a ring.
The foot is hardly taken from the floor, and the progres-
sion is mainly due to a jerking, hitching motion, which
agitates the entire shouter. . . . Sometimes they dance
silently, sometimes as they shuffle they sing the chorus of
the spiritual, and sometimes the song itself is also sung by
the dancers. But more frequently a band, composed of
some of the best singers and of tired shouters, stand at
the side of the room to "base" the others, singing the
body of the song and clapping their hands together or on
their knees.[32]

The third account is extracted from the memoirs of Margaret
Newbold Thorpe, a missionary-teacher in Yorktown, Vir-

[31] Laura M. Townes, Diary, MS, Apr. 28, 1862 entry, Penn School Papers,
Southern Historical Collection, University of North Carolina, Chapel Hill.
[32] Allen, xiii–xiv.

ginia, who, about the year 1866, observed a ring-shout at a religious meeting of ex-slaves. The action, she noted, began just after a prayer:

> When one "gets the power" he usually jumps and shouts, sometimes throwing themselves [sic] so violently that it will take two or three men to keep him (oftener her) from being hurt; this excitement will last for quite a while, ten or fifteen minutes, then suddenly the poor soul [sole] will fall to the floor utterly exhausted and helpless, then near him a circle will be formed with a man standing in the center who is familiar with some of the remarkable hymns they sing. Those in the circle join in the singing swaying backward and forward. [T]he motion gradually increases until they seem like a company of maniacs clapping their hands, jumping about, embracing and crying.[33]

The final account of a ring-shout is taken from an essay, "The Moral and Religious Status of the African Race in the Southern States," written at the close of the Civil War by Rev. John Paris, a Methodist Protestant minister:

> A practice prevails among them that is called the "holy dance." It generally begins just after the conclusion of the sermon, and a prayer has been made. Several persons, both male and female rise to their feet, singing some of their favorite songs; they now join hands forming a circle or ring, and keep time with their feet swaying their bodies, to and fro. [T]his sort of exercise often continues for hours, or until weariness breaks it up.[34]

In these four descriptions of the ring-shout, all of the musical ingredients imperative to African religions are present. There is percussive rhythm manifested in bodily accompaniment and there is dancing, which together results in several of the worshipers "getting the power" or being "filled with the Spirit."[35] The fact that there was culture-wide decorum

[33] Margaret Newbold Thorpe, "Life in Virginia (by a Yankee Teacher)," MS, 1907, 19–21, Special Collections Division, College of William and Mary, Williamsburg, Va.

[34] John Paris, "The Moral and Religious Status of the African Race in the Southern States," MS, 13, Southern Historical Collection.

[35] Although Thorpe mentioned the occurrence of spirit possession in her account, neither Townes nor Paris did. Since spirit possession was a part of the

and form in the ring-shout indicates that the affective responses to rhythm in the music also had been shaped into aesthetic responses.

Observers of the shout, such as Paris and Townes, were clearly ethnocentric. Paris, for example, attributed the rhythmic "behaviors" of black worshipers to their emotional nature: "As the negro is emotional in his nature, it seems to afford him a peculiar pleasure to give vent to his feelings of emotion in his own way, unchecked by conventional rules or regulations."[36] In addition to calling the shout a "savage, heathenish dance" in the earlier diary account, Townes described the same shout to a correspondent in a letter of 1862. She said the shout was "certainly the remains of some old idol worship," and that she had never seen anything so "savage." She continued dogmatically: "They call it religious ceremony, but it seems more like regular frolic to me."[37]

Even James Weldon Johnson, almost three-quarters of a century later, went so far as to define shout songs as "neither true spirituals nor truly religious." Instead, he said, as "semi-barbaric remnants of primitive African dances," they were perhaps at best "quasi-religious."[38] Therefore, when Johnson divides rhythm into nonpercussive and percussive rhythms and says the former implies a spirit of sacredness and the latter a spirit of secularity, it is evident that the specific type and use of rhythm (not the drum) is the decisive factor in his critical judgment:

> In all authentic American Negro music the rhythms may
> be divided roughly into two classes—rhythms based on

shout's choreography, which related it to its African antecedents, then some explanation should be made concerning the absence of references to spirit possession in the Townes and Paris accounts. There are three possible solutions. First, perhaps both observers did not remain at the shout long enough to account for what really did occur. Second, perhaps the worshipers were timid and repressed their ultimate emotional expenditures in the presence of the visitors. And third, although not trance-possessed, the probability that all were at least elated by the Spirit explains the animated emotionalism and physical endurance noted in both narratives.

[36] Paris, 9–10.

[37] Laura M. Townes to Friends, MS, Apr. 25, 1862, 4, Penn School Papers, Southern Historical Collection.

[38] James Weldon Johnson, ed., *The Book of American Negro Spirituals* (New York: Viking, 1925), 33.

the swinging of head and body and rhythms based on the patting of hands and feet. Again, speaking roughly, the rhythms of the Spirituals fall in the first class and the rhythms of secular music in the second class.[39]

Obviously there is no universal unit capable of measuring religion or irreligion in rhythm except the cultural scale established by a particular people. The middle-class culture in which Johnson was entrenched is clearly evident as he further lauds nonpercussive rhythm:

The "swing" of the Spirituals is an altogether subtle and elusive thing. It is subtle and elusive because it is in perfect union with the religious ecstasy that manifests itself in the swaying bodies of a whole congregation, swaying as if responding to the baton of some extremely sensitive conductor.[40]

In pointing out that the sway is essentially a psychological response to rhythm while percussive responses are physiological,[41] Johnson again alludes that the shout is secular in nature. However, a reexamination of the Thorpe, Paris, and Allen accounts of shouting reveals that shouters are also "in perfect union with . . . religious ecstasy . . . as if responding to the baton of an extremely sensitive conductor." That is to say that the holy rhythm of swaying is also a prominent part of the shout's choreography. Thorpe said, "Those in the circle join in the singing swaying backward and forward."[42] Paris said, "They now join hands forming a circle or ring, and keep time with their feet swaying their bodies to and fro."[43] And Allen said, "The glorious shout . . . was struck up, and sung by the entire multitude with a zest and spirit, a swaying of the bodies and nodding of the heads . . . and rhythmical movement of the hands."[44]

To Paris, Townes, and Johnson it was apparently the "primitive" African rhythms of the ring-shout that caused the

[39] Ibid., 28.
[40] Ibid.
[41] Ibid., 31.
[42] Thorpe, 21.
[43] Paris, 13.
[44] Allen, ii.

so-called "savage" dancing and "emotionalism." However, these writers appraised the religiosity of the shout from their privileged perspective as liberated human beings and according to the beliefs and standards of the overculture, rather than according to the beliefs and standards of the oppressed subculture they were criticizing. John Wesley Work responded to such disapproving statements this way:

> Philosophers and learned men have pointed to the Negro's religious outbursts, his shoutings and rejoicings as marks of ignorance, superstition and heathenism. Most assuredly these are not the most approved methods of worship, nor do they measure up to the ideals of the highly cultured, but they at least have an explanation which might lead to a better understanding, and sometimes a better understanding leads to a higher respect.[45]

An explanation that might lead to that better understanding and higher respect is this: "Religion derives from specific human needs and experiences, and it functions in the interests of helping man to cope with the more traumatic aspects of human existence."[46] The ring-shout functions in this "survival interest" spoken of by sociologist of religion C. Eric Lincoln.

This "danced religion," the shout, functioned in the interest of a people attempting to cope with the traumatic aspects of slavery. It was neither "savage" nor "quasi-religious." It was "instant religion" inspired by what Richard Waterman termed "hot rhythm." It was neither "frolic" nor "emotionalism." It was freedom—in rhythm.

Freedom in Rhythm

> It was the therapeutic value of both media that earned the place of music and dance in mystical (religious) rites of man. Although it is no less true today that music and dance bring *catharsis* and *creative inspiration* to the frustrated and anxious, this is no longer accepted as justification for the label of otherworldliness.[47]

[45] John Wesley Work, *Folk Song of the American Negro* (New York: Negro Universities Press, 1969), 18.

[46] C. Eric Lincoln, *Race, Religion, and the Continuing American Dilemma* (New York: Hill and Wang, 1984), 79.

[47] Mary R. Toombs, "Dance Therapy," in Gaston, 330. Emphasis added.

In the ring-shout, freedom through rhythmic activity was attained at two levels—that of *catharsis* and that of *creative inspiration*. At the base level the most fundamental spiritual needs of the oppressed were met through shouting that allowed the release of pent-up anxieties and emotions. This catharsis ran the gamut from mild elation to full spirit possession. Subsequent to satisfying this basic spiritual need, at the second level, the oppressed were able to be creative in their survival and in their emotional expression.

At the base level, Miles Mark Fisher's reference to ring-shouts as "rhythmic exercises" is appropriate, for the shouts were a type of therapeutic calisthenic. The existential result of this "dance therapy" was the purgation of the body, mind, and spirit of the stresses caused by oppressive conditions (much like physical exercise causes bodily release of anxiety and excess energy). Musical and corporeal rhythmic accumulation, being emotional, caused worshipers to respond emotionally:

> Rhythm finds resonance in the whole organism. . . . And, therefore, indirectly it affects the circulation, respiration, and all the secretions of the body in such a way as to arouse agreeable feeling. Herein we find the groundwork of emotion; for rhythm, whether in perception or in action, is emotional when highly developed, and results in response of the whole organism to its pulsations.[48]

John Wesley Work concludes that "rhythm arouses emotion and emotion arouses motion. That is the explanation of the Negro's keeping time with his body while he sings."[49]

Blacks were not emotional beings by nature, as Paris argued. The rhythm in their music was emotional. This emotion-in-rhythm allowed them to exert themselves to full cathartic capacity in a way that was therapeutic. Just as African dancers' concentration on drum rhythms made them oblivious to all other sensations,[50] so did the slaves'

---

[48] Carl E. Seashore, *Psychology of Music* (New York: McGraw-Hill, 1938), 143.
[49] Work, 38.
[50] Zuesse, 195.

involvement in the rhythms of ring-shouts temporarily ele-
vate them from the horrible pit of bondage. Therefore, while
the percussive mode of shouting was a rhythmic stimulant
and the nonpercussive mode of swaying a rhythmic calm-
ative, what is important is that in both states the enslaved
were temporarily able to escape the troubles of the world.

At the second level, "The sense of rhythm gives us a
feeling of freedom, luxury, and expanse. It gives us a feeling
of achievement in molding or creating."[51] Once the spiritual
essentials for survival were met through catharsis, the oppressed could be creative in their methods of survival. They
could create culturally choreographed movement which was
aesthetically satisfying and symbolically meaningful to themselves. What may have commenced as affective responses to
rhythm also developed into aesthetic responses. The shout,
then, was not only an affective response to rhythmic stimuli,
but an aesthetic response—a stylish product of cultural learning, an "acquired response." The aesthetic and affective responses to music produced a greater result combined than the
two apart. Psychologist Robert Lundin explains, "The aesthetic response takes place with an *affective accompaniment*—
thus giving the response importance and significance."[52]

Shouting was certainly therapeutically, theologically,
and symbolically significant to those engaged in the activity
of dancing their religion. The religious validity of the
medium now explained, it is safe to say that the element of
"frolic" was also innate to the aspect of the creative survival
of the enslaved. It is clear what Eileen Southern means when
she says the shout was not to be construed as dance insofar as
observed conventions insured distinct demarcation between
shouting and dancing.[53] "But," says Gilbert Rouget,

> no matter how important its nature as a sign may be, or
> its symbolic function, esthetic power, or ascetic possibil-
> ities, dance is still a motor activity that finds an end in

---

[51] Seashore, 142.

[52] Robert W. Lundin, *An Objective Psychology of Music* (New York: The Ronald
Press, 1953), 171.

[53] Eileen Southern, *The Music of Black Americans* (New York: W. W. Norton,
1971), 161.

itself. Dance is always, at least in part and sometimes despite appearances, the pleasure of dancing, of using one's body in play. . . . In this sense it is already liberation, catharsis.[54]

Consequently, *freedom-in-religion,* which is *rhythm-in-religion* —or rhythm providing the pulse and the Holy Spirit the impulse—is the empowering aspect that enabled the enslaved to survive. It is also the inspirational ingredient that liberated them to create dance and other rhythmic choreography.[55]

[54] Gilbert Rouget, *Music and Trance: A Theory of the Relations Between Music and Possession,* trans. Brunhilde Biebuyek (Chicago: University of Chicago Press, 1985), 118.

[55] The march is another culturally choreographed "dance" that occurred during the religious meetings of the enslaved. In this choreography, the worshipers marched in pairs or in single procession to the beat of the spiritual or hymn they sang. The more rhythmically involved in the music they became, the more elaborate their "dance" became. Ella Clark recollected the marching of ex-slaves in their small plantation church in Georgia and wrote in her memoirs: "I watched the leader as he rose in his dignity and poise. One by one his followers joined him. Perhaps Primus our blacksmith would lead a slow processional. Brer Squire the preacher would 'hist' the tune." (Clark, 43.) Odum and Johnson attempted to look past the external features of the choreography into the minds of the faithful. In doing so they set the spiritual scenery in which the dramatic march took place: "[T]he Negroes often imagined themselves to be the children of Israel, while their marching songs represented Moses leading them out from under the bondage of Pharaoh, or they considered themselves as marching around the wall of some besieged city. Victory would be theirs sooner or later." (Odum and Johnson, 34.) The writers have disclosed a factor quite significant to this freedom-in-rhythm theme. Not only did physical creativity give marchers the sensation of "luxury and expanse," the mental creativity of scene setting, which accompanied it, complemented that feeling of "freedom." While the physical creativity could be visualized in the choreography, the mental creativity could only be deduced from the text of the song. Songs like "March on, for We Shall Find the Day" set the mood of victory and the scenery of battle being waged by Christian soldiers armed with the breastplate of righteousness, the helmet of salvation, and the sword of the Spirit.

7

The Heavenly Anthem:
Holy Ghost Singing in the Primal Pentecostal Revival

T O N G U E - S O N G

*"I will sing with the spirit
and I will sing with the mind also"*[1]

Historians and theologians writing on the genesis of Pentecostalism typically earmark the prolonged Los Angeles revival that commenced at 312 Azusa Street in April 1906. The factor that initially distinguished Pentecostalism from its precursors (the Holiness movement, revivalism, and black religion) was the doctrine of evidential glossolalia (that is, that tongues is the necessary evidence of Spirit-baptism). The activity that further differentiated Pentecostalism was "singing in the spirit" or singing in tongues. Indeed tongue-singing had occurred previously among such religious groups as the Shakers and Mormons, but only during the Second Pentecost did it procure a well-wrought interpretation that secured worldwide promulgation through Pentecostal publications. Yet most scholars have ignored tongue-singing, or have only superficially commented on it. By failing to adequately research the subject they have neglected to identify

---

[1] 1 Corinthians 14:15.

the two fundamental means of glossolalic vocalization and an entire world of Pentecostal thought.[2]

The lack of scholarly attention to the subject is perhaps due to two factors. First, in the Bible Luke did not record tongue-song as an event in Acts. Second, the numerous biblical references to speaking in tongues obscure the one verse about singing in tongues (1 Cor. 14:15b).[3] This biblical passage also eluded theological explanation by early apostolics. "No one had preached it," confirmed Frank Bartleman. His nonempiric clarification of tongue-song: "The Lord had sovereignly bestowed it, with the outpouring of the 'residue of oil,' the 'Latter Rain' baptism of the Spirit."[4] Nevertheless, by assimilating Luke's "history" and Pauline theology with language from spirituals and existent hymnody, a constructive interpretation was derived for the charism of tongue-song that filled the biblical void.

The thirteen issues of *The Apostolic Faith* (September 1906–May 1908), the newspaper of the Azusa Street Gospel Mission, document the acts of the apostolics and the growth of the early Pentecostal church. Here an effort is undertaken to set forth both the event of tongue-song that occurred

---

[2] The following writers are exceptions, because they have given some space to the discussion of singing in tongues. Eddie Ensley in *Sounds of Wonder: Speaking in Tongues in the Catholic Tradition* (New York: Paulist Press, 1977), chap. 5; William J. Samarin in *Tongues of Men and Angels: The Religious Language of Pentecostalism* (New York: Macmillan, 1972), 179–82; Cyril G. Williams in *Tongues of the Spirit: A Study of Pentecostal Glossolalia and Related Phenomenon* (Cardiff: University of Wales Press, 1981), 78–79; Carl Brumback in *"What Meaneth This?": A Pentecostal Answer to a Pentecostal Question* (Springfield, Mo.: The Gospel Publishing House, 1947), 294–95; Bob E. Patterson in *Speaking in Tongues: Let's Talk about It*, ed. Watson E. Mills (Waco, Tex.: Word Books, 1973), 108.

[3] The Apostle Paul in his discussion of tongues says in 1 Corinthians 14:15, "I will pray with the spirit and I will pray with the mind also; I will sing with the spirit and I will sing with the mind also." Most writers, even of biblical commentaries, refer to the "a" section of this verse and skip over the "b" section. Some commenting on the verse do not acknowledge the parallelism in its two parts and fail to realize that Paul was actually referring to singing in tongues. H. L. Goudge was one of the few to understand that "the singing of improvised hymns was evidently one form taken by the gift of tongues." H. L. Goudge, *The First Epistle to the Corinthians* (London: Methuen, 1915), 126–27.

[4] Frank Bartleman, *What Really Happened at "Azusa Street"? The True Story of the Great Revival Compiled by Frank Bartleman Himself from His Diary*, ed. John Walker (Northridge, Cal.: Voice Christian Publications, 1962), 31. As stated earlier, even modern historians and theologians have failed to make the connection between the Pauline idea of "singing in the spirit" and the Pentecostal practice of singing in tongues.

among the earliest Pentecostals and their understanding of that event as documented by eyewitnesses and evangelists of the Apostolic Faith.[5]

"Then our mouth was filled with laughter, and our tongue with shouts of joy"[6]

In an article captioned "Music from Heaven," Jennie Moore, a young black woman, gave her testimony of the Second Pentecost as it first fell upon the saints awaiting the Comforter on 216 Bonnie Brae Street in Los Angeles, April 9, 1906:

> I sang under the power of the Spirit in many languages, the interpretation both words and music I had never before heard, and in the home where the meeting was held, the Spirit led me to the piano, where I played and sang under inspiration, although I had not learned to play.[7]

When the "latter rain" first fell upon those natal Pentecostals, Spirit-baptism was initially evidenced by singing in tongues.[8] Historically, wherever two or three blacks have gathered in God's name, there has been black singing; but in the presence of the Lord what resulted was tongue-song.

Although a black woman was the first to sing in tongues on April 9, 1906, and blacks were the first Pentecostals and continued to constitute the majority at Azusa, any racial distinction was "washed away by the blood." The "new tongue" resulted in a new dialect, a new language, and consequently a "new song" which, according to the Pentecostal interpretation, was the color and culture of the Holy Spirit.

---

[5] Luke defines this type of historicity in the opening verses of his gospel (Luke 1:1–4).

[6] Psalm 126:2.

[7] Jennie Moore, "Music from Heaven," *The Apostolic Faith* (Los Angeles), vol. 1, no. 8 (May 1907), 3. Jennie Moore is the young woman who later married William J. Seymour, the pastor of the Azusa Mission.

[8] The very first issue of *The Apostolic Faith,* just five months after the "latter rain" fell at Azusa Street, contained the doctrine of what was named the Apostolic Faith Movement. Regarding speaking in tongues it stated: "The Baptism with the Holy Ghost is a gift of power upon the sanctified life; so when we get it we have the same evidence as the Disciples received on the Day of Pentecost (Acts 2:3, 4), in speaking in new tongues. See also Acts 10:45, 46; Acts 19:6; 1 Cor. 14:21." See vol. 1, no. 1 (Sept. 1906), 2.

Tongue-song, then, was not "black music," but it was the primal music of the black Pentecostal church.

This Holy Ghost singing, like glossolalic speaking, only occurred after a worshiper had been justified by faith, then sanctified, and finally baptized with the Holy Ghost.[9] This sequence of spiritual passages, referred to as "saved, sanctified, and filled with the Holy Ghost," led to evidential tongue-song:

> A young lady who came into the meeting unsaved, went to the altar during the sermon, under deep conviction, and was saved in about five minutes. Before that evening was over, she was sanctified and baptized with the Holy Ghost and had the gift of the Chinese tongue and was singing in Chinese in the Spirit.[10]

Throughout *The Apostolic Faith* are accounts of speaking, singing, preaching, praying, reciting poetry, conversing,[11] and even writing in foreign tongues and unknown languages. Some believers such as missionary Andrew G. Johnson were even blessed with a combination of glossal manifestations: "I am still talking and writing in tongues. . . . I was singing Chinese one night, a missionary said."[12] Tongue preaching, praying, and singing exhorters were a "triple threat" in the Spirit. Gaston B. Cashwell, a Fire-Baptized Holiness preacher converted to Pentecostalism at Azusa, wrote from his hometown of Dunn, North Carolina: "Some of our preachers have

---

[9] The doctrine of the Apostolic Faith Movement first published in vol. 1, no. 1 of *The Apostolic Faith* (and published sporadically throughout the 13 issues) stated this about justification and sanctification:

"First work.—Justification is that act of God's free grace by which we receive remission of sins. Acts 10:42, 43. Rom. 3:25."

"Second Work.—Sanctification is the second work of grace and the last work of grace. Sanctification is the act of God's free grace by which He makes us holy. John 17:15, 17. . . . 1 Thess. 4:3; 1 Thess. 5:23; Heb. 13:12; Heb. 2:11; Heb. 12:14."

[10] *The Apostolic Faith*, vol. 1, no. 1 (Sept. 1906), 3. The word "saved," here, is synonymous with "justified."

[11] Mrs. Alson Vincent conversed in tongues with her husband. See (Mrs.) Alson Vincent, "Ye Are My Witnesses," *The Apostolic Faith*, vol. 1, no. 8 (May 1907), 4.

Conversing in tongues is seldom documented in the aforementioned newspaper, but its occurrence was verified by William J. Seymour upon his 1907 visit to Zion City, Illinois. Seymour wrote back to Azusa that "some of them converse in tongues." *The Apostolic Faith*, vol. 1, no. 9 (June 1907), 1.

[12] Andrew G. Johnson, "In Sweden," *The Apostolic Faith*, vol. 1, no. 6 (Feb. 1907), 1.

preached, sung, and prayed in unknown tongues, and without speaking a word of English, have awakened sinners."[13]

Praying and preaching in tongues were common occurrences; however, glossolalic speaking and singing, typically mentioned conjunctively, were the usual manifestations in those who had received Spirit baptism. Furthermore, reports of tongue-speaking and tongue-singing published in *The Apostolic Faith* rapidly reached the masses who were hungry for a Pentecostal experience. These served as prototypes for others to follow. As a result, these two glossal vocalizations became the most common religious expressions among the Spirit-baptized of the primal Pentecostal revival.

"An' you jine dat heab'nly choir to see God's bleedin' Lam'"[14]

In spite of the emphasis placed on the tongues doctrine, glossal speaking and singing were not the "message" of the Second Pentecost. They confirmed the message that the Second Coming was imminent. They were not ends in and of themselves but beginnings to the eschatological end, when the Lamb would return and dwell for a thousand years after the rapture, the tribulation, and the restoration of the earth. Therefore, the baptism of the Holy Ghost, not glossae, was to be pursued.

One could have received tongues without the baptism if one had specifically solicited tongues. But by seeking the baptism, the bestowal of tongues was the indisputable evidence of baptism. To appropriate this gift the faithful had to wait upon God to fulfill the Lord's promise to the blood-brought.[15] The vow made by Jesus was that the Comforter, who is the Holy Ghost, would be sent by the Father in the Lord's name (John 14:26).

[13] Gaston Barnabus Cashwell, "Pentecost in North Carolina," *The Apostolic Faith*, vol. 1, no. 5 (Jan. 1907), 1. See his earlier letter from Dunn in which he describes his conversion at Azusa. G. B. Cashwell, "Came 3000 Miles for his Pentecost," *The Apostolic Faith*, vol. 1, no. 4 (Dec. 1906), 3. The Fire-Baptized Holiness Church, in which Cashwell was a minister, converted to Pentecostalism in 1908.

[14] "To See God's Bleeding Lamb" (spiritual). See James Weldon Johnson and J. Rosamond Johnson, *The Second Book of Negro Spirituals* (New York: Viking, 1926), 152–54.

[15] "The Enduement of Power," *The Apostolic Faith*, vol. 1, no. 4 (Dec. 1906), 2.

That promise was fulfilled daily at the Azusa revival, as evidenced by spoken and sung tongues, so the worshipers sang at every meeting "The Comforter Is Come":

> O spread the tidings 'round, wherever man is found,
> Wherever human hearts and human woes abound;
> Let ev'ry Christian tongue proclaim the joyful sound:
> The Comforter has come!

CHORUS

> The Comforter has come, The Comforter has come!
> The Holy Ghost from heav'n, The Father's promise
>   giv'n;
> O spread the tidings 'round, Wherever man is found,
> The Comforter has come![16]

"Give sweeter songs than lips can sing"[17]

Tongue-song "struck awe to all newcomers," said Thomas R. Nickel.[18] To many visitors to the Azusa revival, as to Minnesota preacher H. L. Blake, it was singing in tongues that cut to the core and convicted the heart:

> I had the privilege of being seated in the midst of the assembly at Azusa Street Mission, near the preacher's stand. As the meeting progressed, I became convinced that God was there in mighty power and that this is indeed the work of the Holy Spirit, and that this people had an experience in the Christian life that I had not attained to. It was not so much the speaking in tongues that convinced me, as the heavenly unction that rested upon many as they testified, and as the Holy Ghost sang through them, to the edification of others, and I must confess that before the meeting closed I was hungry for God.[19]

---

[16] That this hymn was sung daily (sometimes in tongues) is documented in "Bible Pentecost," *The Apostolic Faith*, vol. 1, no. 3 (Nov. 1906), 1; and in Frank Bartleman, *Azusa Street* (Plainfield, N.J.: Logos International, 1980), 57. *Azusa Street* is a reprint of Bartleman's *How Pentecost Came to Los Angeles*.

[17] Samuel Longfellow, "Again As Evening's Shadow Falls" (Hymn).

[18] Thomas R. Nickel, "The True Azusa Street Story," *Full Gospel Men's Voice*, Sept. 1956, 9–10.

[19] H. L. Blake, "A Minnesota Preacher's Testimony," *The Apostolic Faith*, vol. 1, no. 6 (Feb. 1907), 5.

Frank Bartleman responded similarly to tongue-song. "When I first heard it in the meetings," he confessed, "a great hunger entered my soul to receive it."[20] So charismatic and alluring was tongue-song that almost all onlookers described it as "sweet" and "beautiful."

Music had already attained a sacred and preeminent place in the cosmos (even before the Holy Ghost used it to communicate to and through its human vehicles). Thus, when cast into a musical setting glossolalia became even more phenomenal and irresistible. Moreover, encased in the universal language of music, glossolalia was more acceptable to some. For instance, Bartleman admitted that he initially feared tongue-speech because it violated human reason;[21] but that he felt tongue-song "would exactly express [his] pent up feelings."[22] For those with a similar fear of glossa, tongues seemed more logical in song; for song, already possessing supernatural qualities, stripped tongues of some of its mystic edge. Hearers were immediately caught up in the sweetness and beauty of its melody.

This sweet and exotic music of the spheres was sung both by soloists and chorally. The Holy Spirit singing a solo through a worshiper was able to induce religious ecstasy in hearers or to bring an audience tearfully to its knees. On the other hand, to Chicago evangelist William H. Durham, who later opened a Pentecostal mission in Los Angeles, it was collective Holy Ghost singing that epitomized the almighty presence of God:

> I never felt the power and glory that I felt in Azusa Street Mission, and when about twenty persons joined in singing the "Heavenly Chorus," it was the most ravishing and unearthy music that ever fell on mortal ears.[23]

Singing in tongues was prompted by a number of spiritual stimuli, which ultimately could be traced back to the Holy Ghost: (1) "Singing in the spirit" often resulted from the

---

[20] Bartleman, *What Really Happened at "Azusa Street"?* 31.
[21] Bartleman, *Azusa Street*, 71–72, 75.
[22] Ibid., 56.
[23] W. H. Durham, "A Chicago Evangelist's Pentecost," *The Apostolic Faith*, vol. 1, no. 6 (Feb. 1907), 3.

singing of human hymns, as evidenced in a letter from Miss Martha Neale to a friend: "'Jesus, Oh, how sweet the name!' . . . is the beautiful hymn the saints sang for three hours the night I received my baptism. . . . I sang it until the Precious Holy Ghost took my tongue and spoke for Himself."[24] (2) Intrigued by tongue-song, some worshipers would freely join the heavenly chorus. For instance, Fred Weiss, having attended a Pentecostal camp meeting in Fairmont, Minnesota, said that a number of people were "singing the heavenly chorus" and that he found his heart wonderfully "in tune with it" so that he was able to join in.[25] Another shared this testimony:

> A little later in the evening, as a young brother was testifying, he began to sing in another language: "O Jesus, Thou wonderful Savior." After a few more words of praise to God in his own language he sang in another [language] beautifully: "Oh, see how the King comes in triumph," upon which the power was so great that many baptized believers arose one after another and joined a mighty chorus in the Spirit, while the young brother went on with his testimony and then sang: "Oh pour out your hearts before Him and bend yourselves in obedience."[26]

(3) Tongue-song also ensued tarrying in silence for the Holy Ghost in a sacred "upper room," a sacrament one termed "Holy quietness." When the Spirit "hushes all flesh," explained the writer, this holy quietness allows it to speak out in praises and shouts and songs.[27]

"Singin' a new song before the throne 'way in de middle of de air"[28]

The melodies the Holy Spirit employed to utter in "unknown tongues" through its human mediums were sometimes extant and other times original.[29] T. B. Barratt, the

[24] (Miss) Martha Neale [to a friend], *The Apostolic Faith*, vol. 1, no. 11 (Oct. 1908), 4.

[25] Fred Weiss, *The Apostolic Faith*, vol. 1, no. 9 (June 1907), 4.

[26] "Missions in Los Angeles," *The Apostolic Faith*, vol. 1, no. 7 (Apr. 1907), 2.

[27] *The Apostolic Faith*, vol. 1, no. 6 (Feb. 1907), 5.

[28] "John Done Saw dat Numbah" (spiritual). See Mary Allen Grissom, *The Negro Sings a New Heaven* (Chapel Hill: The University of North Carolina Press, 1930), 39.

[29] H. H. Goff, "Pentecostal Testimonies," *The Apostolic Faith*, vol. 1, no. 6 (Feb. 1907), 8.

Methodist Episcopal minister and missionary principally responsible for the establishment of Pentecostalism in Scandi-
navia, wrote about the "new song" given him:

> The most wonderful moment though was when I burst
> into a beautiful baritone solo, using one of the most pure
> and delightful languages I have ever heard. The tune
> and words were entirely new to me, and the rhythm and
> cadence of the verses and chorus seemed to be perfect.[30]

Psalm 98:1, the "new song" required by God for God's
people, was typically described by hearers as a "perfect" musical composition. At a family prayer meeting in Los Angeles,
for example, two little girls tongue-sang the identical tune
and text in "perfect harmony."[31] Whether or not the harmony M. B. Forseth heard coming from his daughter and her
playmate was actually acoustically perfect is immaterial.
What is important is that it was perfect to his ears—the ears
of faith. Faith-hearing was a critical compositional element in
the event of tongue-song, for it included not only what was
sung but what was heard. One writer, alluding to the exclu-
sivity of the experience, confirmed its legitimacy in stating
that "bands of angels have been heard by *some* in the spirit."[32]

Furthermore, perfection in tongue-song was probably
relative to the imperfection of "singing in the flesh." In the
mundane, all was tainted and out of tune. Only in the spiritual realm was perfection possible. For that reason old songs
of the flesh were horribly dissonant while "new songs" of the
spirit were perfectly consonant. The imperfection of the
world caused Pentecostals not only to look beyond history to
the imminent second coming, but to listen beyond history for
the "new song" of the Creator.

An even more extraordinary event occurred when
"Hosanna to the Son of David; Blessed be He that cometh in
the name of the Lord" was being sung in tongues in one

---

[30] T. B. Barratt, "Baptized in New York," *The Apostolic Faith*, vol. 1, no. 4 (Dec.
1906), 3.
[31] M. B. Forseth, "A Happy Family," *The Apostolic Faith*, vol. 1, no. 9 (June
1907), 2.
[32] "Bible Pentecost," 1. Emphasis added.

Pentecostal mission while being rendered and interpreted simultaneously and identically at a nearby meeting. "The saints worshiping in these two places were in perfect harmony of spirit," said the writer, "and the Holy Ghost witnessed it."[33] Apparently, tongue-song was not only characterized by "perfect harmony," musically speaking, but also by "perfect harmony of spirit," theologically speaking. It was probably the perfect harmony in the heavenly chorus that resulted from the perfect harmony of spirit. Moreover, the "perfect harmony of spirit" that allowed the glossolalists to sing in "perfect harmony" was the same that allowed the interpreters in the different locations to derive identical translations. All were "with one accord and singleness of heart."

"If I speak [and sing] in the tongues of men and of angels"[34]

"New songs" were sung both in the tongues of men and the tongues of angels (glossolalia). It is documented by hearers of the faith that persons sang in Spanish, Chinese, Native American, and the Gujarati and Hindustani languages of India. One hearer attested that a woman of Salem, Oregon, had received many languages, one of them being that of a Native American tribe, and that she sang some of the Indian chants.[35] Accounts such as this were often verified by others among the faith community who claimed to understand the foreign language being sung.

On the other hand, the language of angels was an "unknown tongue." One interpretation of glossolalic or angelic singing was that the Lord "[gave] the music that [was] being sung by the angels and [had] a heavenly choir all singing the same heavenly song in harmony."[36] A similar interpretation was that God actually placed the Spirit-baptized into God's own heavenly choir to sing celestial songs to God's glory.[37] One writer confirmed, "One of the blessed privileges

---

[33] "The Heavenly Anthem," *The Apostolic Faith*, vol. 1, no. 5 (Jan. 1907), 3.
[34] 1 Corinthians 13:1.
[35] *The Apostolic Faith*, vol. 1, no. 4 (Dec. 1906), 1.
[36] *The Apostolic Faith*, vol. 1, no. 1 (Sept. 1906), 1.
[37] H. M. Turney, "Apostolic Faith Mission in San Jose," *The Apostolic Faith*, vol. 1, no. 5 (Jan. 1907), 1.

conferred upon me was a place in that heavenly choir, the songs of which defy all power of human[s] to imitate."[38] Said George E. Berg, "No one but those who are baptized with the Holy Spirit are able to join in."[39]

The fact that only the Spirit-baptized could participate meant that they were an exclusive group, the spiritual elite among those still tarrying for the power. Neither could those who only spoke in tongues claim membership in the communion of the cosmic choir. Glossolalic-song was the highest glossal gift—for in the heavenly choir of God tongues of men and angels met.

"Let them sing for joy on their couches"[40]

Just as speaking never sufficed humankind, thus necessitating singing, neither did tongue-speaking suffice; there had to be tongue-singing. Nor was it enough for singing to be God-inspired; it had to be Holy Ghost filled.

In religion singing had always functioned as a balm of Gilead, but tongue-singing served an even higher office as a salve of Azusa—an angelic inebriant for the cosmic choristers. Spirit-controlled tongue-singing, requiring no musical recollection, permitted maximum relaxation in song. Ultimate surrender was attainable. Mrs. J. W. Hutchins said, "I was not conscious of singing at all. From seeing others under the power, I had thought it must be a terrible nervous tension, but it was the most perfect surrender and relaxation."[41] Another alluded to the aura of sweetness accompanying tongue-song: "It is so sweet when you are lying down on your bed, and the Lord drops a song from Paradise into your heart, a song you knew nothing about."[42] Still another young lady lay for hours, not comfortably in her bed, but prostrate on the bare floor at the Azusa Mission. Slain in the Spirit, "at times the most heavenly singing would issue up from her lips."[43]

[38] "Editors Receive Pentecost," *The Apostolic Faith*, vol. 1, no. 3 (Nov. 1906), 3.

[39] George E. Berg, "The Heavenly Anthem," *The Apostolic Faith*, vol. 1, no. 5 (Jan. 1907), 3.

[40] Psalm 149:5.

[41] (Mrs.) J. W. Hutchins, "Speeding to Foreign Lands," *The Apostolic Faith*, vol. 1, no. 5 (Jan. 1907), 3.

[42] *The Apostolic Faith*, vol. 1, no. 5 (Jan. 1907), 2.

[43] Frank Bartleman, *Azusa Street*, 61.

Both women (on the bed and on the floor) apparently produced sweet music of equal beauty. The contrasting physical conditions had no affect on the final prophetic composition, for singing in tongues resulted from the indwelling of the Spirit and thus the obliteration of the flesh.

"My tongue shall never tire of chanting with the choir"[44]

Further evidence of the Spirit's control over the flesh was the sheer length of time during which glossa streamed from the singing tongue of the entranced. "One dear sister who had been seeking for a number of days began to sing and sang almost an hour," said Julia Hutchins.[45] Another avouched, "Sometimes I sang for hours and in a new voice and it did not tire me."[46] On one Saturday at the home of H. H. Goff, a Sister Stewart, said Goff, sang nine songs in an unknown tongue.[47] At the Azusa revival Frank Bartleman observed a woman singing and speaking in tongues for five full hours.[48]

The sweetness and beauty that characterized perfectly harmonious tongue-song and the euphoric assuagement it generated in the heart of the glossolalist made it comfortable to continue endlessly.

"Hark! how the heavenly anthem drowns all music but its own"[49]

If Holy Ghost singing was in fact the Spirit caroling "heavenly anthems" through its human mediums, then what was it that the Spirit was proclaiming? Or, in other words, if worshipers singing in tongues were tuned into or were in harmony with the heavenly chorus, then what was it that the angels were declaring? What was the Lord saying?

[44] "When Morning Gilds the Skies." Hymn translated from German by Edward Caswall.

[45] Hutchins, 3.

[46] Clara E. Lum, "Pentecostal Testimonies," *The Apostolic Faith,* vol. 1, no. 6 (Feb. 1907), 8.

[47] Goff, 8.

[48] Bartleman, *What Really Happened at "Azusa Street"?* 65.

[49] Matthew Bridges, "Crown Him with Many Crowns" (Hymn).

The prophesies and exhortations communicated in tongue-song were frequently passages taken from the psalms and other portions of Holy Writ.[50] In an essay on the "Character and Work of the Holy Ghost," a writer explains the threefold importance of Scripture:

> The character of the Holy Ghost is precisely like Jesus the Word of truth, for the Holy Ghost is "the Spirit of truth." [1.] He speaks always of the Word and [2.] makes everything like the Word. . . . [3.] He reveals Christ . . . through the Word.

The essayist concluded, "He witnesses and reveals through the Word, and never gets outside the Word."[51] One sister sang the opening four verses of the eighth chapter of the Song of Solomon in the tongue of the Gujarati language of India.[52] Sister J. S. Jellison joined a Sister Leyden in the Spirit as she caroled "Worthy Is the Lamb" and nearly the entire fifth chapter of Revelations.[53]

The Holy Ghost, able to make everything "like the Word," also communicated through nonbiblical language. "Jesus is coming soon," the key message of early premillennial Pentecostalism, was a typical translation of glossae. For example, a sister in Minneapolis sang in the Spirit and afterwards interpreted the meaning to be: "I am coming soon;/ Be faithful, children/ A little longer;/ I am coming soon."[54]

The Spirit conversed by means of human hymnody with China missionary Antoinette Moomau. This is Christian music that, if not the Word (paraphrased), is much "like the Word." One morning the Holy Spirit revealed that the cross was going to have new meaning in her life. Through and to her the Spirit sang:

> Must Jesus bear the cross alone,
> And all the world go free:
> No, there's a cross for every one,
> And there is one for me.

[50] Berg, 3.
[51] "Character and Work of the Holy Ghost," *The Apostolic Faith*, vol. 2, no. 13, 2.
[52] Berg, 3.
[53] J. S. Jellison, "The Lord Is Speaking in the Earth Today," *The Apostolic Faith*, vol. 1, no. 12 (Jan. 1908), 1.
[54] Ibid., 2.

By reiterating the last line, the Spirit left a burning impression on Moomau's soul. To this provocation she responded,
"By Thy grace I will bear this cross." Again, the Spirit sang,
"Must Jesus bear the cross alone?" She answered, "By Thy
grace, I will." Then the Spirit sang through her:

> The consecrated cross I'll bear,
>   Till Christ has set me free;
> And then go home a crown to wear,
>   For there's a crown for me.

Moomau said the last line was repeated until she could almost
envision the crown.[55]

Other hymns sung in tongues and interpreted in English
were "Praise God from Whom All Blessings Flow," "Holy,
Holy, Holy," "Jesus Is Tenderly Calling You Home," "Under
the Blood," "Heavenly Sunlight," "Down Where the Living
Waters Flow," "Beautiful Beckoning Hands," and "The Comforter Has Come."[56] Christmas carols were also among the
repertoire of the heavenly chorus. "At an all-day meeting on
Christmas," attested one, "we had a Christmas carol in
tongues. . . . It was interpreted by one who knew the language: 'Glory to God in the highest and on earth peace, good
will to men.'"[57]

Those able to translate sung glossae into Scripture,
hymnody, and other prophesy were spiritually double-gifted.
In keeping with the Apostle Paul's precept (1 Cor. 14:13, 16),
they both tongue-sang heavenly anthems and translated the
glossal compositions into the vernacular so that everyone oc-
cupying the room could say "Amen." In a newspaper piece
titled "God Is His Own Interpreter," the intricacies of this
spiritual gift were explained:

> You do not have to strain to interpret. You do not use
> your mind at all. The Lord God uses your vocal organs
> and words come out without your having anything to do

---

[55] Antoinette Moomau, "China Missionary Receives Pentecost," *The Apostolic Faith,* vol. 1, no. 11 (Oct. 1908), 3. Although Moomau said she almost saw the crown, visions, particularly of heaven, were common among the early Pentecostals.

[56] This list is assembled from testimonies published in *The Apostolic Faith* (1906–08).

[57] "The Heavenly Anthem," 3.

with it. . . . Often the Lord sends someone that understands the tongue to verify the interpretation.[58]

"Teach and admonish one another . . . as you sing psalms and hymns and spiritual songs"[59]

In addition to rendering human hymnody in its celestial glossa, the Spirit also prompted the singing of the same in the vernacular. Revealing the versatility of the Spirit, this type of singing was characterized by the same power and perfection as Holy Ghost singing:

> Then for fifteen minutes the whole congregation sings in the Spirit. It comes over us as a wave of sound (not tongues, but in English), a harmony with never a harsh note, a praise in the unity of the Spirit until we are all broken up and lifted into the heavenlies.[60]

While the "heavenly anthem" was subject to translation into premillennial prophecy, vernacular hymns were the basis for more empirical testimony.

> A colored brother arose and sang the verses of a hymn, the people joining in the chorus: "The Blood, the Blood, is all my plea; Hallelujah, it cleanseth me." He then said: "Hallelujah! I am so glad I can testify that the Blood cleanseth me. Oh, the sweetness! My heart is full of love for Jesus. I am so glad I can take up the cross and work with Him now and follow Him. Oh, I know I am leaning on the Almighty's arms."[61]

Mortal hymns in the vernacular were more empirical, but that did not make them any less authentic than glossolalic anthems, for they were among the sanctified repertoire of the Spirit.

The Spirit would also teach mortals the hymns of their faithful foreparents. For instance, when Alberta Hall would

---

[58] "God Is His Own Interpreter," *The Apostolic Faith*, vol. 1, no. 5 (Jan. 1907), 2.

[59] Colossians 3:16.

[60] Stanley M. Horton, "A Day at Azusa Street," *The Pentecostal Evangel*, Oct. 14, 1962, 6. For Horton, as with others, "singing in the spirit" includes more than singing in tongues.

[61] "The Pentecostal Assembly," *The Apostolic Faith*, vol. 1, no. 7 (April 1907), 2. Also alluded to in this testimony is a strain from the hymn, "Leaning on the Everlasting Arms."

raise one of the long-standing hymns, any words she had forgotten the Lord put in her mouth.[62] Laura A. Sims testified that during a prayer meeting the Holy Spirit taught her to sing "A Charge to Keep I Have." She continued to say that upon the verse, "O may it all my powers engage to do my Master's will!" the Holy Ghost filled her heart with joy and she started to sing in tongues.[63] As alluded to earlier in Antoinette Moomau's hymnic dialogue with the Deity, the Holy Ghost taught the words of a hymn, not as a demonstration of omnipotence but to convey a message vital to the spiritual elevation of the singer.

Another type of heavenly anthem, according to evangelist A. E. Stuernagel of San Diego, was the "spiritual song":

> The Psalms are those of the Old Testament, and the hymns those common during the centuries of the Christian church. The "spiritual songs," I believe, are the spontaneous, impromptu songs that are given wholly by the Spirit in these last days. Have you ever known an individual who sang spiritual songs without having learned them? A song of praise and thanksgiving rising from the heart? A young lady about twenty years of age came to our services some time ago, and sang a most wonderful song. . . . Everybody marvelled at the beauty of her songs, and asked her, "Where did you get those songs?" She replied, "Why, the Spirit gave them to me. I have about a hundred of them."[64]

Writing from Lexington, Mississippi, Charles H. Mason, founder of the Church of God in Christ, informed the Azusa Saints (whom he had visited earlier) that the Lord had been singing hundreds of songs there. "I do not have time to go back over one to practice it," he said, "for the next will be new."[65]

---

[62] Alberta Hall, "Pentecostal Testimonies," *The Apostolic Faith*, vol. 1, no. 6 (Feb. 1907), 8.

[63] Laura A. Sims, "Pentecostal Testimonies," *The Apostolic Faith*, vol. 1, no. 6 (Feb. 1907), 8.

[64] A. E. Stuernagel, "Being Filled with the Spirit: The Melodies of Heaven Overflow in the Soul," *The Latter Rain Evangel*, vol. 20, no. 10 (July 1928), 8.

[65] Charles H. Mason, "Testimonies," *The Apostolic Faith*, vol. 1, no. 12 (Jan. 1908), 4. During his five-week stay at the Azusa Street Revival in 1906, Mason was baptized with the Holy Ghost and spoke in tongues.

"Singing and making melody to the Lord with all your heart"[66]

Some psalms, hymns, and spiritual songs, according to evangelist Stuernagel, were inward manifestations privately experienced by individuals:

> The Spirit-filled believer will also be "making melody in the heart." He will have a singing heart. Not everybody can sing with the voice, but everybody can have a whole music-box deep down in the soul. Besides, the vocal song must cease at intervals, but the heavenly heart-song can go on forever. It is the new song of heaven wafted down to earth which will continue through countless ages.[67]

For instance, a Brother Burke asked the Lord to baptize him with the Holy Ghost and the next morning the Spirit was singing in his soul, "The power, the power, the Pentecostal power, is just the same to day." Then Burke said it changed to "The Comforter has come, the Holy Ghost from heaven."[68] Writing from New York, Mrs. J. W. Hutchins said that during worship the saints were kneeling for opening prayer and the vision of Jesus descended upon her with power and the chorus went ringing through her heart: "Jesus' blood covers me,/ I was blind but, hallelujah, now I see."[69] The Spirit not only acted "upon" the baptized but also "within."

"O for a thousand tongues to sing my great Redeemer's praise"[70]

Missionaries worldwide, hungry for a Pentecostal experience, flocked to Azusa in pursuit of a charismatic renewal. Most remained only long enough to receive the Holy Ghost baptism before returning to their domestic and foreign battlefields under the new banner of Pentecost. Others never made it to the Azusan holy land but by hearing the

---

[66] Ephesians 5:19.
[67] Stuernagel, 8.
[68] Burke, "The Holy Ghost from Heaven," *The Apostolic Faith*, vol. 1, no. 3 (Nov. 1906), 3.
[69] Hutchins, 3.
[70] Charles Wesley, "O For a Thousand Tongues to Sing" (Hymn).

testimonies through word of mouth and media were able to participate in the Pentecost. Still others initially inspired by the Holy Ghost took to heart its commission to be witnesses of Jesus "to the end of the earth" (Acts 1:8).

Pentecost spread throughout the world with such speed that the opening caption of the February 1907 issue of *The Apostolic Faith* pronounced boldly, "Pentecost Both Sides the Ocean." From Mukti, India, for instance, missionary Max Wood reported that God had given a young Indian girl the gift of song and that immediately following her tongue-singing she translated the glossa into Marathi.[71] Both tongues and music were "universal languages" which, upon marriage, had far-reaching evangelical effects. For the first time in history thousands of tongues worldwide were "singing in the spirit."

"Sing and rejoice . . . for, lo, I come,
and I will dwell in the midst of you"[72]

Singing did not have to be glossolalic to be authentic; it only had to be prompted by the Spirit rather than by the flesh. Aware of the Awesome Presence, and apparently the manner in which that Presence responded to the blasphemy of Ananias and his wife Sapphira,[73] some Azusans feared being accused of inauthenticity by the Spirit:

> No one dared to get up and sing a song or testify except under the anointing of the Spirit. They feared lest the Holy Ghost would cut them off in their song or testimony. We would wait upon God expecting Him to use whom He would. . . . No one dared to say, "We will now have a song by Brother or Sister so and so," and then as they would come to the front to sing, for the congregation to clap their hands and laud them for their singing.[74]

[71] Max Wood, "Pentecost in Mukti, India," *The Apostolic Faith,* vol. 1, no. 10 (Sept. 1907), 4.

[72] Zechariah 2:10.

[73] Acts 5:1–10. Pentecostals, revealing their fundamentalism, deduced doctrinal truth from narrative accounts in the critical Book of Acts.

[74] Rachel Harper Sizelove, "The Temple: How the Shekinah of God's Glory Fell on the People in the Early Days at the Azusa Street Mission in Los Angeles, California," *Word and Work,* vol. 58, no. 5 (May 1936), 2, 12.

If one had been "singing in the flesh," those with the gift of discernment (1 Cor. 12:10) would have deduced it; for spuriousness not only grieved the Holy Spirit but also the Spirit within human vessels. For example, Martha Neale wrote in a letter to a friend: "Some one got up and sang a hymn (in the flesh), that means, of themselves, and it so grieved the Spirit in me I again gave vent in tears."[75] Frank Bartleman, having opened a new Pentecostal mission in Los Angeles in August of 1906, complained of spiritual grievance. "The devil sent two strong characters one night to sidetrack the work," he said. "A spiritualist woman put herself at the head, like a drum major, to lead the singing. I prayed her out of the church."[76]

The prevailing sentiment among early Pentecostals was that authentic anthems not only had to be prompted by and rendered in the Spirit, they also had to be sung a cappella. Instruments, deemed "worldly," grieved the Spirit. Rachel Sizelove spoke to the subject in her reminiscence of eastern travel during the early thirties. Learning that there was a Pentecostal meeting in the vicinity, she and her husband parked and pitched a tent for the night. Remaining inside that evening, she heard the drums and other instruments in the distance. She said the music sounded so worldly when compared to the heavenly anthem sung at the early Azusa revival. On the following day the pastor of the camp meeting heard that a native Azusite was present and requested her account of the Los Angeles revival:

> I told how they had no piano, drums, or any musical instruments of any kind . . . , they had no strange fire, which typified any use of carnal means to kindle the fire of devotion and praise. Brother Seymour would never say, "All stand to your feet and reach up your hands and praise the Lord. But O how wonderful when the Holy Ghost would raise them to their feet and they would sing in the Spirit. O how could the Holy Ghost

[75] *The Apostolic Faith*, vol. 1, no. 11 (Oct. 1908), 4. The command "do not grieve the holy Spirit of God" is taken from Ephesians 4:30.

[76] Bartleman, *What Really Happened at "Azusa Street"?* 51. In spite of theological similarities, Pentecostals rejected spiritualists, much like Fundamentalists rejected Pentecostals.

have right of way if they had had carnal instruments to depend on?[77]

Testimony after testimony indicate that instruments were disparaged at Azusa; neither formal choirs nor hymnals were necessary since God was bestowing music being sung by the angels. "Many times we do not need these song books of earth," said one writer, "but the Lord simply touches us by His mighty Spirit and we have no need of organs or pianos, for the Holy Ghost plays the piano in all our hearts."[78] Apostle William J. Seymour, the Azusite chief, firmly admonished those who thought it essential to have choirs and trained singers from the conservatories. All of these luxuries, he exhorted, have failed to bring divine power and salvation to our souls.[79] Even Rachel Sizelove, who boasted of the sublimity of the authentic Azusan anthem, had to acknowledge its eventual desecration. She complained, "Instead of the Holy Ghost heavenly choir, they brought in a piano."[80] Bartleman also deplored that "choirs were organized, and string bands came into existence to 'jazz' the people."[81]

*"Upon a psaltery and an instrument . . .
will I sing praises unto thee."*[82]

The schismatic controversy surrounding the use of instruments in the early Pentecostal church was a carryover from the Holiness church (perhaps influenced by the Quakers). However, any argument opposing instruments must be measured against three weighty facts: (1) On April 9, 1906, the first day of the Second Pentecost, Jennie Moore, a black woman, spoke in tongues, prophesied, and then went to the piano and began playing and singing beautiful music when previously she had been unable to play.[83] Similar documented testimonies indicate that her "gift of playing instruments"

[77] Sizelove, 12.
[78] *The Apostolic Faith*, vol. 1, no. 4 (Dec. 1906), 2.
[79] William J. Seymour, "The Holy Spirit: Bishop of the Church," *The Apostolic Faith*, vol. 1, no. 9 (June 1907), 3.
[80] Sizelove, 12.
[81] Bartleman, *Azusa Street*, 89.
[82] Psalm 144:9 (KJV).
[83] Nickel, 7. See Jennie Moore's account in "Music From Heaven," 3.

was no isolated gift among the Spirit-baptized. (2) There are several published accounts of Pentecostals receiving the gift of composing upon musical instruments. One account said:

> While they [the family] were praying in regard to going to Africa, the oldest daughter, Bessie, went and sat down to the piano, and soon called to her mother to bring a pencil and paper, that the Lord was giving her a song from the 16th chapter of Mark. . . . The words and music were both from heaven, and it is inspiring to hear it sung.[84]

(3) In the only clear reference to singing in tongues (1 Cor. 14:15b), the original Greek word for "sing" meant to sing to instrumental accompaniment.[85] To argue that instruments were of the flesh was to say (a) that the Holy Spirit made an error when it led Jennie Moore to the piano on April 9, 1906, (b) that the gift of playing instruments was not a gift of the Spirit, and (c) that the only verse that unquestionably substantiates glossolalic singing is erroneous.

Since it is likely that early Pentecostals would have repudiated these assertions, we can: glean some idea of the intrinsic discrepancy to this controversy; sympathize with those who argued in favor of instruments; and provisionally conclude that the verdict opposing instruments was a mortal judgment rather than a dictate from God.

"Teach me some melodious sonnet sung by flaming tongues above"[86]

A total of eighteen hymns were published in seven of the thirteen issues of *The Apostolic Faith* (December 1906–January 1908).[87] The debut hymn, aptly F. E. Hill's

---

[84] "A Missionary Family," *The Apostolic Faith*, vol. 1, no. 8 (May 1907), 2.

A second instance of the gift of composition was recorded in a piece titled, "San Francisco and Oakland," *The Apostolic Faith*, vol. 1, no. 4 (Dec. 1906), 4.

[85] "The word 'sing' strictly signifies to touch the chord of the instrument, hence to sing with accompaniment. The singing of improvised hymns was therefore one of the principal forms of speaking [singing] in tongues." F. Godet, *Commentary on St. Paul's First Epistle to the Corinthians*, vol. 2 (Edinburgh: T. & T. Clark, n.d.), 280–82.

[86] Robert Robinson, "Come Thou Fount of Every Blessing" (Hymn).

[87] The complete texts are transcribed in Jon Michael Spencer, "The Heavenly Anthem: Holy Ghost Singing in the Primal Pentecostal Church (1906–1909)," *The Journal of Black Sacred Music*, vol. 1, no. 1 (Spring 1987), 17–33.

"Baptized with the Holy Ghost," appeared in the fourth issue of the newspaper (December 1906). Thereafter hymns were published in issues 5 through 9 and 12. All of these pieces, except one, consist of text only. Thomas Helmezhalch's "Jesus Is Coming," first published in issue 4 with text only, reappeared with a musical setting in issue 9.

Comments in the prefaces to several of the hymns indicate that their composition was Spirit-inspired. J. W. Ellison, for example, claimed to have written his "Pentecost Restored" following "Pentecostal anointing." The opening stanza reads:

> O glorious promise of heaven!
> Fulfilled to His people at last;
> The tongues of fire have descended,
> And sealed us as those in the past.[88]

Having witnessed Castilla Reese composing a hymn in the Spirit, one correspondent with the newspaper wrote:

> Mildred composed a piece of music and sat down to play it yesterday. It took my soul almost out of this land, while she played it, and the power came on Sister Reese and she began to sing words, O so sweet and in such harmony with the music. How God flooded our souls as she sang. She could not remember them but yesterday afternoon the power came on her again and she wrote them down. O you could hardly stay here, when they sing and play that piece. It's from the Paradise of God. If nothing else happened but this, it ought to convince people.[89]

In the next month's issue of the paper Sister Reese's piece, "A Song of Prayer," was prefaced with this remark: "Music to which this song is sung, was composed by the little Mildred Crawford, and as she played the piece on the piano, Sister Rees[e] sang the words to it for her, composing as she sang in the Spirit."[90]

"Jesus Christ Is Made to Me," a hymn by Charles Price Jones, was not attributed to an author when published. Its

---

[88] *The Apostolic Faith,* vol. 1, no. 5 (Jan. 1907), 1.

[89] "San Francisco and Oakland," *The Apostolic Faith,* vol. 1, no. 4 (Dec. 1906), 4.

[90] [Signed] Castilla Rees[e], December 2 [1906]. *The Apostolic Faith,* vol. 1, no. 5 (Jan. 1907), 4.

caption was "A new song . . . sung through in the Spirit by all."[91] Another hymn, "Jesus Is Coming," was given by God to the William Cummings missionary family of Los Angeles as they prepared to go to Africa:

> Jesus is coming, is coming;
> Jesus is coming so soon.
> Go into all the world, My saints;
> Tell them that Jesus is coming.
>
> He that believeth and is baptized,
> Tell them that Jesus is coming;
> He that believeth not shall be damned,
> Tell them that Jesus is coming.[92]

In light of these accounts and Pentecostal belief, it is reasonable to assume that all eighteen of the hymns were divinely inspired (if not Holy Ghost wrought) and that they constituted an additional type of "heavenly anthem." A detailed study of these hymns of the Holy Ghost reveals the predominant theological themes of the movement, a wide array of Pentecostal reflection, and historical phenomena.

Two hymns, both titled "Jesus Is Coming," reflect the central theme of the natal Pentecostal revival. "A Message Concerning Christ's Coming" is similarly titled. Altogether, half of the eighteen pieces articulate the premillennial second coming, and two additional ones allude to it. Of these, Alfred Beck's "The Warfare" and C. E. Kent's "The Signs of the Times" are alarmingly apocalyptic. Three of the hymns slant toward the theme of holiness or sanctification, two poeticize the outpouring of Pentecost, two highlight the Holy Spirit, and one expresses missionary zeal. In closing, here are a few stanzas from Kent's "The Signs of the Times," an eschatological response to the traumatic San Francisco earthquake of April 18, 1906:

> The earth is trembling far and near
> With quaking sound,—fills all with fear,
> The rocks are rent with awful power,
> Which causes strongest men to cower.

[91] *The Apostolic Faith*, vol. 1, no. 7 (Apr. 1907), 2.
[92] "A Missionary Family," *The Apostolic Faith*, vol. 1, no. 8 (May 1907), 2.

A sickening feeling fills the air,
And nations tremble yet unaware
That soon will come the awful woe,
When to their dreadful doom they'll go.

All nations feel a crisis near,
Men's hearts are failing them for fear;
Distress of nations now has come,
Soon Christ shall call His people home.

The earth is groaning with its sin,
Which louder grows with awful din,
Until the great triumphant blast,
Shall free from Satan's rule at last.[93]

[93] *The Apostolic Faith*, vol. 1, no. 7 (Apr. 1907), 3.

8

Isochronisms of Antistructure:

Music in the Black Holiness-Pentecostal Testimony Service

HOLINESS-PENTECOSTAL MUSIC

Rite of Intensification

The ritual of testimony commenced when the first black spirituals asked, "Who will be a witness for my Lord?" and someone among that marginal people answered, "I will be a witness for my Lord." Since then the ritual has been principally maintained by and learned from black women who are the bearers of the tradition of "having church."[1]

Testimony service, throughout its historical evolvement, has functioned to prepare the religious community to endure the ways of the world by shaping and rejuvenating its common consciousness. In doing so, the maternal community has carried in its womb the perpetual rebirth of the churched and the larger black community. It is a rite of intensification insofar as this rebirth occurs each week when the churched gather to worship. Testimony service has allowed them through singing, testifying, and shouting to sing, speak, and act the

---

[1] If one looks beyond the male-dominated pulpit, says Cheryl Gilkes, one will doubtless view the Holiness-Pentecostal church as a women's movement. Cheryl T. Gilkes, "The Role of Women in the Sanctified Church," *The Journal of Religious Thought*, vol. 43 (Spring/Summer 1986), 33.

good God has done for them during the past week, thereby strengthening their faith and community for the new week.

By adapting the model of anthropologist Bruce Reed,[2] it becomes apparent that testimony service is not only a rite of intensification but also a rite of transition. Through "creative regression," a healthy form of reversal to the primal source, it transforms the *congregation* of the structural world of experience and intradependence into the realm of worship and extradependence.

Intradependence, Reed explains, refers to the disposition of self-autonomous individuals functioning in the world with their confirmation, protection, and sustenance in their own hands. By the end of the week, individuals are nearly drained of their resources. The "oscillation process" (which Reed has diagrammed) begins with the gathering-greeting of the churched from various walks of life and their "creative regression" (through testimony service) into extradependence.[3] Extradependence, the dependence on God as the source for confirmation, protection, and sustenance, enables individuals to tolerate and begin to eliminate inner disorientation, weakness, and pain. The community is reintensified, enabling it to again transform-engage, breaking up into its

---

[2] Bruce Reed, *The Dynamics of Religion: Process and Movement in Christian Churches* (London: Darton, Longman and Todd, 1978), 73. Reed's original diagram of the oscillatory process is horizontal and contains six parts; here it is circular and is divided into four parts, between which *escape* is conveniently centered. I have placed the testimony and preaching services in brackets to illustrate their location in the process.

[3] Ibid., 32, 34, 15, 35.

individual selves as it reenters the atmosphere of the structural world of intradependence.[4]

This oscillation between intradependence and extradependence is what philosopher Martin Buber refers to as the "two primary metacosmical movements of the world." The movement to extradependence is "reversal to connexion," "the recognition of the Centre and the act of turning again to it;" and the movement to intradependence is the individual's "expansion into its own being." It is in *reversal* that *expansion* is "born again with new wings." Says Buber, "He who truly goes out to meet the world goes out also to God."[5]

When the two major parts of Holiness-Pentecostal worship, the testimony and preaching services,[6] function with the traditional wisdom of the people, even those worshipers seeking escape are inhaled into (through creative regression) and exhaled out of extradependence (transformed) without realizing the dynamics of God's breathing. When testimony and preaching function in this way, "expansion into one's own being" is, as theologian Robert Williams phrases it, "the more enduring experience of sensing that we are being upheld and cradled by strength that is not of our making, something, as Howard Thurman would say, that gives to life a quality of integrity and meaning which we could never generate."[7]

If sacrifice is at the heart of rite, then perhaps testimony is also sacrificial—a sacrificial sharing of one's personal story with the church. It takes courage to share one's story because there is a certain degree of verbal and kinetic evaluation by listeners.[8] Yet by sacrificing it as a testimony many stories are gained in return, stories with which to compare and nourish one's own. "Creative regression to

---

[4] Ibid., 74, 78–79.

[5] Martin Buber, *I and Thou*, trans. Ronald Gregor Smith (Edinburgh: T. & T. Clark, 1937), 116, 100, 95.

[6] Because the *service of the word* functions most powerfully for the purpose of *expansion* (transformation) back into *intradependence*, the *closing service* (altar call, healing, benediction) is not represented in this treatise or in the ensuing model.

[7] Robert C. Williams, "Worship and Anti-Structure in Thurman's Vision of the Sacred," *Journal of the Interdenominational Theological Center*, vol. 14, nos. 1 & 2 (Fall 1986/Spring 1987), 171.

[8] Elaine J. Lawless, "Making a Joyful Noise: An Ethnography of Communication in the Pentecostal Religious Community," *Southern Folklore Quarterly*, vol. 44 (1980), 17.

extra-dependence," confirms Reed, "entails a conscious act, on the part of the individual, of placing himself in the hands of another, with due appreciation of the risks involved, but with hope derived from satisfactory experience."[9]

Testimonies also benefit the larger unchurched community by the rejuvenated churchgoers effusing God's "breathing," the "anointing," into the community. Those engaging in "representative oscillation" (infrequent in their church attendance but dependent on the attendance of a relative or friend) and "vicarious oscillation" (neither attending nor having individual representation, yet dependent on worship happening),[10] are carried in the womb of those women and upon the shoulders of those men who engage in "personal oscillation" (attend church regularly). Personal oscillation is God's regular inhaling and exhaling of the ritually synchronized community, while "representative" and "vicarious" oscillation comprise God's breath upon the represented. God breathes in weekly cycles on the churched and the unchurched.

The Superstructure of Testimony

The testimony service (usually preceded by the song service) is the climactic segment of the devotional service, which includes opening song, scripture, and prayer (occasionally preceded by prayer requests).[11] Typically there are one or two (two men or two women) "devotional leaders" who lead the testimony service, which lasts between fifteen and sixty minutes. The devotional leader may open the service by saying something like: "The testimony service is open to testify as to the glory of God. Let's have church saints."[12]

That the "regression" or "reversal" of testimony service is "creative" is illustrated by the many ways used to expedite time. In very large churches a time limit may be placed on testifying—one minute, for example (although most tend to go overtime). Occasionally a testifier will "ride on the back" of the hymn raised by the previous speaker, repeating its

---

[9] Reed, 35.
[10] Ibid., 54.
[11] For a basic liturgical model see Arthur E. Paris, *Black Pentecostalism: Southern Religion in an Urban World* (Amherst: University of Massachusetts Press, 1982), 54.
[12] In one Pentecostal church the person who reads the scripture opens the service with a testimony, while the one who lines the hymn closes with a testimony.

words so the participant-listeners can make the thematic connection. Whereas the "saints" usually stand one at a time to testify, in some churches all who wish to speak stand and await a cue from the devotional leader. In one particular church the worshipers know that at a given time the choir will sing and following the chronological testifying of each of its members (to the background of the music), any of the worshipers who have not yet spoken may stand and "testify in one voice."

The completed testimony service does not dubiously flow into the service of the Word via some "spontaneous" activity that shifts the course of events. The devotional leader usually says something like, "This ends our testimony service and we now turn the service over to our pastor." Although the testimony service has a specific time, place, duration, and prescribed entrance and exit, testimony is occasionally interjected at places outsiders would perceive as inappropriate. On one occasion the benediction had been given, the music for the recessional was about to commence, and one woman stood up raising her hand informing the pastor that she had something to say. What followed her testifying was shouting (holy dancing), which spread as the fire shut up in their bones ignited. However, Arthur Paris assures us that the typical Pentecostal service is not chaotic. He says, "There is never cacophony; participants always know what 'score' is being played that night and what 'key' and which 'instrumentation' will be used."[13]

Hymnody-Testimony and Community

The means by which testimony service functions to intensify individual faith and the church bond are multifold. First, testifying is a response to the biblical command for the redeemed (Ps. 107:2) to make known the doings of the Lord (Ps. 105:1). By making known God's doings, others going through similar experiences are encouraged to endure. Testimony also comprises the sharing of problems and petitioning of special prayer from the saints. Confessional testifying, where one confesses neglect to respond to the calling of the Spirit to speak with or pray for that distressed person during

[13] Paris, 79.

the week, may follow such petition. A particularly talented singer may use testifying as a practical and "creative" means of employing their gift for the exhortation and edification of the congregation. Or if one of the ministers misses the gathering-greeting part of service, he or she might "check in" with a testimony.

Singing plays a crucial part in the process of synchronization in all of these instances. It is the congregation's channel of entrance into the antistructural realm of testifying— the spiritual realm of God doings, problem solving, faith building, and communal confessing. For instance, if a testimony indicates that a person is mourning, any one of the "saints" may raise a hymn of consolation. In one case the pastor led the singing of this chorus three times:

> Jesus will fix it for you
> He knows just what to do;
> Whenever you pray let him have his way,
> Jesus will fix it for you.

As a "watchman on the wall" (Isa. 62:6), the minister knows when and what kind of hymn to help soothe the individual and to simultaneously intensify the community bond. The genius of testimony service is that it "creatively" applies healing, massages courage, and generates expansion.

The dynamics at work in the testimonial rite of intensification would be described by Martin Buber as an "I-Thou" relation:

> Community is the being no longer side by side (and, one might add, above or below) but *with* one another of a multitude of persons. And this multitude, though it moves towards one goal, yet experiences everywhere a turning to, a dynamic facing of, the others, a flowing from *I* to *Thou*. [14]

When many selves *feel* their persons singing, thereby becoming aware of their own being,[15] it is not to the obliteration of

---

[14] Quoted in Victor Turner, *The Ritual Process: Structure and Antistructure* (Ithaca: Cornell University Press, 1969), 127.

[15] Gilbert Rouget, *Music and Trance: A Theory of the Relations between Music and Possession*, trans. Brunhilde Biebuyck (Chicago: Chicago University Press, 1985), 120.

the relation *I-Thou*. It is not *I* feeling *I* without also being *with Thou*. And even though the hymns selected as the entrance into testifying tend to be textually *I*-centered, the singing congregation transmuted into the testifying of the individual creates such a strong relation that it is best described as an *essential We*. Anthropologist Victor Turner explains with reference to Buber:

> Buber does not restrict community to dyadic relationships [*I* and *Thou*]. He also speaks of an "essential *We*," by which he means "a community of several independent persons, who have a self and self-responsibility. . . . The *We* includes the *Thou*. Only men who are capable of truly saying *Thou to* one another can truly say *We with* one another."[16]

This *essential We* is what Turner terms "communitas"—that higher form of community relation "creatively" entered into through testimony, which initiates the antistructural movement out of the structured community. This *essential We*, communitas, which "transgresses or dissolves the norms that govern structured and institutionalized relationships and is accompanied by experiences of unprecedented potency," is often momentarily superseded by "spontaneous communitas," which is "a phase, a moment, not a permanent condition." "Spontaneous communitas," defines Turner, "has something 'magical' about it. Subjectively there is in it the feeling of endless power."[17] When these potent spiritual moments latent in antistructure (the realm of extradependence) are revealed, the *essential We* spontaneously becomes an *ultimate We*, what Buber refers to as the Self, delivered from all being conditioned by *I*, merged in God such that the saying of *Thou* ceases for lack of twofold being. Buber himself admits that there is a state beyond *I* and *Thou*, as in ecstasy, wherein the *I* is swallowed up by the *Thou*, which is no longer *Thou*, but "that which alone is."[18] The *ultimate We* is *that which alone is*.

---

[16] Cited in Turner, 129.
[17] Ibid., 128, 139–40.
[18] Buber, 83–84.

The Isochronism of Singing-Testifying

Opening one's testifying with singing is part of a long-standing tradition that may have started with the singing of spirituals. The isochronism[19] singing-testifying certainly was a practice in postbellum black Protestant and Holiness churches that found its way into early Pentecostalism. Sounding nearly identical to the contemporary accounts to be examined shortly, a 1907 report of "a colored brother" testifying at the Azusa Street revival is proof of the persistence of the tradition:

> A colored brother arose and sang the verses of a hymn, the people joining in the chorus: "The Blood, the Blood, is all my plea; Hallelujah, it cleanseth me." He then said: "Hallelujah! I am so glad I can testify that the Blood cleanseth me. Oh, the sweetness! My heart is full of love for Jesus. I am so glad I can take up the cross and work with Him now and follow Him. Oh, I know I am leaning on the Almighty's arms."[20]

That testimony typically begins with and is thematically built upon a hymn is partly because the meter, rhyme, and melody of hymns make them more memorizable than scripture. Consequently, hymnody has become a key source of lay theology, further functioning as a means of distinguishing the language of testimony from that of secular talk. Of course this stylistic application of hymnody has received sanctioning from the black preacher who has traditionally prefaced preaching with the singing of a hymn.

The use of a testimony hymn is not merely stylistic; it is usually a piece that alights upon one's life and addresses God's doings during the period of intradependence. Sometimes a single hymn remains with an individual one oscillatory cycle after another as a means of comfort and healing during a particularly trying period in life. In such instances

---

[19] An *isochronism* (or *isochron*) comprises chronological moments in a single event, for example, gathering-greeting or singing-testifying. Testimony service is in many respects a link between these chronological yet holistic events (isochronisms).

[20] "The Pentecostal Assembly," *The Apostolic Faith* (Los Angeles), vol. 1, no. 1 (Apr. 1907), 2.

the testifier will often say before singing the hymn, "The Lord put this song in my heart" or "I was led to sing this song," or following its singing, "Bless your name Lord, that song was really deep down in my heart." Some hymns have a long emotional history. A person may remember that a particular song was the favorite that a mother or grandmother used to sing when she testified or that a father or grandfather liked to sing when he lined the hymn. Perhaps little attention was paid to these hymns while growing up until some crisis caused them to take on special meaning (possibly the crisis point at which one's "representative" or "vicarious" oscillation became "personal"). "Nothing is more laden with emotional associations than music," confirms Gilbert Rouget; "nothing is more capable of recreating situations that engage one's entire sensibility."[21]

Unless a hymn is original or the testifier specifies, "*I*'ve got a song ringing in my soul and *I* want to try singing it to the Lord," the group joins in the singing as a means of entering into the testifying.[22] Most often the testifier will lead a round or two of a chorus (some of the hymns have no known verses and are comprised solely of a chorus). Usually beginning in an unmetered way, a hymn picks up tempo and rhythmic regularity as the congregation joins in and begins to clap and the musicians begin to play. The singing continues until the one who raised the hymn (frequently the one who is singing the loudest) stops to testify.[23] If the individual gets caught up in the song, it may continue incessantly. "A few times I can remember starting a song and never getting around to testifying," one woman attested.[24] If testifying is

[21] Rouget, 123.

[22] One woman from the Virgin Islands was able to sing solo because she set a mixture of familiar hymn texts to a tune indigenous to her homeland and unknown to the congregation. In another instance, a young woman sang an original song, reading her words from a piece of paper.

[23] The success of the song can be measured in terms of intensification (e.g., tempo and volume), kinetic involvement (e.g., shouting), and verbal interjections (e.g., tongues).

[24] Cited in (and interviewed by) William T. Dargan, "Congregational Gospel Songs in a Black Holiness Church: A Musical and Textual Analysis," Ph.D. dissertation, Wesleyan University, 1982, 79. This and all subsequent citations from this dissertation are results of interviews carried on by Dargan.

not to follow the singing, the speaker may simply say, "I thank God for that song" and be seated.

Since testifying (speaking) tends to open with singing, then the structure of the service is balanced between these two parts. Singing smoothly connects one act of testifying to the next and often prompts the spoken part to be musical. This results in greater fluidity between testimonies. Because music is "laden with emotional associations," a hymn is able to speak to the former testimony and the ensuing one, thereby providing the required emotional transition between "stories." Bennetta Jules-Rosette, in her study of an independent Apostolic church in Africa, terms this the "coherence factor."

> The "coherence factor" that seems to be consistently realized is that singing, whenever it takes place, follows speech without an appreciable gap in time. This factor does not determine what will be sung or the length of time allowed for singing. In this way, the ceremony is maintained as a continual flow of sound of which the components are negotiable.[25]

In testimony service the continual flow of sound, the "coherence factor," enables the stories to comprise one disconnected narrative.

Cadential Rite in Testifying

The rite of entering into the performed action of testifying commences with singing, which is followed by salutation that "gives honor" to the Lord, the clergypersons, on down to the members and friends. The rite of "entering out" is more theologically and symbolically substantive. The formula consists of three parts.

(1) The first segment of the cadential rite, in its simplest form, is "I'm saved, sanctified, and filled with the Holy Ghost." This basic formula is variously embellished as "I'm saved, sanctified, and have the baptism of the Holy Ghost," or "I'm saved, I'm sanctified, Holy Ghost filled and fire-baptized," or "I'm saved, sanctified, baptized and filled with

---

[25] Bennetta Jules-Rosette, *African Apostles: Ritual and Conversion in the Church of John Maranke* (Ithaca: Cornell University Press, 1975), 132.

the Holy Ghost and fire." One woman (perhaps not yet Spirit-baptized) really individualized the saying with "I'm saved, I'm sanctified, and I'm satisfied." Another started off by saying "I'm saved from sin." Pre-formula words also personalize the saying: "I thank God this morning that I can say without a doubt that I'm saved, sanctified and have the Holy Ghost fire deep down in my soul."[26] There was a time when Holiness-Pentecostal worshipers regularly recited an extended version of the formula: "I'm saved, I'm sanctified, I have the baptism of the Holy Ghost and fire, have the walking-hallelujah, fire burning in the flesh, joy unspeakable." The "walking-hallelujah" and the "fire burning in the flesh," still occasionally referred to by the older members, are the *dynamos* of the Spirit.[27]

(2) Inner spiritual experiences tend to overflow outward to participate in the empiric meanings and applications they generate. Here, the threefold formula (saved, sanctified, and Spirit-baptized) is immediately followed by a statement of intention and application—antecedent and consequent. The intention (the antecedent) is stated as, "I got a mind to live right." After leading the congregation in the singing of "I'm gonna serve the Lord" (*4X*), a worshiper testified that "having a made-up mind" (intention) is for the purpose of service:

> I thank God for that little song of praise, "I'm Going to Serve the Lord." My heart is fixed and my mind made up, and it makes it easy for you to serve the Lord. You cannot serve unless you have a fixed heart and a made-up mind.

It is feasible that this segment of the cadential rite was derived from one of the hymns the saints sometimes sing:

[26] Black Pentecostal scholar Leonard Lovett wrote in the seventies that some of the young black Pentecostals were comfortable saying "saved, sanctified, baptized with the Holy Ghost for liberation." Lovett explained, "They point to such texts as, 'God anointed Jesus of Nazareth with the Holy Ghost and with power; who went about doing good, and healing all that were oppressed of the devil; for God was with him'" (Acts 10:38). Leonard Lovett, "Black Origins of the Pentecostal Movement," in *Aspects of Pentecostal-Charismatic Origins*, ed. Vinson Synan (Plainfield, N.J.: Logos International, 1975), 140.

[27] The doctrine of the Holy Spirit is so important to Pentecostalism that instead of concluding a prayer in the customary way, "in the name of Jesus," one deacon ended his intoned prayer "in the name of the Holy Ghost—Amen."

> I've got a mind to live right (2X)
> I've got a mind to live right every day.
> I tell Jesus, give me a mind to live right
> I've got a mind to live right every day.

Following the singing of two more verses (in which the words "do" and "talk" replaced "live") one woman testified: "I thank God this morning for that little praise, for that's my testimony—I have a mind to talk right and I have a mind to do right. Truly I thank God for that this morning."

The consequent is a statement of will, for example, "I feel like going on." The antecedent and consequent may be stated together as: "I got a made-up mind (or "My mind is made up") to go through with the Lord." Some stress that the isochronism *going-on/going-through* (with the Lord) is life-denying passage: "I made up my mind years ago that I'm determined to go to heaven if it cost me my life" or "I have a deep determination today to run for my life as never before." Whereas the statement of determination naturally implies intention, to state one's intention without confirming one's determination seems to be an incomplete formula. Though saved, sanctified, and Spirit-baptized, one must have both the *mind* (intention) to "live right" and the *will* (determination) to "run on" in order to truly "fight the good fight of faith."

(3) After announcing one's salvation, sanctification, and Spirit-baptism, and one's mind and will to "live right" and to "run on," what follows is petition for prayer. Usually this is stated as "I desire your prayers," or "Pray my strength in the Lord," or "Pray much for me." The most potent cadential petition has mutuality and is able to maintain the heightened experience of community:

> I'm saved, I'm sanctified,
> Holy Ghost filled and fire-baptized;
> *Pray for me,*
> *I'll be praying for you.*

The following example casts the cadential petition in the context of the complete rite:

> I'm yet saved and I'm sanctified
> Holy Ghost filled and fire-baptized.
> I have a deep determination in my soul

To press my way on up
To meet the soon-coming king.
I desire your prayers
To pray my strength in the Lord.

Movement into Testifying

Singing is the channel by which worshipers are brought into the experience of testifying. If a testimony is to be mournful, then a mournful hymn best addresses the speaker's remorse and "coherently" brings the congregation into the experience of the speaker. If a testimony is to be celebrative (as most are), then the hymn raised is appropriately jubilant. Upon "coherently" entering into the singing, the speaker (*I*) and congregation (*Thou*) are liminal, neither *I-Thou* nor the *essential We;* they are truly betwixt and between. Once carried through singing into the *essential We* of testifying, the congregation (*Thou-We*) is able to offer the speaker (*I-We*) its authentic verbal and kinetic support—applause, tongues, shouting; or, in instances of tribulation, its meta-prayerful glossal moans.

Although singing transmutes the church into the narrative experience of the speaker, it is equally important in bringing the speaker to the point of readiness to sacrifice her or his testimony with the marginal group. One of the saints explained it this way:

> Some songs automatically break down walls and barriers. I don't know if you've ever experienced being burdened or tied up in knots so that you don't even know what to say. Certain songs can open you up, so that by the time you've finished that song, you're down at the altar and you're ready to talk.[28]

The Coherence Factor in Practice

The following isochronisms of singing-testifying illustrate the dynamism of the "coherence factor." The first example was led by the musician of a small storefront Pentecostal church. Following a verse sung solo to his own guitar accompaniment, all joined in the chorus:

---

[28] Cited in Dargan, 78.

> Hold to his hand, God's unchanging hand (2X)
> Build your hopes on things eternal;
> Hold to God's unchanging hand. .

After another verse and two choruses, he began testifying:

> Praise God—hold to God's unchanging hand. Praise
> God—That's part of my testimony this morning, saints.
> Praise God—I've made up my mind to hold on to God's
> unchanging hand. Praise God—Sometimes the road
> gets hard—Praise God—and it seems like there's just no
> end to anything—Praise God. But I just gotta continue
> to hold on to God's unchanging hand; realizing—Praise
> God—as long as we—Praise God—keep our hand in the
> master's hand—Praise God—after a while—Praise
> God—everything will be alright—Praise God.[29]

While some testifying makes only brief reference to the
introductory hymn, the coherence factor is most evident
when, as the next example illustrates, the testifying is built
around the hymnic theme.

> I'm blessed, better than blessed, praise the Lord (2X)
> When I'm tossed round at sea, O the Lord watches me;
> I'm blessed, I'm blessed, O praise the Lord.

Succeeding a second verse (and introductory salutation), the
speaker storied:

> I praise God for that song, "I'm Blessed, Better than
> Blessed". . . . I praise the Lord because that song was
> ringing in my heart. Yesterday afternoon we went to a
> nursing home, and we went around and sung Christmas
> carols—some of the girls and I from the job—and I tell
> you, it really touched my heart because I looked around
> and saw how blessed I really am. And I'm here to praise
> God, because I don't care how young you are or how old
> you are, you can still be in that condition. And I'm here
> to praise God because we are blessed, better than
> blessed! And if we just look around and see how blessed
> we really are, we can really give God the praise;
> because God deserves all the praise that we've been

---

[29] Testimonies are often interspersed with the words "hallelujah" or "praise
God," and sometimes with tongues. For many testifiers, such ejaculations function
as commas, semicolons, and periods, or as introductory exclamations to sentences.

giving him this morning. I praise God because I feel
good on the inside. I praise God for being saved, sanctified, and have the Holy Ghost and a mind to live right. I
desire your prayers.

One way of gauging the coherence of the congregation's at-
tainment of the higher community relation of communitas is
when another worshiper is moved to "ride on the back" of the
singing-testifying of the speaker. "I thank God for that song,"
a worshiper responded in this instance, "that I too can look
around and say that the Lord has been good to me."

Some testifying is more on the order of exhortation than
testimony, more of a "watchman" sensibility. Quite consistent
with the nature of the position, it is often the devotional
leader who gives an exhorting testimony and is "creative" at
using it to lead the worshipers into brief potent religious
experiences such as shouting or speaking in tongues. The
speaker may occasionally exhort first and then drive the message home with a hymn, but in the ensuing instance the devotional leader opened with singing (begun slowly in a free
style, with the organist "tuning in" a sustained accompaniment):

> Just another day that the Lord has kept me (2X)
> He has kept me from all evil with my mind stayed on
> Jesus
> Just another day that the Lord has kept me.

Against the backdrop of softly sustained chords, the devotional leader then exhorted:

> You know, we might think it's for something good that
> we've done that the Lord has kept us. But I can say by
> his grace it is he that has kept us, and not we ourselves.
> I'd like somebody to just help me sing that song.

In the same drawn-out style the devotional leader had the
congregation join her in singing verses one and two. Having
led the group to this depth of antistructure, she increased the
tempo to a double time (twice as fast), and the second verse
was thrice sung to the accompaniment of the drums, tambourines, and clapping. Shouting ensued and the *essential We*
"spontaneously" burst into ultimacy.

Marginality, Liminality, and Seminality in Musicianship

Before defining the meaning of shouting, it is important to investigate the part musicians play both in facilitating and debilitating the height of community relation conduced by the devotional leader. The dynamics in the tension between facilitation and debilitation include *marginality, liminality,* and *seminality.*

The musical engagement of musicians in the singing, testifying, and shouting of the congregation may give the impression that they, and not just their music, are members of the intense worshiping congregation rather than simply the mechanical means to heightened forms of community. On the one hand, Melvin Williams finds that the spirited involvement of the musicians in their music is contagious and inspires worshipers, especially those who identify and interact closely with the musicians, to react and participate.[30] This is often true, but Arthur Paris finds that musicians usually do not testify or otherwise participate in the service, so that what is important about them is their music.[31] In testimony service, marginal musicians generally function like marginal ministers, as "watchmen on the wall," veritably as music *ministers.* As "watchmen" it is important for them not to get caught up in their own spiritual experiences but rather to keenly "sense the presence or flow of the Spirit in the service."[32]

Wherever musicians are intricately involved in sensing and responding to the ebb of the Spirit in the antistructural activities of the singing-testifying event, the church depends on their seminal engagement in extradependence. When the biblical patriarch Saul was ill, an organist storied, he would call *a musician,* David, to play upon his lyre and Saul's troubled soul would be refreshed and healed (1 Sam. 16:23). The David of Holiness-Pentecostalism is the organist, and his lyre is the organ. While some Davids would undoubtedly admit that they marginally function as "watchmen," others,

[30] Melvin D. Williams, *Community in a Black Pentecostal Church: An Anthropological Study* (Prospect Heights, Ill.: Waveland Press, 1974), 150.
[31] Paris, 77.
[32] Cited in Dargan, 106.

according to one musician's opinion, would contend that their shouting and moaning is done on their lyre:

> Perhaps the only difference in the anointing on the person in the pew and on me is that they just don't have an instrument before them on which it can be expressed. I praise the Lord on the instrument; whereas that individual might praise the Lord by clapping the hands or patting the feet or doing the holy dance or saying "Hallelujah."[33]

Typically the organist is marginal, but she or he is by no means liminal, for the position is a seminal one. When an *I* raises an old slow and mournful spiritual as entrance into testifying, the organist may feel self-led to respond as an *I* rather than as a *Thou* and ride that piece in a gospel idiom for an extended period. And the instrumentalists in their enthusiasm often play so loudly that the words of the singing cannot be heard, occasionally causing *I* to forfeit her or his testifying. It is perhaps because of these kinds of *interruptions* that instrumentation was controversial in the early Holiness and Pentecostal movements.[34]

In the absence of the regular organist in one Holiness church, a talented nine-year-old girl sometimes substitutes, and there is a world of difference in the achievement of the heightened form of community. While *the* organist was seminal-marginal, the nine-year-old was marginal-liminal, neither a regular worshiper nor *the* organist. Here, Turner's categorical delineation between liminality and seminality is revealing. Of his partial list, several are particularly relevant in comparing *the* seminal organist to the liminal neophyte: absence of status versus status, absence of rank *vs* rank, humility *vs* just pride of position, unselfishness *vs* selfishness, total obedience *vs* obedience only to superior rank, silence *vs* speech, simplicity *vs* complexity, heteronomy *vs* degrees of autonomy, sacredness *vs* secularity.[35]

---

[33] Ibid., 107.
[34] See Rachel Harper Sizelove, "The Temple: How the Shekinah of God's Glory Fell on the People in the Early Days at the Azusa Street Mission in Los Angeles, California," *Word and Work*, vol. 58, no. 5 (May 1936), 12.
[35] Turner, 106–7.

In many respects the nine-year-old's marginal-liminal qualities were more conducive to the heightened form of community than the seminal-marginal predisposition of the organist. "Communitas," says Turner, "breaks in through the interstices of structure, in liminality; at the edges of structure, in marginality; and from beneath structure, in inferiority."[36] In observing the distinction between the seminal and the liminal, it appears that the Holy Spirit is better able to breathe life into the community that produces heightened forms of community through the innocence of a child.

The Meaning of Shouting

Shouting refers interchangeably to praising the Lord with a loud voice and holy dancing.[37] Shouting—"getting happy," "getting religion," or "having church"—"it's like 'fire shut up in my bones'" (Jer. 20:9) the people say. It is "joy unspeakable and full of glory" (1 Pet. 1:8 KJV). The classical Pentecostal view of shouting involves an "anointing" from the Holy Ghost, but shouting in obedience to the ordinance to praise the Lord with dance (Ps. 150:4) is no more the result of an anointing than clapping in compliance to the command for the people to clap their hands (Ps. 47:1). "Sometimes I just feel like praising Him in the dance," said one woman. "But when the anointing does come on me to dance—when it comes on me this way I go for days! This really doesn't happen very often, it's like a special occasion."[38] Unless the "watchman" stops the music in order to check for "dancing in the flesh" (response to the music), there is no plenary means to check for "dancing in the Spirit" (response to the Spirit).

When the fire of the Holy Ghost descends, some dance in the pews while others move into the aisle. Those who identify and closely interact with the organist are perhaps drawn toward the instruments where they can better "bathe in the music." Some sojourn to their favorite corner, their closet, while others gravitate toward the sacred center before the altar. This inner center is the principal place of visibility

---

[36] Ibid., 128.
[37] See Zora Neale Hurston, *The Sanctified Church* (Berkeley, Cal.: Turtle Island, 1983), 91–94, for an ethnography of the various manifestations of shouting.
[38] Cited in Dargan, 79.

and authority where testimony is led, scripture read, prayer rendered, healing delivered, solos sung, tongues spoken, and conversion is ritually consummated. If shouting is in fact a renewal of the initial conversion crisis, such that conversion and shouting are "different moments in a single experience"[39] (an isochronism), then perhaps gravitation toward the sacred center is a form of "creative regression." As such, shouting is not the dysfunctional attempt to return to the womb that Reed disparages, in which the individual attempts to escape by obliterating her or his "estranged" past. Rather, the past remains but is transformed.[40]

Danced Religion

Singing-testifying about victory over travail frequently functions as spiritual, mental, and physical transmutation into the most trenchant form of ritual celebration—"danced religion." Shouting, using Rouget's language, is "dancing the music" or "acting the music."[41] Insofar as it is stylized celebration in the testimonial rite of intensification, "dancing the music" is ritual dance.

Music is a means of drawing worshipers into the realm of ritual dance. Music functions for the purpose of allowing the self to experience and envisage its entire person worshiping God, thereby revealing its primordial bond with the creator of that creature. *Singing the music* also strengthens the community bond, but *dancing the music* is more religiously essential because it allows the worshiping community to realize its spiritual power. Furthermore, in terms of expressing what it means to be saved, sanctified, and Spirit-baptized, *dancing the music* is more symbolically substantive than song, whose words inadequately represent the power of the Spirit.

What is finally being communicated to God and about the worshiping community is not that which is sung but that which is ritualized in shouting. That shouting forcefully stories the ultimate gospel is evidenced in the fact that it is usually twice as trenchant and thrice as long as its introductory

---

[39] James H. Cone, *Speaking the Truth: Ecumenism, Liberation, and Black Theology* (Grand Rapids: Eerdmans, 1986), 26.
[40] Reed, 38.
[41] Rouget, 91.

singing-testifying isochronism. E. Franklin Frazier alludes to this when he says "singing is accompanied by 'shouting' or holy dancing which permits the maximum of free religious expression on the part of the participants." In Holiness-Pentecostal churches, says Frazier, shouting is the "chief religious activity."[42]

It will be illustrated below that shouting is a point of transmutation from singing-testifying into even greater ultimacy. But first it is important to show that one's reception, not only of the initial ability to shout (at conversion for instance), but of a personalized style of shouting[43] is a rite of passage. In the medium of testifying, one woman announced the occasion and led in its ritual celebration:

> He gave me the dance last Sunday—Praise God. I didn't even know it till I went home—Praise God. When I was dancing in my feet something said, "look down"—Hallelujah. I was so excited—Hallelujah Jesus. I didn't even realize he gave me the dance—Praise God. Hallelujah Jesus! (*3X*) Hallelujah! (*2X*) . . . I didn't even realize when I got home—Praise God—that he gave me the dance in my feet—Praise God. . . . I always wanted to dance for the Lord—Hallelujah.

Spontaneously she began demonstrating for the church the dance that the Lord had given her feet, to which the organist (who had been sustaining chords in the background) and instrumentalists responded with the appropriate "shout" music, while the community clapped, stomped, and beat its tambourines.

Slain in the Spirit

> A man has not become truly religious until he has humbled himself before the Lord by [falling] on the floor, unashamed in the dust and dirt.[44]

[42] E. Franklin Frazier, *The Negro Church in America* (New York: Schocken Books, 1974), 59, 61.

[43] The idea that being given the dance by the Lord means receiving a particular charismatic choreography is further alluded to when another woman said, "Yes, the Lord has given me a shout and it has changed over the years." Cited in Dargan, 79.

[44] Quoted in G. Norman Eddy, "Store-Front Religion," *Religion in Life*, vol. 28 (Winter 1958–59), 73–74. The original word replaced here was "rolling" (which

This was the language used by a black Pentecostal preacher around mid-century to describe the religious significance of being "slain in the spirit."

When one is "agonizing in the spirit" (travailing or making strong supplication and prayer to the Lord) and the Spirit is making intercessory groanings, the flesh is trying to bring itself under submission to the Spirit. When one is "slain in the spirit" it is believed that God's Spirit has taken dominance over the human spirit (trance) and that one is literally overwhelmed (collapse): *dance* ⟶ *trance* ⟶ *collapse*. As worshipers lay slain, it is said that they are experiencing the euphoric afterglow of the anointing—God is refilling them, giving them visions, or bringing them internal peace. Being "slain in the Spirit" is to "enter out" of a powerful spiritual experience with divine imperative. It is to revitalize the worshiping community with even greater effusing power than if one had "entered out" by one's own accord. It is, in the language of John 7:38, the flowing out of one's belly living rivers of water.

has a history of negative connotation), for what was being referred to is one "falling" to the floor "slain in the spirit."

9

Christ against Culture:

Anticulturalism in the Gospel of Gospel

G O S P E L   M U S I C

The Meaning of Gospel Music

Gospel music derives its name and theology from the gospel of Jesus Christ. Among the composers and practitioners of the genre it is generally agreed that the "gospel of gospel" is "good news" amidst "bad times." "Black music is called gospel," defines Louis-Charles Harvey, "because it attempts to relate the 'good news' of Jesus Christ primarily to the existence of black folk in this country."[1] For blacks who encountered oppression and desolation upon migrating to Southern and Northern cities following Reconstruction, this jubilant music has been, according to Wyatt T. Walker's assessment, "a song of faith which rallies the hope and aspiration of the faithful in the face of devastating social conditions."[2] Irene Jackson concurs that gospel songs "deal with the immediate problems affecting Blacks and are specifically designed to help Black people to surmount immediate circumstances of their lives."[3]

[1] Louis-Charles Harvey, "Black Gospel Music and Black Theology," *The Journal of Religious Thought* 43, no. 2 (Fall–Winter, 1986–87), 26.
[2] Wyatt T. Walker, *"Somebody's Calling My Name": Black Sacred Music and Social Change* (Valley Forge: Judson Press, 1979), 127.
[3] Irene V. Jackson, ed., *Afro-American Religious Music: A Bibliography and a Catalogue of Gospel Music* (Westport, Conn.: Greenwood Press, 1979), 74.

While Jackson further defines "gospel" as reflecting the same "existential tension" found in the spirituals,[4] Lawrence Levine points out that the "tension" in gospel is not quite as unyielding. The reason is that while the Jesus of the spirituals is a "warrior," the Jesus of the gospel songs is "a benevolent spirit" who promises a restful, peaceful, and just afterlife.[5] Therefore, if there is any "tension" it is not so much in the existential aspect of gospel as in the paradox that Jackson and Levine, in their opposing views, are both correct.

Some theological thinkers are not as sympathetic to gospel as Harvey, Walker, Jackson, and Levine. Calling gospel "the most degenerate form of Negro religion," Joseph Washington sharply criticizes the weakening of the theology of the spirituals. "Gospel music is the creation of a disengaged people," he says. "Shorn from the roots of the folk religion, gospel music has turned the freedom theme in Negro spirituals into licentiousness. It is . . . sheer entertainment by commercial opportunists."[6] Washington wrote this in 1964, and eight years later there was no change in his opinion: "Blacks created a whole new religious music in gospel songs which revolutionized music in the black congregations through the leadership of jackleg preachers and evangelists who went from rags to riches by means of bringing the secular world of blues and jazz into worship."[7]

The intention here is not to measure the theology of gospel music against that of the spirituals and certainly not against the best theories of Christian ethics. (Such comparisons probably led to Washington's disgruntlement.) Rather, the aim is to take gospel as it is and determine just where it stands theologically. It will be helpful to review the studies of Charles Copher and Mary Tyler in order to be informed as to the characters, events, places, images, and means used to propagate the theology of gospel.

[4] Ibid., 73.

[5] Lawrence W. Levine, *Black Culture and Black Consciousness: Afro-American Folk Thought from Slavery to Freedom* (New York: Oxford University Press, 1977), 175.

[6] Joseph R. Washington, Jr., *Black Religion: The Negro and Christianity in the United States* (Boston: Beacon Press, 1964), 51.

[7] Joseph R. Washington, Jr., *Black Sects and Cults: The Power Praxis in an Ethnic Ethic* (Garden City, N.Y.: Anchor/Doubleday, 1972), 78.

Charles Copher's investigation of characters, events, places, and images in 300 gospel songs defines the distinctiveness of the genre. Copher found relatively few references to biblical characters and events in the fifty songs of Tindley and his counterparts (1895–1935). In these songs God is simply addressed as Father, occasionally as God Most High and Rock of Ages, whereas references to Jesus are far more numerous and varied. Not only is Jesus addressed as King and Savior (seven times each) and Lamb, Lily of the Valley, Son of God, Truth Divine, and Word of Life (once each), but the few references to events almost always deal with his life: his teaching (three times), his trial before Pilate and crucifixion (two times each), and his walking on water, last supper, prayer in Gethsemane, and declaration of the great commission (once each). The places catalogued by Copher include heaven (six references), the Jordan River and Calvary (two references each), the Red Sea, wilderness, Sea of Galilee, and New Jerusalem (one reference each).[8]

In the 250 gospel songs covering the period 1930 to the present, Copher found that references to characters predominate over events. Naturally Jesus is the principal personage with ninety-eight of the 250 songs being about him. Fourteen of those ninety-eight deal with his second coming. In comparison with the spirituals, twice the number of gospel songs address the crucifixion, resurrection, and final triumph of the Lord. While God is addressed simply as Father or God (twenty references), Jesus is referred to by a variety of interesting names: Bread of Heaven, Cornerstone, Fortress, King, King of Kings, Lamb, Lily of the Valley, Lion of Judah, Lord of All, Master, Rock of Ages, Solid Rock, Rose of Sharon, Savior, Shepherd, Shield, Son of God, Bright and Morning Star, Sword, Way, and Wonderful. The places of reference catalogued are twenty-five accounts of heaven (one-tenth of the 250 songs examined), eight accounts of Calvary, four each of the Jordan River and Beulah Land, three of Zion, two

[8] Charles B. Copher, "Biblical Characters, Events, Places and Images Remembered and Celebrated in Black Worship," *Journal of the Interdenominational Theological Center* 14, nos. 1 & 2 (Fall 1986/Spring 1987), 75, 85, 78.

each of Canaanland and New Jerusalem, and one each of
Bethany, Galilee, Promised Land, and Bethlehem.[9]

In Mary Tyler's study of the 104 gospel songs of Charles
Henry Pace, five categories are used to characterize the variety of Pace songs: (1) personal testimonies, (2) questioning
belief and introspection, (3) scriptural messages, (4) dialogue
with God, (5) personal counsel to listeners.[10] Adjacent to the
reflections of Harvey, Walker, Jackson, and Levine, the studies of Copher and Tyler copiously complete a general definition of gospel.

Theological Typologies for Anatomizing Gospel

The reason for citing the following studies of William
T. Dargan, Louis-Charles Harvey, and Henry H. Mitchell
(and Nicholas Cooper-Lewter) is that each gives additional
information about the inner theological meaning of gospel
music. These particular studies will help prepare for the
adaptation of H. Richard Niebuhr's typology in his book
Christ and Culture (1951), which will address the finer issue of
where gospel stands theologically amidst Christian pluralism.

Dargan's examination of 104 gospel songs sung at a single Holiness church in Washington, D.C., concludes that the
four most prevalent theological themes in gospel music are
power, praise, salvation, and *struggle.* The aspect of *power,* he
says, includes the three subcategories of "cross-bearing,"
"crown-wearing," and "crown-wearing" in the course of
"cross-bearing" (sometimes referred to by believers as "joy in
the midst of sorrow" or "victory in the valley"). The primary
power symbols that authorize and enable believers to carry
out the will of God are the "name" and the "blood" of Jesus
(the latter being invoked in moments of crisis). The theme of
praise, continues Dargan, includes the aspects of celebration
and thanksgiving, means by which believers encounter and
attest to the *power.* The theme of *salvation* is comprised of
three subcategories—witness to the unsaved, the saving

[9] Ibid., 78, 85.
[10] Mary A. L. Tyler, "The Music of Charles Henry Pace and Its Relationship to
the Afro-American Church Experience," Ph.D. dissertation, University of Pitts-
burgh, 1980, 101.

deeds of the Savior, and the believer's quest for or response to her or his own salvation. The theme of *struggle* includes such aspects as trouble, battle, danger, fear, judgment, desperation, determination, and steadfastness. Dargan concludes that the common threads running through all of these concepts are human frailty and dependence and the severity of the eschatological teachings of Jesus.[11]

In Henry H. Mitchell and Nicholas Cooper-Lewter's book, *Soul Theology* (1986), an extensive typology is constructed in which gospel songs and other black musical genres are categorized theologically. The first six of the ten types deal with attributes of God, the remaining four with humanity: (1) the Providence of God, (2) the Justice of God, (3) the Majesty and Omnipotence of God, (4) the Omniscience of God, (5) the Goodness of God and Creation, (6) the Grace of God, (7) the Equality of Persons, (8) the Uniqueness of Persons: Identity, (9) the Family of God and Humanity, and (10) the Perseverance of Persons. The authors' thesis is that black people intuitively select songs that provide them with the nourishment and therapeutic affirmation they need to endure.[12]

Louis-Charles Harvey's study, "Black Gospel and Black Theology," based on an assessment of 1,700 gospel songs, found that nearly a third of the number (452) are centered around the person of Jesus Christ. The remaining include 393 references to the Christian life, 354 to heaven, 237 to God, 154 to humanity, 32 to Satan, and 29 to the Holy Spirit. This Christocentrism led Harvey to derive as his thesis that "The most fundamental statement made about Jesus Christ is that he is Everything. He is Everything because he is *Friend, Protector,* and *Liberator.*" It is in these ways that Jesus is regarded as the answer to the problems of black life.[13]

Of the theological typologies of Dargan, Mitchell, and Harvey, it is Harvey's that seems most useful for the present

---

[11] William T. Dargan, "Congregational Gospel Songs in a Black Holiness Church: A Musical and Textual Analysis," Ph.D. dissertation, Wesleyan University, 1983, 112, 115, 122, 127–28, 131.

[12] Henry H. Mitchell and Nicholas Cooper-Lewter, *Soul Theology: The Heart of American Black Culture* (San Francisco: Harper & Row, 1986), 95, 4.

[13] Harvey, 27.

study. Part of the reason is that it distills and translates into the jargon of gospel music the essential matter of the other two typologies, that in gospel music Jesus Christ is "Everything"—Friend, Protector, and Liberator. If Harvey's typology is sufficiently comprehensive, then the more numerous categories in Dargan's and Mitchell's typologies ought to reduce to the three categories in Harvey's typology; and they do. In Dargan's typology songs of *power* and *salvation* coincide with Jesus as Liberator, songs of *struggle* with Jesus as Protector and Friend, and songs of *praise* with Jesus who is all three concurrently—"Everything." In Mitchell's typology *The Goodness of God and Creation* coincides with Jesus as Friend, *The Justice of God* with Jesus as Protector, *The Grace of God* with Jesus as Liberator, and *The Providence of God, The Majesty and Omnipotence of God,* and *The Omniscience of God* with Jesus as "Everything."[14] Having checked Harvey's typology, and imbuing it with the implicit meanings of the other two typologies, it will become a point of reference as the theological history of the gospel music movement is examined.

The Christ-Culture Dilemma in Gospel

Gospel music is the creation of a people who exist amid the absurdity of American race conventions and thus is a music that constantly raises questions about the relationship of faith and culture or society. Therefore, H. Richard Niebuhr's historically derived typology seems to be a useful context for theological analysis. In *Christ and Culture* Niebuhr delineates five principal ways Christians have attempted to address the water and oil of Jesus Christ and human culture. He terms these five types: (1) Christ against Culture, (2) Christ of Culture, (3) Christ above Culture, (4) Christ and Culture in Paradox, and (5) Christ the Transformer of Culture. While theological types such as Dargan's, Mitchell's, and Harvey's examined gospel music itself, what is presently attempted is an analysis of gospel music in the context of an extraneous matrix. The objective critique Niebuhr's typology promises

---

[14] The remaining aspects of *The Equality of Persons, The Uniqueness of Persons,* and *The Family of God and Humanity* (which in Mitchell's book have no gospel song references) coincide with Jesus as Reconciler—an atypical attribute for the Lord in almost all of gospel music.

to yield makes its application even more provocative. A brief word shall be said about the theological implications each of the five types has for gospel music in general.

1. That gospel music is basically of the "Christ against Culture," or radical anticultural, type is implied in Mitchell and Cooper-Lewter's study, in that all their categories reference gospel songs except "The Equality of Persons," "The Uniqueness of Persons," and "The Family of God and Humanity." Gospel music does not encourage individuals to be truly *unique* (or equal in their uniqueness) in order to apply their particular vocations to converting the world for the good of the family of God and humanity; rather individuals are taught to lose their identities in Christ's. "Do not love the world or the things in the world" is obviously a scriptural tenet to which they ascribe. "*If any one loves the world, love for the Father is not in him*" (1 John 2:15). Levine agrees that in regard to long-term solutions for the problems of human beings the space between the here and the hereafter has widened. "There [are] . . . few songs portraying victory in this world," he says. "Ultimate change when it [comes takes] place in the future in an otherworldly context."[15] It is actually through gospel's denial of the world that it makes the "news"—friendship, protection, and liberation—seem unequivocally "good" and a convincing alternative, not only to the world, but to one's friends, family, and neighbors.

2. By interpreting culture through Christ, the "Christ of Culture" advocates regard those aspects of the world that are in accord with Christ as most essential; and by interpreting Christ through culture, they distill from Christianity those teachings that seem most congruent with the best culture the world has to offer.[16] In such a cultural Christology human martyrs are often regarded as the apostles of Christ insofar as they prophetically aid human beings into bringing the gospel to bear in the world;[17] whereas in gospel music Christ who is far-removed from culture is "Everything," so that everyone else of culture is nothing. A charge against

[15] Levine, 176.

[16] H. Richard Niebuhr, *Christ and Culture* (San Francisco: Harper & Row, 1951), 83.

[17] Ibid., 102–3.

these Christians is that their love of culture has so qualified devotion to Christ that the Lord has been displaced by an idol called by his name.[18] However, inasmuch as gospel music predicates the antithesis of cultural Christology— irreconciliation between church and world, the gospel and social law, grace and human effort—it cannot be accused of the idolatry of serving two masters.

3. The *synthesists* of the "Christ above Culture" type hold that both Christ and culture are to be affirmed in that the Lord is holistically human and divine, concurrently of the here and the hereafter.[19] On the other hand, advocates of gospel almost entirely neglect the human aspect of Jesus Christ, including his ascription to Jewish culture[20] and his careful distinction between the culture of the oppressors and that of the oppressed. Furthermore, whereas for the synthesists salvation does not presuppose the destruction of God's creation,[21] in gospel God's creation is perceived as coalescent with human culture and subject to destruction upon the apocalypse. While the synthesists believe in having all this world and heaven too,[22] gospel advocates can be accused of nothing but faith in "Jesus only."

4. The *dualists* of the "Christ and Culture in Paradox" type are also anticulturalists but contend that human laws prevent humanity from worsening its perpetually fallen condition.[23] In gospel music the paradox of "the lesser evil" is the consequential synthesis of several theses and antitheses. First, gospel condones human denial of the world insofar as it is a social commentary revealing what it means to be black and oppressed[24]—*thesis.* Yet it is an evangelical music that makes no direct claim on the need for human liberation and social reconciliation—*antithesis.* Second, amidst socioeconomic oppression, blacks have made a decision to be themselves in a way that gospel is a means of "identity awakening" and

---

[18] Ibid., 110.
[19] Ibid., 120–21.
[20] See Matthew 5:17–19; 22:21; Romans 12:1, 6.
[21] Niebuhr, 143.
[22] Ibid., 144.
[23] Ibid., 165–66.
[24] Harvey, 26.

"identity nourishing"[25]—*thesis.* Yet gospel music enjoins Christians to lose their individual identities in Christ's—*antithesis.* The *synthesis* of these theses and antitheses, the paradox, is that that which is cultural or "worldly"—human oppugnancy toward oppression and identity nourishing—is being utilized as a "lesser evil" to lead the worldly to the Ultimate Alternative, Christ. That is to say that the entire gospel music movement is a dualistic statement that *it is better to sing gospel than to burn.*

5. The *conversionists* of the "Christ the Transformer of Culture" type are also anticulturalists. However, in believing that the world is perverted rather than inherently evil, they maintain that creation (which includes human culture) can be transformed to its original good. This notion, suggested at several points in the Gospel of John,[26] is misconstrued when interpreted by gospel songwriters. According to "the gospel of gospel," it is not so much that *"God so loved the world that he gave his only begotten son,"* as it is that which follows—that *"whoever believes in him should not perish but have eternal life"* (John 3:16). In gospel music the individual, not the world or the vocations of the worldly, are evangelized and transformed by love. Moreover, Christ may be Friend, Protector, and Liberator in gospel music, but the one thing the Lord essentially is not portrayed as is Reconciler. Customarily gospel does not command individuals to love those who despitefully use them but rather to turn away from them. This turning away from the world heavenward to the Ultimate Alternative is an end in itself rather than serving as a means of turning back toward friend, kindred, and neighbor in reconciliation. If Jesus as "Everything" is the "ideal symbol of wholeness in gospel music,"[27] it is more the wholeness of each individual's spiritual self than of the family of God and humanity.

In summary, the Niebuhrian "Christ and Culture" typology has illustrated that the entire history of gospel music is an anticultural *movement.* Of the three historical epochs in gospel—the Transitional Period (1900–30), Traditional

---

[25] Walker, 144.
[26] See John 1:29; 12:32, 47.
[27] Harvey, 27.

Period (1930–69), and the Contemporary Period (1969–present)—all but a few gospel songwriters of the modern era are of the "Christ against Culture" type. The few conversionists of the "Christ the Transformer of Culture" type are also anticulturalists, but less radical. With this overview, the next step is to closely examine each of the three periods of the gospel music movement in order to determine the specific ways in which anticulturalism is manifested.

Anticulturalism in Transitional Gospel

The Transitional Period, or Pre-Gospel Era (1900–30), commenced with the gospel hymns of Charles Price Jones, the founding bishop of the Church of Christ (Holiness) USA, and Charles Albert Tindley, a Methodist minister of Philadelphia. While Tindley, author of some thirty gospel hymns, has been credited as the first black to publish an original collection in 1901, Jones, the more prolific poet and musician and composer of over 1,000 songs, was actually the first with his *Jesus Only No. 1* (1899), which was followed by his *Jesus Only Nos. 1 and 2* (1901).[28]

The songs of Jones consider the "traditions of men" to be "unworthy of authority,"[29] and they depict the world as an evil realm wherein "ev'ry trusted friend forsake[s]," "kindred drive thee from their door," "thou art despised and lone," and "none will speak a word of cheer." Life, he lyricizes, is an "open sea" swept over by "raging storms of sore affliction," and those who ascribe to its ways are woefully wicked:

> From the malice of the wicked I will hide,
> From their tongues deceitful slander, from their pride;
> From the evil that they do, From their worldly pomp and show—
> In Thy presence I will happily abide.

In another song Jones speaks not only of being hidden from the likes of malice and slander, but also from the temptations thereof: "Hide me from the world's alluring," he implores.[30]

---

[28] In 1906 Jones published a third songbook titled *His Fullness*.

[29] Cited in Otho B. Cobbins, ed., *History of Church of Christ (Holiness) U. S. A.* (New York: Vantage Press, 1966), 407.

[30] See Jones, "The Time Will Not Be Long," "None But Christ," "I Will Hide," "Precious Savior."

To Jones the "world of sin" is nontransformable. He almost sounds like a conversionist in one of his songs when he says, "Yes, there's a fountain deep and wide to cleanse the world from sin." But in another he explains that all is not lost, not because human beings can change things, but because it is "abundant grace" that "God bestows upon a sinful race." Moreover, the nations are "perishing in sin," implying that sin in the world will remain untransformed to the destructive end. When the "King of glory" comes, "the nations, long so sinful, shall approach their awful doom." Simply seeking to endure in what Jones often refers to as "a lost world" and "a land of woe," Christian believers typically assume a passive role in their human destiny. Their principal vocation is not itself transformative of the world, but spiritual warfare against the "foe," the world, under the spiritual protection of Jesus. Only once does Jones speak more trenchantly, albeit figuratively, of helping level the carnal land of licentiousness:

> There are cities great and high, Hallelujah!
> Strong and wall'd up t'ward the sky, Praise the Lord!
> But by faith we'll bring them low, Hallelujah!
> And Jehovah's pow'r we'll show, Praise the Lord![31]

For the most part believers are not Samsons or Joshuas. They are, in Jones's words, "weary pilgrims toiling through a world of woe." The only means of liberation from this toilsome pilgrimage is for them to "keep on looking away to Jesus" so that the Holy Ghost will "a citizen of heaven make [them] while on earth below." This turning away from the world heavenward to Jesus is what Jones denotes the "heavenly calling":

> I am so glad of the heavenly calling,
> Calling away from the world and its charms;
> I am so glad I have fled for a refuge,
> Into the Savior's strong arms.[32]

It was Jones's lifelong intention to convince his people of the value and beauty of holiness, for he was sure that worldly

[31] See Jones, "Go, Wash, and Be Clean," "Hear, O Hear the Savior Calling," "O Tarry for the Power," "O Sinner, Where Will You Stand?" "There's a Happy Day at Hand."

[32] See Jones, "The Fount Is Flowing," "The Time Will Not Be Long," "Praise Ye the Lord in Faith and Hope," "Saving Me Wholly By Grace."

gain would only promote robbery, engender pride, breed strife, and cause fatality. The appropriate response to the "heavenly calling" is surrender to Jesus by subverting man-made tradition and exalting the Lord:[33]

> I have surrendered to Jesus,
> Conquered by weapons of love;
> I have forsaken earth's treasures
> Seeking a treasure above.

In order to withdraw from the world of lust and pleasure, which Jones calls the world of the flesh of Satan, one has to "surrender all." Probably drawing from Luke 14:26, he implies that surrendering all not only means denying one's father, mother, wife, children, brothers, and sisters, but also one's own life. Only if the Christian disciple has denied self can she or he sing, "I am wholly sanctified."[34]

Another song predicating the idea of surrendering all to Jesus is "I'm Happy with Jesus Alone." Jones writes about this piece: "I would know nothing but Jesus. No name but His. No master but Him. No law but His word. No creed but Jesus. I [have] to be 'Happy with Jesus alone.' All else [is] trash to me."[35] While the worldly are "the enemies of holiness" and the very "trash" of humanity, the holy "citizens of heaven" are in a sense the enemies of "the world." In his probing song, "Are You a Christian," Jones exhorts, "The noblest men the earth has known, and the noblest women too . . . forsook the world and served the Lord." Reflecting the radical eschatological ethic of Jesus, Jones writes in another song that "Friends and kindred, earthly honor, wealth and ease I all would flee." Except for Jesus, he claims, "I would count all else but loss." The title song of Jones's first and second collections of gospel hymns, *Jesus Only*, is a further explanation of what it means to surrender oneself to the Lord:

> Jesus only is my motto,
> Jesus only is my song,
> Jesus only is my heart-thought,
> Jesus only all day long.

[33] Cited in Cobbins, 24, 28.
[34] See Jones, "I Have Surrendered to Jesus," "I Am Wholly Sanctified."
[35] Cited in Cobbins, 409.

> Then away with ev'ry idol,
> Let my Lord be all to me;
> Jesus only is my Master,
> Jesus only let me see.[36]

Three important theological threads (all related to *surrender*), which have weaved through the history of the gospel music movement, clearly coalesce in the above piece. The first is the espousal of the nontrinitarian formula for evoking spiritual authority and power—the "name" of Jesus, stated here as "Jesus only." The second is that Jesus is "Everything," stated by Jones as the Lord being "all to me." And the third is the desire to see Jesus face to face: "Jesus only let me see."

Although most of Jones's songs are eschatological in calling for converts of holiness to renounce their kindred, some of the gospel songs of his era contain an empirical element by reflecting the tragedies of urban life during the first quarter of the twentieth century. For instance, the following song may be referring not just figuratively to a daughter or son spiritually forsaken by worldly relatives but actually physically abandoned by abusive parents:

> Should father and mother forsake me below,
> My bed upon earth be a stone,
> I'll cling to my Savior, He loves me I know,
> I'm happy with Jesus alone.

Not only will Jesus speak a word of cheer to make the spiritually forsaken and physically abandoned happy, he will also give individuals rest from their daily concerns of subsistence:

> Have you cares of business, cares of pressing debt?
> Cares of social life or cares of hopes unmet?
> Are you by remorse or sense of guilt depressed?
> Come right on to Jesus, He will give you rest.

Notwithstanding the empiricism, ultimate rest is rewarded in heaven, which is the Christian's principal endeavor in life. The world is unjust and unhappy, but heaven is a place of justice and joy:

[36] See Jones, "Can You Stand?" "God Forbid That I Should Glory," "Jesus Only."

> There's a happy time a-coming,
> There's a happy time a-coming,
> When oppressors shall no longer sit on high,
> When the proud shall be as stubble,
> For their sins receiving double;
> There's a happy time a-coming by and by.[37]

The gospel hymns of C. A. Tindley are also the "Christ against Culture" type. Anyone familiar with Tindley's sermons, particularly his sermon "The World's Conqueror," is probably already convinced that the theology of this Methodist minister is the type "Christ the Transformer of Culture." In this great sermon Tindley contends that love is the principal force God uses to conquer evil and lead human beings, their vocations, and all of their possessions back to God, their primal source. Alluding to the conversionist theme in 1 John 3:16, Tindley says that it was only after Jesus Christ came into the world that love was "harnessed and adjusted to the lifting of this old world from hell to heaven."[38] Tindley, as the pastor of socially active East Calvary Methodist Church in Philadelphia, also carried out a strong social advocacy and welfare ministry.

In spite of the conversionist motif in this sermon, there is little that distinguishes the Tindley gospel hymns from those of C. P. Jones. Tindley does not espouse the tenets of holiness or sanctification, but like Jones he complains in his songs that the human domain is a "world of sin" and a "world of tears," a "wilderness" from which, he writes, "I shall be free some day." Whereas Jones tends to generalize about the spiritual transgression of the world, Tindley typically specifies social aspects of its decadence, as the following verse illustrates:

> Our boasted land and nation, Are plunging in disgrace;
> With pictures of starvation Almost in every place;
> While loads of needed money, Remains in hoarded piles;
> But God will rule this country, After a while.

Tindley also grimaces about modernism: "The world of forms and changes is just now so confused, that there is found some

---

[37] See Jones, "I Am Happy with Jesus Alone," "Come unto Me," "There's a Happy Time a-Coming."

[38] Cited in Ralph H. Jones, *Charles Albert Tindley: Prince of Preachers* (Nashville: Abingdon Press, 1982), 157–58, 161–62.

danger in ev'rything you use." In one of his most celebrated songs, "We'll Understand It Better By and By," Tindley further specifies the dilemma of impoverishment as one that makes the nation so repressive to his people:

> We are often destitute of things that life demands,
> Want of food and want of shelter, thirsty hills and
>   barren lands,
> We are trusting in the Lord, and according to his
>   word,
> We will understand it better by and by.[39]

The life Tindley depicts in song is not only one of worldly destitution for Christian disciples but also one of sheer loneliness. There are no decent persons to be found in the world, and even Christians' friends misunderstand them and are never around when they are needed. In Tindley's response to these "trials dark on ev'ry hand" and to being "tossed and driv'n on the restless sea of time," he most resembles the radical anticulturalism of Jones's millenarianism. Tindley's reaction is to divest himself of the world and seek a better "home" in heaven:

> By and by when the morning comes,
> When the saints of God are gathered home,
> We'll tell the story how we've overcome:
> For we'll understand it better by and by.

Because the world is no friend to Christians, Tindley looks away to heaven in his song "I'm Going There":

> Although a pilgrim here below,
> Where dangers are and sorrows grow,
> I have a home in heaven above,
> I'm going there, I'm going there.[40]

Spiritualizing the kingdom of God idea in the Sermon on the Mount, Tindley claims that those who are already in heaven are the little ones who "lived and suffered in the world," whose "hearts [were] burdened with cares," and whose "bodies were full of disease" because "Medicine nor doctor could give them much ease." They were the "poor and

---

[39] See Tindley, "Some Day," "After a While."
[40] See Tindley, "We'll Understand It Better By and By," "I'm Going There."

often despised," he says, who "looked to heaven through tear-blinded eyes." However, until the "morning" comes ushered in by Christ Liberator Jesus, those who suffer in this world are exhorted to endure, a charge attainable only if Christ Friend and Protector Jesus is standing by:

> When the storms of life are raging, Stand by me (2X)
> When the world is tossing me, like a ship upon the sea,
> Thou who rulest wind and water, Stand by me.[41]

Anticulturalism in Traditional Gospel

The Traditional Period, or Golden Age of Gospel (1930–69), dominated by the Baptists, gained momentum under Thomas A. Dorsey, a Baptist songwriter influenced by the gospel hymns of Tindley. Other gospel composers and arrangers of the era are Doris Akers, J. Herbert Brewster, Lucie Campbell, James Cleveland, Theodore Frye, Dorothy Love, Roberta Martin, Sallie Martin, and Kenneth Morris. Together these musicians transformed the congregational *gospel hymn* of the Transitional Period into the solo, quartet, and choral *gospel song* of the Traditional Period.

Akin to Jones's and Tindley's hymns, Dorsey's songs also disparage the "world of sin" and "worldliness" and complain adamantly about life being full of despair and heavy burdens, sorrow and troubles, earthly trials, and battles with foes pressing in on every side. Dorsey, in portraying the friendship of Jesus as an ultimate alternative, reveals further distrust of and detatchment from the world. When you cannot share personal secrets with your mother, father, friend, or neighbor, he says, you can always tell Jesus in confidence. And when friends and kindred "forsake you and cast you aside," he advises, "There's a Savior who's a friend all the way." Thus it is that gospel's portrayal of friends and families, which is the very best of culture, is one full of shade and shadow and no light.[42]

Dorsey's "good news" about Christ Liberator, Friend, and Protector Jesus is that "When satan oppresses me His

---

[41] See Tindley, "What Are They Doing in Heaven," "Stand By Me."
[42] See Dorsey, "Tell Jesus Everything," "Someday, Somewhere."

grace will caress me" and that "When troubles depress me He won't fail to bless me." And because Jesus is present, figures Dorsey, "God is not dead":

> The times may get hard/Your way may be drear
> The road may be dark/The storm is severe
> But don't forget the name of Jesus.
> Your way may be lost/You grope in despair
> God is not dead/And Jesus is there
> Now don't forget the name of the Lord.

That "God is not dead" is sublimely lyricized in the image of God taking one's hand in Dorsey's time-honored master-piece, "Precious Lord, Take My Hand":

> Precious Lord, take my hand,
> Lead me on, let me stand
> I am tired, I am weak, I am worn,
> Through the storm, through the night,
> Lead me on to the light,
> Take my hand precious Lord,
> Lead me on.[43]

Dorsey portrays the Christian's principal vocation as one of mere "watching and waiting" for the Savior's return because he finds that life is "uncertain" and full of "confusion." It is then that one's "tired and weary work" will yield to the "real life"—an existence of comfort and rest in a heavenly home:

> Watching and waiting singing my song,
> Darkness all fading shadows most gone
> Jesus will greet me it won't be long
> Real life awaits me when I get home.

According to other Dorsey songs the "real life" is not only an entity of peace and joy with "riches to share" in "a city so fair" far away from "burdens and cares," but a reality in which real justice rules:

> By and by, by and by
> When we reach that home beyond the sky,

---

[43] See Dorsey, "I'll Tell It Wherever I Go," "Don't Forget the Name of the Lord," "Precious Lord, Take My Hand."

There the wicked will cease from troubling
And the weary will be at rest
And ev'ry day will be Sunday by and by.[44]

When Dorsey expresses the desire to "do some good
thing every day" in order to "help the fallen by the way" and
to "bring back those who've gone astray," it implies that "life"
in the world is also "real" and that its transformation into the
kingdom of God is perhaps a motif hidden behind the front
of his apparent radical anticulturalism. However, any hint of
conversionism is obliterated when Dorsey implies that good
deeds for the victimized of the world are but for the sake of
earning salvation and the congratulations "Well done." In this
regard, human life is not really "real," it is a mere "race" on a
"highway" to "the glory land," in which "when the last mile is
finished" the saved "shall receive a crown."[45]

The gospel songs of Rev. W. Herbert Brewster are theologically indistinguishable from Dorsey's. Brewster's songs
also portray the earthly realm as "a world of sin." In living
amidst this "mean and sinful" world, Brewster murmurs that
one's life is incessantly gloomy and burdensome. Until those
who are saved by grace ascend into an eternity of sor-
rowfree, painfree, and carefree existence, Jesus makes life's
toilsome pilgrimage more bearable. Brewster's "good news"
is that the troubled, discouraged, oppressed, wounded, sick,
and sore who have broken and bleeding hearts, weary souls,
longings, trials, aches, and conflicts should come unto Jesus.
"Weeping may endure for a night," he solaces, "but joy will
come in the morning":

Take up your cross, and follow Him,
Through failing and through great sorrow,
Through stormy night and valley dim,
And joy will come tomorrow.[46]

Jesus can make this futile life more bearable because while
the world wears a frown the Lord wears a smile.[47]

[44] See Dorsey, "Watching and Waiting," "Someday, Somewhere," "Every Day
Will Be Sunday By and By."
[45] See Dorsey, "My Desire," "When the Last Mile Is Finished." See also "That's
All That I Can Do."
[46] Brewster, "Weeping May Endure for a Night."
[47] See Brewster, "Just over the Hill," "Make Room for Jesus in Your Life,"
"Weeping May Endure for a Night," "I Want the World to Smile on Me."

The songs of James Cleveland are also homologous with the theology of radical anticulturalism. They are distinct from the songs of Dorsey and Brewster only because they highlight the aspects of "cross-bearing" and Christ-dependence. Cleveland attempts to console the distressed by admonishing that "cross-bearing" is a prerequisite to salvation—believers must weather the storms and rains of life if heaven is to be their final resting place. "If you can't stand it when your so-called friends put you down," he taunts, "Just remember No Cross . . . No crown!" The second prominent theme in Cleveland's music is the contention that Christian disciples must completely depend on Friend, Protector, and Liberator Jesus. Joining his counterparts in declaring that Jesus Christ is "Everything," Cleveland carries the idea further in decreeing that the Lord is also to *do* "everything" for the believer. In a song appropriately titled "Take Them and Leave Them There," he exhorts that you must carry your burdens to Jesus, for "You know you cannot solve your own problems." In another song Cleveland subjects his audience to examination: "Who will make all my decisions for me?" he questions; the choir answers, "Jesus will."[48]

Anticulturalism in Contemporary Gospel

The Contemporary Period, or Modern Gospel Era (1969–present), is dominated by Pentecostal artists of the Church of God in Christ, particularly Edwin Hawkins, Walter Hawkins, Andrae Crouch, Sandra Crouch, and the Clark Sisters. The era commenced with the Edwin Hawkins Singers' recorded arrangement of the old Baptist hymn "O Happy Day" in 1969.

In the music of Edwin Hawkins, the last quarter of the twentieth century remains replete with toils, snares, burdens, cares, and friends that forsake friends. As the Ultimate Alternative, Jesus is of course Friend, Protector, and Liberator

---

[48] See Cleveland, "I'll Do His Will," "No Cross, No Crown," "Take Them and Leave Them There," "Jesus Will." To elaborate on the theology in the songs of Lucie Campbell, Dorothy Love, Roberta Martin, Sallie Martin, Kenneth Morris, and others of this period is basically to rehearse all that is typical in the music of Dorsey, Brewster, and Cleveland.

of those who walk "with" or "in" him. The distinction is that Hawkins is far more optimistic about the world than his predecessors, resulting in a music with less heavenward polarity. Moreover, not only is Jesus savior of those who choose to follow him, but also "of this world He is Savior," affirms Hawkins. For the first time in the history of the musical movement, "the gospel of gospel" is more than merely a petition for the oppressed to turn away from the world heavenward. Under Hawkins's ministry the songs exhort Christ's followers to apply their love-transformed vocations toward the conversion of the world to its coming good:

> If you want the world to be a better place to live in (3X)
> Try real love, Try real peace,
> Don't put it off, Try the Real Thing today.[49]

The importance of this solicitation to "Try the Real Thing" is that practicing "real love" in order to make the world "a better place to live in" is for the sake of love itself, rather than for the singular end of seeing Jesus' face. "It's not by works that I'm saved today, through many good deeds that I've done," confesses Hawkins. Hence, to the conversionist Jesus is "Everything" when he is Friend, Protector, and Liberator, plus Reconciler:

> Where there's hatred try a little love in its place.
> Where there's sadness, try a little happiness.
> Where there's madness, try a little kindness.
> Where there's confusion try a little peace.
> Give your brother a smile as you're passing by.
> Try to do, try to do something good.[50]

No longer are Christians enjoined to turn heavenward from hatred, sadness, madness, and confusion, but rather to be reconciliatory, to "do something good" by applying "real love." And no longer is Jesus the Ultimate Alternative—a smile—to a world that perpetually wears a frown, but rather the Lord is active in the world reconciling it unto himself. In Hawkins's music Jesus' love shines through the

---

[49] See Hawkins, "Jesus," "Have Mercy," "Try the Real Thing."
[50] Hawkins, "Have Mercy."

world as neighbor gives neighbor a smile when passing by. Rather than being the Ultimate Alternative to the world, the Lord is the Ultimate Source of its transformation.

With blacks making substantial gains in their quality of life during the final quarter of the twentieth century it fits that the music of Edwin Hawkins has responded with a more positive worldview—the conversionist or "Christ the Transformer of Culture" type. However, there remain those, such as Hawkins's brother Walter Hawkins, for whom Jesus Christ is still the Ultimate Alternative. In terms of its anticulturalism, the music of Walter Hawkins is not quite as radical as that of transitional or traditional gospel. Yet it still depicts human beings as cross-bearing hoboes rambling through a destitute land engaging in whatever charity they can muster up in order to at long last hear the Lord say, "Well done." So-called friends are still not friends at all: "Just when you need a friend," Hawkins lyricizes, "they're not around at all, they just watch you fall."[51] The "good news" Hawkins has for his audiences is not to simply "be grateful" because "a little pain makes [one] appreciate the good times," but to be grateful because a little friendlessness helps one to appreciate the Ultimate Alternative:

> If you ever need a friend that sticks closer than a
>   brother,
> I recommend Jesus because He's that kind of friend.
>
> He'll walk right in front of you to always protect you
> So the devil can't do you no harm.
> He is faithful ev'ry day to help you along the way,
> He's that kind of friend.[52]

The music of Andrae Crouch occasionally characterizes life as full of sleepless nights, burdens, and wickedness. Crouch also applies the customary means of consoling the disconsolate by heralding the virtues of cross-bearing:

> I thank God for the mountains
> And I thank Him for the valleys,

---

[51] Walter Hawkins, "Love Is God." See also "Try Christ."
[52] See Walter Hawkins, "Goin' to a Place," "I'm a Pilgrim," "Love Is God," "Try Christ," "Be Grateful," "He's That Kind of Friend."

> I thank Him for the storms he brought me through,
> For if I'd never had a problem
> I wouldn't know that He could solve them,
> I'd never know what faith in God could do.

Nonetheless, in highlighting the entity of power in the Holy Ghost and in the "name" and the "blood" of Jesus, Crouch places far greater emphasis on the joy of "crown-wearing" than on the sorrow of "cross-bearing." This substantially depletes the radical edge of anticulturalism in Crouch's music. There are no definite conversionist motifs, like the songs of Edwin Hawkins, but Crouch depicts God's created humanity in a much more positive light. For instance, in "Somebody Somewhere Is Praying Just for You," he characterizes human beings as capable of something other than deceit—as capable of caring ("the real thing"). In another song he confidently exclaims, "I've got a whole lot of friends and I'm thankful." Crouch's hope is that heaven will be his "final home," and he urges believers to be ready for Christ's return—to "walk right" and "talk right" in preparation for the "great celebration." But again, there is neither a sense of anticulturalism being radical in his music nor of urgency to get to heaven at the earliest opportunity.[53]

Similar to the music of her brother Andrae, a large number of the compositions of Sandra Crouch are songs of praise. Pieces like "Magnify the Lord with Me," "He's Worthy," "My Soul Loves Only You," "Glorify the Lord," and "My God How Excellent Is Your Name" are of a "crown-wearing" rather than "cross-bearing" type. In spite of her joyous praise for the Creator, Sandra Crouch nevertheless recognizes the reality of a world that is destructive. In her song "We Need to Hear from You," she beckons God for his "perfect way." "There is no other way that we can live," she pleads:

> Destruction is now in view,
> Seems the world has forgotten all about You,
> And children are crying,
> People are dying;

[53] See Crouch, "Through It All," "Living This Kind of Life," "No Time to Lose (I Wanna' Be Ready)."

> They're lost without You,
> So lost without You.

In Sandra Crouch's music the world is not characterized as inherently evil, but as "a world that needs the Lord." However, unlike true conversionism, the reason the world needs God is not for it to be transformed presently, but so it might be prepared for the transformation to occur in the hereafter. In songs like "Souls for the Kingdom" and "We're Waiting" there is a strong sense of expectancy in terms of Christ's early return and a sense of urgency for believers to be ready. Yet Crouch's repeated beckoning, "Come, Lord Jesus," never implies that the urgency is due to this world being so irreparably destitute and devoid of inherent reconciliation.[54]

Christ-Everything the Ultimate Alternative

The single stream of thought that issues through the history of the gospel music movement is the notion that Jesus Christ is "Everything." For instance, Jones says, "Christ is all," or further, "all and all." Tindley also claims Jesus as his "all," adding that his allness is such that "there's nothing between." Morris sings, "Christ is all, all and all this world to me." The Lord is "all and all" to Brewster because he is friend to the friendless, mother to the motherless, and father to the fatherless. Dorsey lyricizes, "He's ev'rything to me cause he saved me." To Cleveland Christ is also "Everything," in fact, *everything* that anyone will ever need. And Sandra Crouch prayerfully proclaims, "You are my ev'rything, dear Lord, You are the source that I draw from; My joy, my strength, Oh Lord, is in You."[55]

In gospel music Jesus Christ is Everything—Friend, Protector, and Liberator—because he is portrayed as the Ultimate Alternative to a world that is essentially nothing, that is, no friend, offering no protection, and conditioned by

---

[54] See Sandra Crouch, "Souls for the Kingdom," "Come, Lord Jesus."

[55] See Jones, "All I Need," "Is Thy Life Too Good for Jesus?" "Jesus My All in All"; Tindley, "Nothing Between"; Dorsey, "I'll Tell It Wherever I Go," "I Know Jesus"; Morris, "Christ Is All"; Brewster, "Surely God Is Able"; Cleveland, "I Can't Stop Loving God," "He's Everything You Need," "He's Got Everything You Need"; Crouch, "I'll Always Love You."

captivity. It becomes acutely evident that nothingness, the condition of human nonbeing, is the oppressive aspect of culture causing black people to look away heavenward to Everything through gospel music. Everythingness is the light at the end of the human tunnel which is just bright enough to allow human beings to see the alternative to the light—the irreconcilable darkness of nothingness. What highlights the depiction of Jesus Christ as the Ultimate Alternative is the fact that the Lord is not customarily characterized as Reconciler. The fact that in gospel music Jesus Christ is Everything but Reconciler is basically what makes him stand over against culture, which to the conversionists is nothing but creation in need of reconciliation.

Each gospel song and each gospel composer captures only a minute part of a Lord who is Everything, but the entire gospel music movement draws a more composite picture of the Savior. Of course these characterizations are mere interpretations that generally seem to satisfy millennialists who customarily subscribe to radical anticulturalism. But for other Christians who have experienced the Lord as "Christ of Culture," "Christ above Culture," "Christ in Paradox with Culture," or as "Christ the Transformer of Culture," the picture gospel music paints is quite partial. If gospel music is theologically problematic, it is not because it captures the "hard times" God's little ones have faced in the twentieth century and that it offers alternative "good news," which is to look away heavenward from nothing to Everything. If the "gospel of gospel" is problematic, it is because the individuals who are its preachers and its audience may be irreproachably convinced that Jesus Christ is no more and no less than the Everything gospel music pictures him as. Not even Roberta Martin escapes this critique in denoting the Lord "more than all,"[56] for insofar as Jesus Christ is not generally characterized as Reconciler in gospel, he is not "more than all" because he is not *all* at all.

In the final analysis Jesus Christ is more than the Everything gospel music casts him as. The Lord is Everything

[56] Martin, "More than All."

beyond the world's wildest imaginations. Nevertheless, the power and potency of the gospel music movement in history is the unanimity of its anticulturalism as a profound critical measure for balancing the other more positive views of culture amid Christian pluralism.

10

Sermon and Surplus:
Musicality in Black Preaching

The Spirituals of Black Preaching

A close correlation exists between black preaching and the antebellum spiritual, for it is most likely that a substantial number of spirituals evolved via the preaching event of black worship. Although it is probable that slave preachers, apart from worship, worked at composing pleasing combinations of tune and text in order to teach spirituals to their congregations, it is believed that spirituals more frequently developed from extemporaneous sermonizing that crescendoed little by little to intoned utterance. This melodious declamation delineated into quasi-metrical phrases with formulaic cadence was customarily enhanced by intervening tonal response from the congregation. Responsorial iteration of catchy words, phrases, and sentences resulted in the burgeoning of song to which new verses could be contemporaneously added. Spirituals created in such a manner were sometimes evanescent, while favorable creations were remembered and perpetuated through oral transmission. Contemporaneous "songs" evolving from the musical preaching of contemporary black preachers and the intervening responses from their congregations can also be understood as "spirituals."

That preaching was and remains the channel through which "spirituals" evolved is quite consistent with preaching being a "kratophany," a word Mircea Eliade defines as a manifestation of power.[1] William Turner, who uses the word to describe the power behind black preaching, says:

> Within the tradition of the Black Church, preaching is truly a manifestation of power, or (in a word used by Eliade) a "kratophany." As in a "theophany," which is a manifestation of deity, some object is present which opens to the transcendent while simultaneously being rooted in the world of tangible, historical reality. With a theophany, the object many be a tree or a stone, as in African traditional religions, while with preaching the kratophany is spoken word and rendered gesture. Further, within the context of the culture that sustains black preaching, there is no modality more indicative of the presence of deity, power, and intrusion from another order than that of the preached word entrenched in musicality.[2]

Because preaching is "a word coming from another world," Turner contends that "human beings have found it difficult to utter in ordinary speech the extraordinary pronouncements which preaching requires."[3] The musicality in black preaching is in a sense a glossal expression beyond the literal word:

> The music of black preaching can be understood as a sort of "singing in the spirit," for there is a surplus (glossa) expressed in music which accompanies the rational content (logos) expressed in words. The rational portion is contained in the formal structure of the sermon which reflects the homiletical soundness and the doctrinal tradition in which the preacher stands. For the glossal portion, the preacher becomes an instrument of musical afflatus: a flute through which divine air is blown, a harp upon which eternal strings vibrate. For

---

[1] Cited in William C. Turner, Jr., "The Musicality of Black Preaching: A Phenomenology," *The Journal of Black Sacred Music*, vol. 2, no. 1 (Spring 1988), 27.
[2] Ibid., 27–28.
[3] Ibid., 23.

the sake of the audience, the preacher becomes an oracle through which a divinely inspired message flows.[4]

An examination follows of the various ingredients of this music which enhance the communication of the "surplus" of "a word coming from another world." The prime ingredients to be considered are melody, rhythm, call and response, and polyphony, as well as the structural and antistructural aspects of the chanted sermon—the form (the rational content) and the improvisation (the glossal content).

Melody

Melody is essentially that which is variously referred to as whooping, intoning, chanting, and tuning. This particular mode of melody is definable as a series of pitches that have continuity, tonality, quasi-metrical phraseology, and formulaic cadence. Turner, a typical preacher in the black tradition, says, "The spectrum of musical expression ranges from the sonorous delivery, which has a pleasant melodiousness, meter, and cadence, to the full-blown chant or song." Furthermore, says Turner:

> To those who are a part of the tradition in which musical delivery is normative, such a form often emerges as the criterion for preaching. This valuation categorizes other styles of delivery as mere speech, address, or lecture; but hardly as preaching.[5]

The use of melody in sermons and prayers is a long-standing tradition[6] of which a kratophany was the spontaneous creation of black spirituals. A correspondence of 1862 describes the "tuning" of a prayer at a religious meeting of Louisiana slaves:

> He kneels on the ground and pours out a stream of words as fast as he can utter them, or rather *sing* them, for the voice rises and falls in the cadence of a rude song, the congregation accompanying his voice, the

---

[4] Ibid., 22, 29.
[5] Ibid., 21.
[6] See Willis Laurence James, "The Romance of the Negro Folk Cry In America," *Phylon*, vol. 16, no. 1 (1955), 15–30, particularly 19.

men in a groaning voice and the women and children in
all sorts of wailings and whinings.[7]

An 1864 account of preaching in Warrenton, Mississippi, is
additional documentation of intoned declamation:

> The black preacher in the Methodist Church at [the]
> opposite corner [of the plantation] by his loud tone, rise
> and fall of voice, and tune, with earnest manner, re-
> minded me of some of our Quaker Preachers. I could
> not hear the words, but the sound came all the way into
> my chamber window very distinctly.[8]

Further, the observer of a 1938 open-air revival and baptism
in New Orleans noted that a Brother Carter "fell on his knees
with his starry eyes up to the skies, and gave one of his
singing prayers."[9]

The fact that black preachers intoned their sermons and
prayers is historically normative, for their African ancestors
chanted their oral history and folk stories, and Africa's North
American progeny moaned bluesy hollers and vendors
whooped street cries. Additionally, just as Africans chanted
tribal laws, stories, and proverbs, so have black preachers
intoned biblical laws and stories. Moreover, as Africans have
preserved their history and theology in song, so have black
preachers perpetuated African-American experience and religious belief in their "spirituals."

There are also similarities between the melodic style of
black preaching and West African folksinging. They both
alternate and combine speaking and singing. Both fluctuate
in pitch due to the voice being used as a practical tool of
expression rather than an instrument of *bel canto*. And both
use repetitive cadential formulas melodically, rhythmically,
and textually. Furthermore, in black preaching, as in African
recitation, it is impractical to sing for extended periods, so
that chanting is a more economical method of uttering the
word and its "surplus."

[7] Simeon A. Evans to Mother, MS, Aug. 21, 1862, Department of Archives and
Manuscripts, Louisiana State University, Baton Rouge.

[8] Isaac Shoemaker, Diary, MS, May 8, 1864, entry (p. 74), Manuscript Department, Duke University, Durham, N.C.

[9] "River Baptism," MS, 1–2, Louisiana Collection (Louisiana Writers Program,
WPA, 1935–43), Louisiana State Library, Baton Rouge.

The principal melodic mode employed in chanting or "tuning" is the pentatonic, a scale that found its way into black preaching and black spirituals through African folk-song.[10] The preacher who masters this five-note scale has an appealing pitch vocabulary to enhance textual proclamation. Further embellishment of the pentatonic and fuller expression of the "surplus" is attainable by customary vocal inflections such as the lowering, bending, scooping, and wavering of pitches. The pentatonic is the principal mode shared by all black preachers who "whoop," so that extensive musical variety is uncommon between preachers. The same was true of antebellum spirituals; their composers also remained within limited modal and stylistic boundaries. Yet within these boundaries their poetical ingenuity burgeoned, fueled by the intrusion of power from another order, producing "spirituals" that were distinctly individual creations.

Rhythm

Rhythm is the "residue" that gives black preaching motion and momentum. Without it there would be no kratophany, no means of giving the "surplus" locomotion. The various forms of rhythmic manifestation in preaching are the most primordial means of expressing "surplus."

The validity of the notion that rhythm lies at the base of black preaching is well supported. Those who have studied it concur that rhythm is its fundamental musical component. Bruce Rosenberg's coast-to-coast study of the South emphatically deduced that rhythm is probably the most vital part of the black preacher's musical art.[11] William Pipes's research in Macon County, Georgia, specifically found that black preachers customarily fit sentences into metrical units by squeezing together and stretching out words, while simultaneously accompanying their delivery by striking the lectern or stomping the foot.[12] In addition, ministers often drum

---

[10] From the tonic, the ascending intervals of this scale are a minor third, two major seconds, and another minor third. Many of these modern spirituals employ only a portion of the scale, with heavy emphasis on the tonic (reciting tone).

[11] Bruce A. Rosenberg, *The Art of the American Folk Preacher* (New York: Oxford University Press, 1970), 42.

[12] William H. Pipes, *Say Amen, Brother* (New York: William-Frederick, 1951), 152–53.

upon the podium to stress important words in key sentences, so that percussive rhythmic variations evolve syntactically. Other times the beating is a syncopated counterpoint to the preaching.

However, Turner, who thoroughly traces the black preacher's use of rhythm back to Africa, says:

> The connection between rhythm and life is the primal nexus from which the manifold expressions of culture flow. In its unity, rhythm/life surges forth in the multifarious forms through which the world is known: language, art, society, religion, government, and so forth. It is therefore only a short step to the realization that the very force of life that pulsates through individuals and communities is given objective tangible expression in rhythmic motion and music, and that musical rhythm is the aesthetic signification of the force sustaining the people.[13]

Among the Africans taken to America, says Turner, every effort was made to preserve the primal connection with the spiritual world:

> However, the surplus of deep stirrings, intensity, and zeal within the African spirit, easily expressed in African languages by means of rhythm, tone, and pitch, found little correspondence in the vocabulary of the strange land. And drumming, a precise means of communicating with human beings and the deities, was strictly forbidden in the slave regime. But, alas, rhythm and musicality were sustained within the worship of the slave community, a portion of its residue being deposited in black preaching.[14]

When preaching becomes extra-rhythmical during the sermon's climax, when the "surplus" is being profoundly effused, it often prompts outbursts of applause. As willing vessels, black preachers allow the "surplus" enveloped in rhythm to invigorate them and to evoke the enthusiastic involvement of the congregation in the moment of kratophany.

---

[13] Turner, 26.
[14] Ibid., 26.

Increasingly the worshipers respond to the preaching percussively with clapping, stomping, and shouting (holy dancing). The resulting texture is a contrapuntal matrix of African-like cross-rhythms. "Replete with drama and musicality, its performative power is expected to move people and to cause reaction," says Turner. "Nodding the head, shedding a tear, holy dancing, speaking in tongues, singing, humming aloud, and saying 'amen' are responses to the power manifested in effective black preaching."[15]

An account of worship at Jerusalem Temple Baptist Church in New Orleans, around 1939, captures an incident of the rhythmic expression of "deep stirrings, intensity, and zeal within the African spirit." As a worshiper offered up a prayer, the writer noted that "feet were heard on the floor with a very definite beat. There was groaning . . . the sisters started rocking and the brothers started swinging their bodies. The church got hot!"[16] Moreover, just as the most marked part of a spiritual's refrain was sometimes iterated until it burst into a ring-shout, so does the contemporary preacher reiterate a sermon's phrase until it climaxes in shouting. This typically occurs in Holiness-Pentecostal churches where shouting is a customary expression of the "surplus" or the "anointing."

It was the rhythmic use of language that enabled black preachers such as Martin Luther King, Jr., to communicate the power beyond the literal word. One of King's favorite literary "licks" consisted of parallel syntax with similar word endings, which resulted in a rhythmic cadence.[17] This syntactical parallelism, also common to biblical psalmody, is exemplified in the closing three lines of the following quatrain excerpted from his sermon "The Drum Major Instinct":

> Yes, if you want to say that I was a drum major,
> say that I was a drum major for justice;

[15] Ibid., 28. See also Harold Dean Trulear, "The Sacramentality of Preaching," *Liturgy*, vol. 7, no. 1, 15–21, particularly 19–20.
[16] McKinney, "The Jerusalem Baptist Church, Father Joseph, Pastor," MS, 4, Louisiana Collection, Louisiana State Library.
[17] Hortense J. Spillers, "Martin Luther King and the Style of the Black Sermon," in *The Black Experience in Religion*, ed. C. Eric Lincoln (New York: Anchor/Doubleday, 1974), 83–84.

> say that I was a drum major for peace;
> I was a drum major for righteousness.

By no means the first to use parallel construction, King was following a tradition of long standing. The identical kratophany is found in a sermon preached by a black preacher in Chapel Hill, North Carolina, around 1935:

> I kin see God settin' up dere in ol' glory
> shakin' his golden locks and a-
> stampin' his lightnin' foot an'
> sayin' "Preach it, brother."[18]

Another customary literary "lick," also favored by King, is comprised of aphoristic iterations. Just as the resounding of a musical theme establishes the theme's rhythmic character in the ear of the listener, so does repetition of a sermon's theme establish its rhythm and the power in its words. The aphorisms "I have a dream" and "Let freedom ring," periodically repeated with the Kingian beat, created such a memorable rhythm and kratophany. Continuing in the footsteps of his cultural forebears, the drum major King was adept at using words to beat out the "surplus" in rhythmic patterns.

The reference to black preaching as "hitting-a-lick" (cited as early as 1855)[19] also alluded to vocal percussiveness. Although the voice is basically a lyrical instrument, it is quite capable of percussiveness in its punctuation of pungent consonants, particularly alliterative Ps. Also, as consonants arise during sentencing and are accented, percussive syncopations evolve syntactically. Some preachers prefer to employ rhythmic motives that accent such consonants as a strong "c" or "k." The power and action latent in the meaning of such words as "com-ing," "knock-ing," "ask-ing," "seek-ing," "claim it," and "thank you" are released through the punctuation of percussive consonants.

Not only is the vocal line of homiletical delivery percussive and syntactically rhythmical, so are the accompanying

---

[18] Frank Clyde Brown, Folk Sermons, MS, "Broadcastin' Station," 17. Manuscript Collection, Duke University.
[19] Julia Lord Loveland, Journal, MS, Mar. 25, 1855, entry, Manuscript Department, Duke University.

theatrics of the preacher. The kratophany is not only in the spoken word but, as Turner has said, in rendered gesture.[20] Grace Holt described the initial steps of a preacher's movement and gesture as "slow-moving" and "funky." This, she said, prompts the physical involvement of the congregation in the preaching event.[21] A vivid portrayal is drawn by one attending a camp meeting in Chinquepin, North Carolina, around 1922:

> One Sunday the preacher was getting into a weaving way speaking loudly and slightly swaying his body. Out in the congregation they were saying "Uhoo he's walkin'. Walk, brother, walk." Then he got louder and swayed more and they said, "Uhoo, he's running now, run, brother, run."[22]

Notwithstanding the caricature, it is evident that the "surplus" finds release, not only in the singing of a sermon, but in the rhythmic dancing of it.

Call and Response

"In Alabama dey had de Sheep Callin' Baptists, whar de preacher dress as a shepherd an' call his congregation like de shepherd call his sheep an' de congregation answer back, 'baa, baa?'"[23] To this unusual account of call and response, told by a Texas ex-slave, is added a more conventional (but no less humorous) example excerpted from a sermon preached at a New Orleans revival by Louisianian Rev. W. Scott Chinn:

You all ain't got no religion . . .

Amen, brother!

You all ain't got no more religion than the white folks . . .

At's right, brother!

You all ain't got no more religion than the Jews . . .

[20] Turner, 28.

[21] Grace S. Holt, "Stylin' Outta the Black Pulpit," *Rappin' and Stylin' Out*, ed. Thomas Kochman (Urbana: University of Illinois Press, 1972), 191.

[22] Brown, Folk Sermons, MS, "A Holy Dance," 5.

[23] George P. Rawick, ed., *The American Slave: A Composite Autobiography*, vol. 7, pt. 6, suppl., ser. 2 (Westport, Conn.: Greenwood Press, 1977), 2783.

Amen! Tell it to 'em straight!

Why, ef you was livin' in Jerusalem when Jesus was
bawn, you wouldn't of believed it onless you got a en-
graved announcement readin' "Mary and Joseph announce the birth of Jesus. Mary is his mammy, and he
ain't got no pappy."

Amen, preacher . . . ain't it de truf![24]

During this call and response or responsorial event, worshipers engage in more than acknowledging the kratophany
of the preacher's "spoken word and rendered gesture," they
actually preach back. Therefore, there is reciprocity through
which preacher and congregation commune in the spontaneous creation of song.

This reciprocity is important, for seldom is song spontaneously produced by a preacher during the sermon without
the participation of the congregation. It is congregational
response that inspirits climactic "celebration," which Turner
defines as "that point to which the preacher leads the congregation in moments of thanksgiving and transport—wherein
the skills of musical delivery are unsurpassed in attaining the
exalted moment."[25] Celebration is the stage at which sustained musical expression of the "surplus" results in song.
Correspondingly, it has been proven repeatedly that the
black preacher who "lectures" to an unresponsive congregation is the one who "sings" in a responsive setting. Spontaneous intoning takes courage, so a preacher will not "let go
and let God" before a comatose congregation. There is the
constant threat of appearing irrational (glossal) at points of
spiritual satiation by allowing oneself to react freely to the
Spirit. This intimidation is obliterated when pulpit and pew
progress dialogically toward doxology.

Call and response or "call and recall," as it is sometimes
termed in the black church, is a practice deeply rooted
in African folk song. Yet Henry Mitchell says that, aside
from this cultural aspect, there is a logical or biological

[24] Miriam Brown to John E. Canaday, MS, Oct. 7, 1929, Miriam Brown Papers, Special Collections, Tulane University, New Orleans.
[25] Turner, 21.

explanation for its occurrence during preaching. He states that extended intoning naturally requires pauses for breath, at which points a congregation responds.[26] In addition, Joseph Johnson gives a theological interpretation. He defines the responsorial event as "a trilogy, in which the Holy Spirit moves the black preacher, and the black preacher speaks to the congregation and the congregation responds with 'Amen.'"[27] This is exactly what Turner denotes "a direct link between the spirit within the preacher, the word being uttered, and the worshiping congregation."[28] Olin Moyd adds to these estimations that congregational dialogue with the preacher also includes nonverbal responses,[29] or what Gerald Davis terms "sound-absent sermonphones."[30] Analogously, just as a conductor is an unvoiced but integral part of the music during a symphonic performance, so are sound-absent sermonphones unvoiced but integral elements of musicality in the expression of "surplus."

Finally, an extension of the responsorial event is the antiphonal event. Here, a spatial polychoric effect is attained in an acoustical polarity between the deaconesses and missionaries in the "hallelujah corner" and the deacons in the "amen corner," or in churches where the seating arrangement is segregated by gender. In such a setting the blocks of male "sermonphones" and contrasting female "sermonphones" create quasi-antiphonal song.

Polyphony

Homophony (harmony) occasionally results when a preacher's intoned delivery is accompanied by a homophonic instrument, principally the organ. In fact some preachers do their best "tuning" when an organist is intricately engaged in the "song." However, the preaching event,

[26] Henry H. Mitchell, *Black Preaching* (San Francisco: Harper & Row, 1979), 166.
[27] Joseph A. Johnson, *Proclamation Theology* (Shreveport, La.: Fourth Episcopal District Press, 1977), 41.
[28] Turner, 25.
[29] Olin P. Moyd, "The Word in the Black Church," *Freeing the Spirit* 1, no. 4, 26.
[30] Gerald L. Davis, *I Got the Word in Me and I Can Sing It, You Know: A Study of the Performed African-American Sermon* (Philadelphia: University of Pennsylvania Press, 1985), 99.

due to congregational involvement, is characterized more by polyphony (counterpoint) than homophony.

Polyphony is what Henry Mitchell calls "culturally choreographed counterpoint, with the preacher's intoned Gospel cast in a continuous context of congregational chant."[31] Intertwining lines of sung "phrase sermonphones" —"Tell it, Rev," "Help yourself," and "Go ahead, brother preacher"—and "nonarticulated sermonphones"—moaning and humming—establish a dense polyphonic texture. For instance, the musical threads of polyphonic fabric are so intricately interwoven that when a preacher dramatically breaks off the chant, a congregational response is sometimes present to complete the cadence.

Congregational involvement in the contrapuntal kratophany in black preaching is historically normative. For instance, a Mississippi ex-slave vividly recalled a religious meeting of slaves whose humming, praying, and singing produced a soft contrapuntal accompaniment to the sermon: "Dey would hum deep and low in long mournful tones swayin' to an' fro. Uders would pray and sing soft while de Broder Preacher wuz a deliverin' de humble message."[32] A Texas ex-slave recalled that when they prayed they made a circle and would "git to moanin' low and gentle: 'Some day, Some day, Some day, this yoke gwine be lifted offen our shoulders.'"[33] An 1855 account of the praying of Sam Drayton, a black Georgia preacher, is similar. The writer recorded that "While they were praying a low moaning sound would be heard, gradually growing louder until it became a perfect wail."[34] Ethnomusicologist Natalie Curtis Burlin also witnessed a song spontaneously evolve from a prayer delivered by a black Virginia clergyman during the early 1920s:

> Minutes passed, long minutes of strange intensity. The mutterings, the ejaculations, grew louder, more dramatic, till suddenly I felt the creative thrill dart

[31] Henry H. Mitchell, *The Recovery of Preaching* (San Francisco: Harper & Row, 1977), 117.
[32] Rawick, vol. 10, pt. 5, suppl. ser. 1, 2247.
[33] Ibid., vol. 5, pts. 3 & 4, 133.
[34] Ella Gertrude (Clayton) Thomas, Journal, MS, July 12, 1855, entry (p. 49), Manuscript Department, Duke University.

through the people like an electric vibration, that same half-audible hum arose,—emotion was gathering atmospherically as clouds gather—and then, up from the depths of some "sinner's" remorse and imploring came a pitiful little plea, a real Negro "moan," sobbed in musical cadence. From somewhere in that bowed gathering another voice improvised a response: the plea sounded again, louder this time and more impassioned; then other voices joined the answer, shaping it into a musical phrase; and so, before our ears, as one might say, from this molten metal of music a new song was smithied out, composed then and there by no one in particular and by everyone in general.[35]

The strange intensity, creative thrill, gathered emotion, the real Negro moan—these things were the "surplus" of spiritual repletion being shaped like molten metal into song.

Heterophony, a contrapuntal texture prominent in folk music of African descent, is also an element of musicality in black preaching. Heterophony resulted when each person in a group of slaves rendered the melody of a spiritual in her or his own way or when the blues singer attempted to duplicate the melody he was moaning on his guitar. It currently results when worshipers join the preacher in the intoning of familiar scripture, hymnody, "phrase sermonphones," and iterated aphorisms. Attentive worshipers, familiar with the style and form of traditional black preaching and linked up with the spirit within the preacher and the word being uttered, are able to anticipate sermonic phraseology and heterophonically preach along. As Rosenberg put it, they "anticipate the preacher's music."[36] As each strays intentionally or unintentionally from the unison melody, exotic harmonies result—heterophonically.

In review, the range of polyphonic texture during symphonic black preaching and prayer runs the gamut from a melody/countermelody relationship, where the preacher's intoning is accompanied by one or more simple "sermonphones," to a more complex cross-rhythmic dialogue between

---

[35] Natalie Curtis Burlin, "Negro Music at Birth," *The Musical Quarterly* 5 (Oct. 1919), 88.

[36] Rosenberg, 39.

preacher and congregation. The responsorial event is partly moderated by the talented preacher through calculated phraseology that intentionally leaves space for response. The more complex polyphonic and heterophonic dialogue is controlled by the congregation as they allow themselves to express the "surplus" of spiritual repletion.

Form

Sermonic intoning does not necessarily result in the creation of song. There are isolated episodes that are insufficiently continuous and complete to be considered musical. Rhythm, call and response, homophony, polyphony, and heterophony give melody personality, but *form* shapes the "strange intensity" of individual and communal musicality into song. It is in song that the kratophany is concretely captured, with the possibility of its surplus being perpetuated in the oral tradition.

Well-wrought sermons and prayers have cohesive literary form, but it is a superstructure not relative to the "spirituals" that evolve as units. The "spirituals," which exist as formulaic segments within the sermonic superstructure, are constructed of repetition, extension, variation, differentiation, modulation, thematic recapitulation, and transition. These are structural means of capturing the countless nuances of antistructural "surplus." For example, as a preacher is intoning and engaged in the spontaneous formation of song, there are three creative choices to be made that determine form. When given a word, phrase, or sentence, the preacher can repeat it, vary it, contrast it, or extend it. Further, when a word, phrase, or sentence is repeated verbatim, the preacher can stress the same syllables and words, emphasize other syllables and words, deliver the material with the same rhythmic pattern, superimpose a different pattern, or sing the text to the same tune, vary it, or intone a new tune.

Bruce Rosenberg and Gerald Davis have examined the intermediate means of building form within sermonic superstructure. Rosenberg adds three points of interest. First, he says the preacher sometimes uses metrical word patterns in formulaic verses (strophes) that may consist of parallel syntax. Second, the theme, as the gravitational center of the overall sermonic composition, when varied systematically results in a theme and variation form. Last, a sermon is comprised of compound form, the units of which are connected via textual transition.[37] Davis further defines formulaic transition and the important part the sermonic theme plays contextually:

> In this discussion the thematic bridge mechanism is a category of formula that has the specialized function of bridging the sermon's independent units through restatements of the sermon's theme and by providing temporary closure for the preceding formula and entry into the next formula.[38]

This "coherence factor" essentially allows for maximum fluidity in the effusing of the "surplus."

One of several formulaic masterpieces transcribed from intoned preaching is found in a collection of preached "spirituals" titled *Sacred Symphony* (1987).[39] The piece is "Come On and See a Man" and comprises intriguing passages of responsorial format, extension, recapitulation, and repetition, all of which give the preacher a broader means of solidifying (in form) part of the power of the eternal word. Verse one reads:

> Come on and see a man
>   that read my history.
> Come on and see a man
>   that will be your companion.
> Come on and see a man
>   that will save your soul.
> Come on and see a man
>   that can pull you from a burning hell,
>   place your feet on a solid rock.
> Come on, come on and see a man.

Obviously the fourth couplet was extended in a way that penultimately prepared for the recapitulation, which was also

[37] Ibid., 10, 17, 66.

[38] Davis, 56.

[39] Jon Michael Spencer, *Sacred Symphony: The Chanted Sermon of the Black Preacher* (Westport, Conn.: Greenwood Press, 1987), 78.

extended with the twice-stated "come on." Following this is a
section that seems to function as a chorus with its use of
repetition in the second and third lines:

> A burden bearer, a heart regulator, a mind fixer,
> He's alright. He's alright.
> Come on. Come on.

Verse two is identical to verse one in its responsorial format
and use of recapitulation. The difference is that the solicitation to "come on" comprises the consequent rather than the
antecedent of the musical sentence. This syntactic twist and
shortening of "Come on and see a man" to simply "Come on"
results in verse two being a variation of verse one:

> If you're down, come on.
> If you're weary, come on.
> If you're friendless, come on.
> If you're broke, come on.
> If you're lonely, come on.
> Come on and see a man.[40]

In this example it should be obvious that the expression
of the "surplus" through the glossa of musicality does not
necessarily result in glossolalia. In fact, Turner contends,
"Not only does such celebration enhance the understanding
and retention of the gospel; it is, as Henry Mitchell asserts,
essential to faithful communication of the gospel." Turner
says further: "This is not to diminish the significance of the
cognitive aspect, for celebration does not stand independent
of responsible exegesis, careful penetration of the teachings
of the church, and sensitive theological insight."[41] In short,
kratophany does not transcend form; it contemporaneously
creates its own form amidst spontaneity.

Hymnody, psalmody, traditional spirituals, and gospel
songs are important text sources for the contemporary
preacher's "spirituals." Not only does the preacher spontaneously select passages from these sources at points of

---

[40] It is fascinating that the form of this song can be analyzed as a rondo (A B A'
C A''), in that brief verses carry the listener back to a responsorial variation of the
refrain (A') and then returns to the opening sentence (A'').

[41] Turner, 21.

intoning the "surplus," but the forms themselves demand musical delivery due to their formulaic and lyric musicality. The form of a particular hymn, psalm, spiritual, or gospel song, when quoted at length, becomes the form of that particular segment of the performed "spiritual." In addition, quotations from these sources evoke a musical disposition in the listener, not only due to the poetic form of these genres, but because familiarity with the lyric prompts recollection of the music. And the listeners' emotional responses to the music and its meaning impact the vitalization of the kratophany and the contemporaneous form of the preaching. To be sure, the congregation, as an integral component of musicality capable of directing the course of the preaching event and of making or breaking the "song," is a conduit of the "surplus" and has direct bearing on contemporaneous sermonic form.

Hymns, psalms, spirituals, and gospel songs, used thematically in a sermon, aid further in the creation of musical form. For instance, the thematic hymn recited early in a discourse may permeate an entire sermon like a musical theme permeates a symphonic composition.[42] An introductory quotation from a familiar hymn or psalm immediately catches the attention of listeners and prompts musical consciousness. Intermittent reference to the lyric allows the preacher to maintain and build upon the level of musicality. The ideal invitational hymn is the one quoted during the discourse, whether the hymn is thematic or is introduced at the point of sustained "singing" of "surplus." The preacher's intoning not only serves as a "coherent" transition between spoken declamation and invitational hymn but also as spiritual transition whereby the congregation is led to the altitude of musicality required to involve them in an ardent singing of the consummative song:

| spoken discourse | $\longrightarrow$ | free intoning | $\longrightarrow$ | intoned hymn | $\longrightarrow$ | invitational hymn |

It is in this way that the "surplus" finds its fullest release.

[42] For further discussion of the use of hymnody in black preaching, see Michael A. Battle, "The Kerygmatic Ministry of Black Song and Sermon," *The Journal of Black Sacred Music*, vol. 1, no. 2 (Fall 1987), 17–20.

In preaching, the "surplus" is also expressed through key modulation. Just as the spiritual "We Are Climbing Jacob's Ladder" ascends by semitones verse after verse, so are some black preachers able to modulate the tonal center of their chanting in order to facilitate the most potent kratophany.

Improvisation

Melody, rhythm, call and response, homophony, polyphony, and heterophony help construct sermonic form; however, the structure of a performed sermon is actually the result of the antistructural element of improvisation. Preaching is improvisatory because there is neither any way for the human vessel to contain the "surplus" nor of knowing beforehand how the "surplus" is going to be released. One fact is certain, says Turner. "The preacher who genuinely enters this state of spirituality is able to deliver discourse far exceeding that which has been prepared."[43]

The most intensive examination of improvisation in black preaching is a comparative study with jazz improvisation found in the work of Henry Mitchell. Mitchell's inquiry led him to conclude that ideal improvisation is characterized by freshness and relevance. With reference to jazz bassist Charlie Mingus, he explains:

> Charlie was saying that jazz " improvisation" was, in fact, often the very opposite. Instead of a solo riff or improvisation related (in a subtle black way) to the theme of the musical composition, the most frequent "ride" or riff is a repetition of something used every time the player is given the opportunity to solo improvise. . . . But preachers are perhaps the worse offenders. . . . Many simply have not had a chance to learn more than 3 or 4 "riffs" with which to climax a sermon.[44]

As Clarence Rivers plainly put it, "Spontaneity takes a great deal of practice."[45]

---

[43] Turner, 28.
[44] Henry H. Mitchell, "Black Improvisation," *Freeing the Spirit* 2, no. 4 (Winter 1973), 37–38.
[45] Clarence J. Rivers, "To Train a Preacher . . .Train a Performer," *Freeing the Spirit* 1, no. 4, 50.

There are additional comparisons between sermonic and jazz improvisations. First, the musical theme in jazz is akin to the textual theme in a sermon: both are simply motifs requiring further improvisatory development. Second, both jazz and sermonic compositions tend to have superstructure, inside of which intermediary form is created by the antistructural means of improvisation. Third, the art of preaching, like the art of jazz soloing, is characterized by improvisatory vocal inflection, such as the bending and lowering of pitches, sliding from tone to tone, grace notes, and tremolo. In preaching these are subtle means of expressing the multifarious nuances of the "surplus." Last, just as enthusiastic applause from an audience can impel a jazz artist to return to the stage for an encore, so do exuberant responses from a congregation inspire a minister to stand back up and "whoop" just a little longer. Some preachers are known for improvising two or three "encores," each of which, as it crescendos to a higher climax, more profoundly expresses the "surplus."

In summary, the ultimate act of sermonic composition takes place in the pulpit during delivery, just it takes place on stage for the performers of gospel, blues, and jazz. As the gospel singer's song is characterized by a freely melismatic melodizing and the jazz singer's song by a creatively syncopated sentencing, so is the preacher's song distinguished by an unrestrained and extemporaneous outpouring of the "surplus" executed with the finesse of a poet. "When preaching attains the level wherein rhythm and musicality are unrestrained—wherein the preacher 'let's the Lord have his way'—it is customarily said that the preacher is 'under the anointing' and is 'being used of God.' In the vernacular of the culture, we say, 'the preacher has come.'"[46]

---

[46] Turner, 29. The "preacher" Turner refers to is the Holy Ghost.

BIBLIOGRAPHY

1

The Spiritual

Cone, James H. *The Spirituals and the Blues.* New York: Seabury Press, 1972.

Proctor, Henry Hugh. "The Theology of the Songs of the Southern Slave." *The Southern Workman,* vol. 36 (1907), 584–92, 652–56.

Thurman, Howard. *Deep River: Reflections on the Religious Insight of Certain of the Negro Spirituals.* New York: Harper, 1955.

————. *The Negro Spiritual Speaks of Life and Death.* New York: Harper, 1947.

Washington, Joseph R., Jr., *Black Religion: The Negro and Christianity in the United States.* Boston: Beacon Press, 1964.

2

Antislavery Hymnody

Betker, John P., comp. *Miriam's Timbrel: Sacred Songs, Suited to Revival Occasions; and also for Anti-Slavery, Peace, Temperance, and Reform Meetings,* 2d ed. Mansfield, Ohio: [The Wesleyan Methodist Church], 1853.

Chapman, Maria Weston, comp. *Songs of the Free and Hymns of Christian Freedom*. Boston: Isaac Knapp, 1836.

Eaklor, Vicki L. *American Antislavery Songs: A Collection and Analysis*. Westport, Conn.: Greenwood Press, 1988.

Garrison, William Lloyd, comp. *A Selection of Antislavery Hymns, for the Use of the Friends of Emancipation*. Boston: Garrison & Knapp, 1834.

Hatfield, Edwin Francis, comp. *Freedom's Lyre: Or, Psalms, Hymns, and Sacred Songs for the Slave and His Friends*. New York: S. W. Benedict & Company, 1840.

3

Social Gospel Hymnody

Coffin, Henry Sloane, and Ambrose White Vernon, eds. *Hymn of the Kingdom of God*. New York: A. S. Barnes, 1911.

Mussey, Mabel, ed. *Social Hymns of Brotherhood and Aspiration*. New York: A. S. Barnes, 1914.

The Survey, vol. 31, no. 14 (January 3, 1914).

Williams, Mornay, ed. *Hymns of the Kingdom of God*. New York: n. pub., n.d.

4

Civil Rights Song

Carawan, Guy, and Candie Carawan, comps. *Freedom Is a Constant Struggle: Songs of the Freedom Movement*. New York: Oak Press, 1968.

————, comps. *We Shall Overcome! Songs of the Southern Freedom Movement*. New York: Oak Press, 1963.

Lift Ev'ry Voice: The NAACP Songbook. New York: NAACP, 1972.

Reagon, Bernice Johnson. "Songs of the Civil Rights Movement 1955–1965: A Study in Cultural History." Ph.D. dissertation, Howard University, 1975.

Songs of the Spirit Movement. Chicago: The Ecumenical Institute, 1968 (*Image*, no. 6, January 1968).

5

The Blues

Cone, James H. *The Spirituals and the Blues*. New York: Seabury Press, 1972.

Garon, Paul. "Blues and the Church: Revolt and Resignation."
    Living Blues, vol. 1, no. 1 (Spring 1970), 11–23.
Gruver, Rod. "The Blues as a Secular Religion." *Blues World,* no.
    29 (April 1970), 3–6; no. 30 (May 1970), 4–7; no. 31 (June
    1970), 5–7; no. 32 (July 1970), 7–9.
Neal, Larry. "The Ethos of the Blues." *Black Scholar,* vol. 3, no. 10
    (Summer 1972), 42–48.
Oliver, Paul. *Conversation with the Blues.* New York: Horizon Press,
    1965.

6

The Ring-Shout

Allen, William Francis, et al. *Slave Songs of the United States.* New
    York: Peter Smith, 1951.
Epstein, Dena J. *Sinful Tunes and Spirituals: Black Folk Music to the
    Civil War.* Urbana: University of Illinois Press, 1977.
Genovese, Eugene D. *Roll, Jordan, Roll: The World the Slaves Made.*
    New York: Vintage Books, 1976.
Raboteau, Albert J. *Slave Religion: The "Invisible Institution" in
    the Antebellum South.* New York: Oxford University Press,
    1978.
Southern, Eileen. *The Music of Black Americans.* New York: W. W.
    Norton, 1971.

7

Tongue-Song

The Apostolic Faith (Los Angeles), 1906–1908.
Bartleman, Frank. *What Really Happened at "Azusa Street"? The True
    Story of the Great Revival Compiled by Frank Bartleman Himself
    from His Diary.* Ed. John Walker. Northridge, Calif.: Voice
    Christian Publications, 1962.
Brumback, Carl. *"What Meaneth This?": A Pentecostal Answer to a
    Pentecostal Question.* Springfield, Mo.: The Gospel Publishing
    House, 1947.
Ensley, Eddie. *Sounds of Wonder: Speaking in Tongues in the Catholic
    Tradition.* New York: Paulist Press, 1977.
Patterson, Bob E. "Catholic Pentecostals," in *Speaking in Tongues:
    Let's Talk About It.* Ed. Watson E. Mills. Waco, Tex.: Word
    Books, 1973.

Samarin, William J. *Tongues of Men and Angels: The Religious Language of Pentecostalism.* New York: Macmillan, 1972.
Williams, Cyril G. *Tongues of the Spirit: A Study of Pentecostal Glossolalia and Related Phenomenon.* Cardiff: University of Wales Press, 1981.

8

Holiness-Pentecostal Music

Cone, James H. *Speaking the Truth: Ecumenism, Liberation, and Black Theology.* Grand Rapids: Eerdmans, 1986.
Dargan, William T. "Congregational Gospel Songs in a Black Holiness Church: A Musical and Textual Analysis." Ph.D. dissertation, Wesleyan University, 1982.
Hollenweger, Walter J. *The Pentecostals.* Minneapolis: Augsburg Publishing House, 1972.
Hurston, Zora Neale. *The Sanctified Church.* Berkeley, Calif.: Turtle Island, 1983.
Paris, Arthur E. *Black Pentecostalism: Southern Religion in an Urban World.* Amherst: University of Massachusetts Press, 1982.
Williams, Melvin D. *Community in a Black Pentecostal Church: An Anthropological Study.* Prospect Heights, Ill.: Waveland Press, 1974.

9

Gospel Music

Copher, Charles B. "Biblical Characters, Events, Places and Images Remembered and Celebrated in Black Worship." *Journal of the Interdenominational Theological Center,* vol. 14, nos. 1 & 2 (Fall 1986/Spring 1987), 75–86.
Harvey, Louis-Charles. "Black Gospel Music and Black Theology." *The Journal of Religious Thought,* vol. 43, no. 2 (Fall–Winter, 1986–87), 19–37.
Jackson, Irene V., ed. *Afro-American Religious Music: A Bibliography and a Catalogue of Gospel Music.* Westport, Conn.: Greenwood Press, 1979.
Levine, Lawrence W. *Black Culture and Black Consciousness: Afro-American Folk Thought from Slavery to Freedom.* New York: Oxford University Press, 1977.

Mitchell, Henry H., and Nicholas Cooper-Lewter. *Soul Theology: The Heart of American Black Culture.* San Francisco: Harper & Row, 1986.

Walker, Wyatt T. *"Somebody's Calling My Name": Black Sacred Music and Social Change.* Valley Forge, Pa.: Judson Press, 1979.

10

The Chanted Sermon

Davis, Gerald L. *I Got the Word in Me and I Can Sing It, You Know: A Study of the Performed African-American Sermon.* Philadelphia: University of Pennsylvania Press, 1985.

Mitchell, Henry H. *Black Preaching.* San Francisco: Harper & Row, 1970.

————. *The Recovery of Preaching.* San Francisco: Harper & Row, 1977.

Rosenberg, Bruce A. *The Arts of the American Folk Preacher.* New York: Oxford University Press, 1970.

Spencer, Jon Michael. *Sacred Symphony: The Chanted Sermon of the Black Preacher.* Westport, Conn.: Greenwood Press, 1987.

Turner, William C., Jr. "The Musicality of Black Preaching: A Phenomenology." *The Journal of Black Sacred Music,* vol. 2, no. 1 (Spring 1988), 21–29.

GENERAL INDEX

MUSIC INDEX

Song Titles and Hymnbooks

259